Hospitality
Information Systems and E-Commerce

RENEWALS 458-4574.

Hospitality
Information Systems and E-Commerce

D. V. TESONE

University of Central Florida

WILEY

JOHN WILEY & SONS, INC.

Library of Congress Cataloging-in-Publication Data:

Tesone, D. V. (Dana V.)
    Hospitality information systems and E-commerce / D. V. Tesone.
        p. cm.
    Includes bibliographical references and index.
    ISBN 0-471-47849-0 (pbk.)
  1. Hospitality industry—Data processing. 2. Management information
systems. 3. Electronic commerce. I. Title.
    TX'11.3.E4T47 2005
    647.94'068—dc22

2004014936

Printed in the United States of America

10 9 8 7 6 5 4 3 2 1

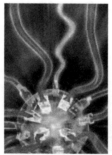

Contents

CHAPTER 4

Computer Networks and Telecommunications for Hospitality   71

CHAPTER 9

Preface

Hospitality Information Systems and E-Commerce is intended to provide students with the ability to converse intelligently with technology professionals providing end-user services to hospitality industry managers who use technology to enhance organizational productivity. Many current texts on hospitality information systems are too narrowly focused on hotel information and transaction-processing systems. Traditional business administration texts are too technically focused on management information systems issues geared toward Chief Information Officer (CIO) training. The purpose of this text is to empower the student with management awareness and terminology comprehension as it relates to the hospitality industry and its managers. In keeping with the interpersonal nature of the hospitality industry, *Hospitality Information Systems and E-Commerce* provides a primary approach to the use of technology to enhance human interactions.

Overview of the Text

The book is divided into three parts, each representing a different aspect of hospitality information systems. Part I includes chapters that represent the linear systems aspect of information technology and information systems. Part II deals with electronic business that opens the linear internal process of information systems to electronic interfaces from outside a hospitality organization. Finally, Part III discusses the business functions of the hospitality industry that are used to provide products and services for all organizational constituency groups. Figure 1 is a graphical representation of the text and each of its parts. Part I is represented by the linear input–transformation process–output model presented in Chapter 1. The diamond surrounding the linear model represents e-business interfaces that include intranets, extranets, and the Internet (Part II). The outer circle represents the functions of hospitality organizations that are described in Part III.

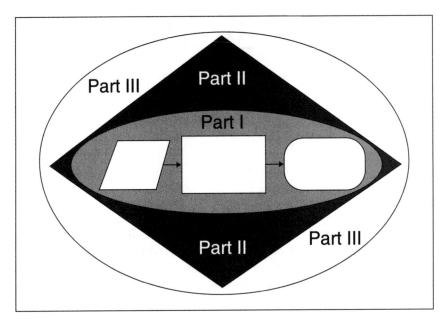

Figure 1

PART I

Chapter 1 presents an overview of the systems approach to working with technology, and Chapters 2 and 3 discuss the computer hardware and software that are used for general and more specific applications at home and in the office in organizations (see Figure 2). Chapter 4 provides a snapshot of computer networks from the smallest to the largest linkages and prepares us to enter the realm of electronic business, which is the theme of Part II.

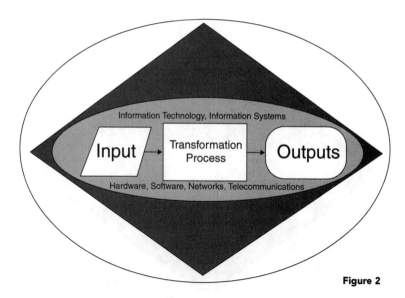

Figure 2

PART II

Part II begins with a description of electronic commerce (e-commerce), the practice of conducting business through electronic linkages consisting of constituency groups relative to a specific hospitality organization (Chapter 5). In Chapter 6, the discussion considers the information technology and information systems required to perform e-commerce functions. The final aspect of Part II is a discussion of the contemporary marketing implications of e-business for the hospitality and tourism industry, as presented in Chapter 7. The diamond portion of the model shown in Figure 3 represents Part II of the text.

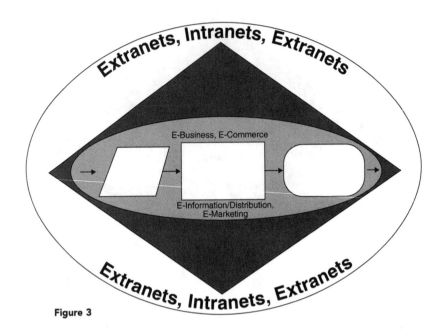

Figure 3

PART III

Part III takes us past the basics of information technology and information systems into the realm of the actual functions performed by individuals in the hospitality industry. Chapter 8 provides an overview of property management systems and centralized reservation systems, which gives us the interfacing mechanism of other systems, such as point-of-sale and other retail and catering management systems, as discussed in Chapter 9. Next, we shift to administrative systems for marketing, accounting, human resources management, and hotel systems in Chapters 10 and 11. Chapter 12 provides an overview of safety, security, and physical plant systems, along with a few conclusions. Notice the completed model in Figure 4 that highlights the outer circle that represents the functions performed by individuals and teams in hospitality organizations.

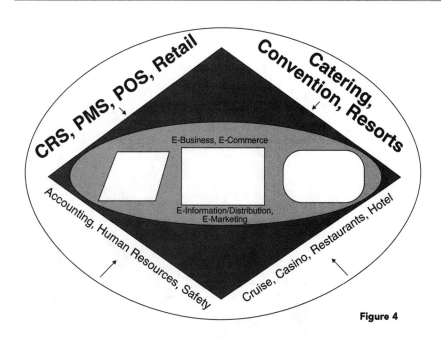

Figure 4

Supplementary Materials

An *Instructor's Manual* (0-471-69606-4) is available to qualified adopters of this textbook. Among the features of the Instructor's Manual are lecture notes, answers to the discussion questions, and test questions. Contact your Wiley sales representative for details.

The Instructor's Manual can be downloaded from the text's companion website at wiley.com/college/tesone.

ACKNOWLEDGMENTS

Thank you to the reviewers of the original proposal for this book and the reviewers of the manuscript for their insightful and helpful comments. They are:

Adekunle A. Fagade, University of Massachusetts, Amherst
Don St. Hilaire, California State Polytechnic University, Pomona
Robert Wahl, Johnson & Wales University

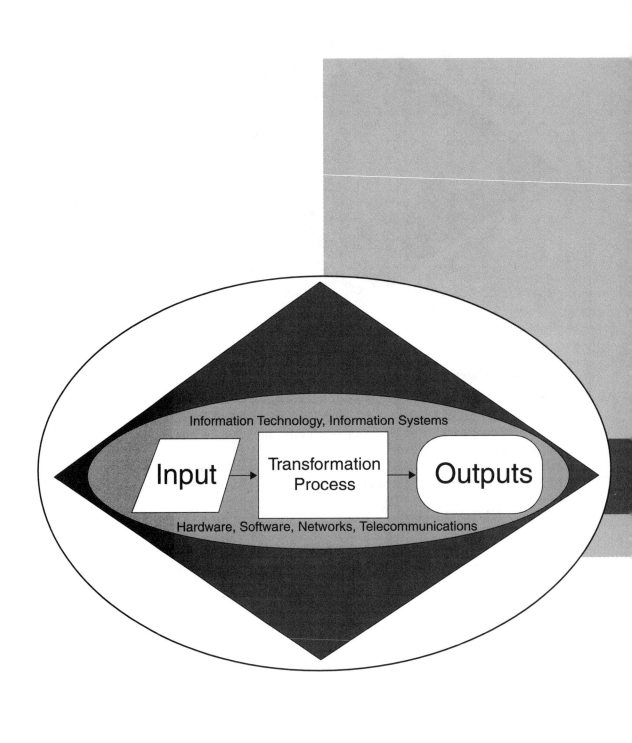

PART I

General Applications

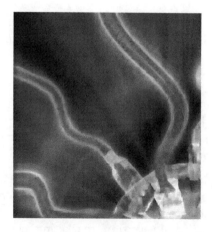

Understanding Hospitality Information Systems and Information Technology

CHAPTER OBJECTIVES

In this chapter you will learn to:

1. Describe hospitality organizations from a systems-oriented perspective.
2. Identify the components of the productivity chain in a nonlinear model.
3. Explain the relationships that constitute systems and subsystems.
4. Describe the relationship between internal and e-business processes.
5. Identify the manager's role in working with system processes.

On-the-Job Training

You are working as an intern at the corporate office of a large restaurant chain. Lately, you have been working with the chief information officer (CIO) for the firm. You are assisting the CIO with a project that identifies how the restaurant management teams have been using the technology that has been installed at each of the restaurant units (stores).

In the past the CIO campaigned vigorously to finance the installation of state-of-the-art point-of-sale (POS) systems in each restaurant. The CIO believed that the restaurant managers could use those systems as tools for administration, marketing, customer relations, management reporting, and enhanced productivity levels in each store.

The systems have been in place for about three months. Before their installation each restaurant manager was trained thoroughly in the use of each system, which handles all the internal transaction processing and has telecommunications interfaces with the Internet for automated guest and corporate office interactions.

Your task is to conduct a field study and identify the levels at which each restaurant uses each component of this interactive system.

To be continued . . .

INTRODUCTION

Information technology (IT) Hardware and software used to process information for organizations.

Information system (IS) Relationship of the IT components used to produce, store, share, and distribute information for use by the people affiliated with an organization.

This chapter introduces the concept of systems thinking as it is applied to **information technology (IT)** and **information systems (IS).** It is important for hospitality managers to understand the broad realm of systems thinking and know how to apply it to all *hospitality information systems (HIS)* and technology. This overview of systems theory provides the foundation for understanding everything you need to know about management and technology. All systems are frameworks of relationship patterns. Systems thinking provides templates that permit one to take apparently complicated concepts and simplify them. Thus, it is in every hospitality manager's interest to understand systems thinking.

UNDERSTANDING THE COMPONENTS OF SYSTEMS THEORY

Before discussing systems theory, it is appropriate to identify the role of a few of the components you will learn about in this book:

- *Theories:* A theory is an underlying principle or an explanation of something scientific or philosophical.[1] Theories explain why things happen.
- *Practices:* A practice is based on a set of theories. Thus, a practice explains how to do things, based on why things happen.
- *Tools:* A tool is something used to perform a practice. A tool is something we use to do things, whereas the things we do are based on why things happen. Table 1.1 will give you a picture of these relationships.

Theories drive practices, and practices use tools. Thus, philosophy and science give us management principles, which guide us in the practice of management. Management practices require the use of tools such as technology. Therefore, management is a practice, not a science, as some people would have you believe. Furthermore, technology is a tool that helps managers practice management, not a science or a practice, as others would have you believe. *Systems thinking* is a theory from science and philosophy that describes patterns of collaborative energy called relationships.[2] More specifically, this theory bases its findings on the hard sciences and includes computer science.[3]

Analyzing Systems Theory in General

Based on general systems theory, the management and technology systems approach views every entity as a system with interdependent parts that function as a whole.[4] Each entity is also a subsystem in relation to a larger system, and so on, throughout the universe. The outside environment does not influence **closed systems.**

Closed system An entity consisting of related parts that is not influenced by outside forces.

Table 1.1 Theory Tools		
Why Things Happen	*How Things Happen*	*What I Need to Make Things Happen*
Theory Science/philosophy	Practice Management	Tools Technology

Open system An entity consisting of related parts that is influenced by outside forces called the external environment.

The external environment of the world influences hospitality organizations, which are **open systems.** These organizations must interact constantly with the external environment for survival and evolve in order to keep up with the changes in the world around them. For instance, the Internet revolution that is occurring in today's environment influences hospitality organizations to create systems that permit electronic entry by potential guests and customers, something that was not a concern 20 years ago. Hospitality organizations that fail to respond to this situation in the external environment will find themselves at a competitive disadvantage.

A person is a biological system, as are trees, plants, and animals, which all interact with the universal laws of biology that come from the environment. If a person is a system and that person is a member of a family, then the system called "that person" is a subsystem of the family. The person is a unique and complete system, but when that person is interacting with the other people in the family unit, that relationship makes each person a subsystem of the family system. The same is true for organizations, which are composed of people, with each person being a biological system. When the people in an organization interact with others, they become subsystems of the organization: Work units, departments, and divisions divide them. The organization may be one unit in a chain of organizations, which makes it a subsystem of that chain. If the chain is in the business of providing hospitality services, that chain is part of a larger system called the hospitality industry.

What Are the Differences between Mechanistic and Organic Systems?

Subsystems, which are interrelated and reflect the whole, influence other subsystems as well as the larger system. Each subsystem plays a role that is relevant to the general system. Therefore, each part is interrelated and must take into consideration the impact of change on other subsystems and the whole system. Since the integration of all subsystems represents the general system collectively, **interdependence** is a key factor in analysis and decision making when one is planning technology systems.[5]

Interdependence The mutually beneficial relationship among systems and subsystems.

Mechanistic systems are closed systems with definitive life spans and continuously atrophy into nonexistence. An electronic computer, for instance, eventually will burn out and stop working. Environmental factors may quicken the process. For instance, if one removes the fan from a computer unit and places it in a very hot room, that computer will die a premature death. Keep the computer fan working and place it in a cool room, and the computer eventually will stop working because of wear and tear over time (the normal life span of a machine). We may use some of its components for spare parts and probably will haul the rest of the computer to the junkyard. If the computer parts are not usable, they will exist as rusty junk. Because a computer is a machine, it does not have the capacity to adapt to environmental changes. In a hostile environment it will wear out quickly and in a compatible domain it will wear out slowly, but in either case it will wear out and stop working. In addition, as a result of the rapidly developing nature of computer technology, a machine probably will become outdated before it ceases to operate. The laws of Newtonian physics explain the concept of wearing out perfectly.[6] Since energy creates heat, extreme environmental change will cause the entity to throw off more energy than it can generate until it has no more energy left (entropy). Once it runs out of energy, the parts stop working and the entity stops doing things (dies).

Organic systems have the capacity for infinite life because of their ability to evolve. For instance, a biological plant or animal will generate offspring during its lifetime and will feed the earth after the end of its biological life. During its life span the animal or plant will adapt to the environment for survival. It will pass the genetic adaptive code to the next generation, which will begin its new life as an evolved entity. The plant or animal will know that it is time to evolve when it becomes uncomfortable as a result of changes in the environment. This escalating level of discomfort will cause confusion and energy dissipation (anxiety) on the part of the plant or animal. If minor adaptations do not work, it will experience more anxiety until it thinks it is going to die. At that (bifurcation) point the plant or animal must escape the discomfort imposed by the environment. It has two choices: stay the way it is and give away the rest of its energy (entropy) or mutate into another life form (evolve). Scientists call this environmentally induced anxiety chaos.[7] Now we have conflicting conclusions—a paradox.

One scientific theory supports entropy (death), and the other supports evolution (mutation). Which one is correct? One scientist eventually came along to settle this paradox. His solution was that both death and evolution are true because of chaos.[8]

Here is the explanation. All matter, regardless of density, is composed of energy.[9] As the environment becomes more complex, mechanistic entities give off more energy than can be generated and thus atrophy into oblivion (like an overheated computer). When organic systems enter into chaos, they can expend all their energy on managing the chaos or can use some of the energy for an evolutionary escape (negentropy).[10] In the first scenario, the organic system eventually will use up all its energy and die because of the stress from the chaotic event. However, in the second scenario, the organic system has a chance to escape with some of its energy. Once the organic system escapes from the chaos, it may begin to replenish its energy. However, to do this, the entity ceases to be what it once was as it takes on a new form of "life." Either way, the plant or animal ceases to exist in its original form. It has been changed forever. If the plant or animal were able to mutate, the scientists would say that it created "new order" out of "disorder," and as a result it could be said that the mutated plant or animal died and survived at the same time.

For example, let's say there is a certain type of toad that hops on the ground and likes to eat things found on the ground. All of a sudden another animal develops a taste for these toads. The toad-eating animal is fat and slow but is quick enough to catch a toad. The next thing you know, most of the toads in the forest are disappearing. Nevertheless, the remaining toads will be very stressed out. One toad learns to climb trees and adapts her diet to things she may find in those trees. A few other toads witness this behavior and replicate it. Eventually the animals will eat the toads remaining on the ground and then will have to find something else to eat because they are not physically able to adapt to tree-climbing behavior.

A group of scientists walks into the forest and quickly determines that the ground toads are extinct. They discover, however, a new breed of tree toad that is very similar to the species that used to live on the ground. Although the scientists believe that the ground toads have died, nature knows that they have died only in their role as ground toads and that the same toads have evolved into tree toads. Therefore, they are dead yet are still alive. The conflict between the second law of thermodynamics and chaos theory has been solved.

What does this have to do with management and technology? At this point let's just say that what is good for the toad is good for the person. In addition, because organizations include people, they are organic systems. Since managers manage organizations, which are organic systems that use machines as tools, it is good for them to know how toads evolve so that they will be able to use the tools to do the same thing for organizations during times of chaos that the external environment imposes on them.

What Are Linear Systems?

Empirically, we are taught to believe what we can see. Thus, most systems that are taught to us are linear in nature, which means they are two-dimensional, with a start point on the left side and an end point on the right side. Figure 1.1 shows a linear process for management and technology processes.

The management perspective of Figure 1.1 is quite broad, whereas the technology perspective is somewhat narrow. Management inputs include all the resources that are used to create a product or service. These could be material resources, human resources, financial resources, and

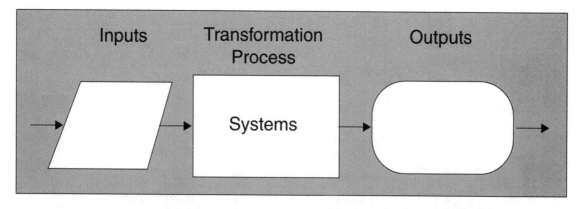

Figure 1.1 Linear Management and Technology Process

technology resources. The people, equipment, technology, and machines convert the raw materials during the transformation process. The final product or service is the output that results from that process. The output function always interfaces with a customer or guest directly. An internal customer is someone who is providing a service for a guest. The external customer is the guest. Therefore, a worker who provides products and services to another employee is serving the internal customer, and one who provides them to the guest is serving the external customer. Everyone in the organization is serving someone either internally or externally.

The more narrow technology perspective in Figure 1.1 demonstrates the process of information technology and information systems. IT is a resource consisting of hardware, software, and people. IS describes the process relationships (networks) of IT. For instance, a hotel installs a new computer system (hardware and software) at the front desk; this is an example of IT. The new system interfaces with the *property management system (PMS)* that performs many front-office and back-office functions; this interconnectivity (network) is an example of IS. Figure 1.2 provides a more detailed picture of the linear management and technology process.

Figure 1.2 shows management and technology processes in combination. In addition, there are measurements for both inputs and outputs. Inputs are measured in terms of efficiency—doing things right, or minimizing the cost of resources—and effectiveness—doing the right things, or maximizing products and services in terms of quality and quantity for guests and internal customers. If a manager continuously improves efficiency and effectiveness, she is enhancing *productivity,* which adds *value* to the organization. The organization considers a manager who is responsible for adding value to the organization a *value-added manager.* It is the prime directive for each manager to enhance productivity every day,

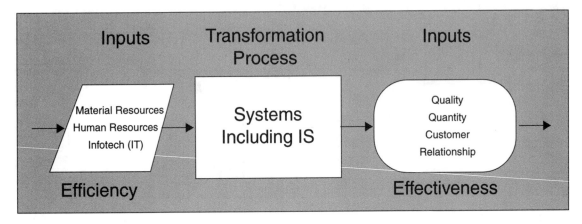

Figure 1.2 A More Detailed Picture of the Linear Management and Technology Process

which makes him a value-added manager. This activity will guarantee career success in the fields of management and entrepreneurship.

When we view Figure 1.2 from a technology perspective, it identifies resources applicable to IS processes and outcomes. In the world of IS, people, hardware, software, and networks are resources that result in data, which are converted into information (transformation process); this results in information products (useful information for members of the organization and its guests) (outcomes). This process provides a simple definition of **management information systems (MIS):** the conversion of data (more than one datum) into information for use by the members of the organization to serve its guests. In a **client/server architecture,** end users as well as information specialists provide data input as well as information; this is known as the *user interface.* Storage devices maintain outputs for use by end-user applications. The organization measures outputs in terms of quality (accuracy, timeliness, usability) and quantity (volume and accessibility).

Management information system (MIS) The conversion of data into information for use by the members of an organization to serve its guests or customers.

Client/server architecture Network configuration that permits data input and exchange by end users as well as information specialists.

Since all systems are open systems, Figure 1.2 shows a model that is surrounded by boundaries to the external environment, which influence the production system. The organization influences the management and information systems, and the outside environment influences the organization; hence, the outside environment influences management and IS functions.

Figure 1.3 identifies the organizational boundaries that invisibly drive the management and technology process. Factors in the external environment constantly influence the organizational boundaries.

The *meaning system* consists of the organizational culture, including variables such as the values, attitudes, and beliefs of shareholders, employees, and guests that constitute the unwritten norms for behavior within the organization.[11] The *learning system* is a feedback loop that

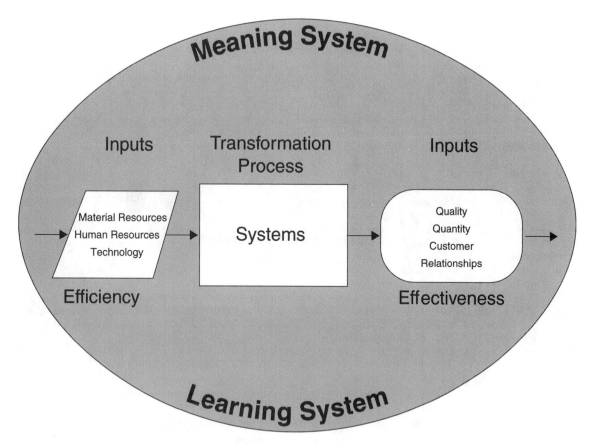

Figure 1.3 Productivity Model

converts shared experiences into knowledge that it uses to enhance productivity further. Figure 1.4 describes the learning process used to drive a *knowledge management systems (KMSs).*[12]

One classification of IS that helps accomplish organizational development objectives is called knowledge management systems. These systems use internetworked databases to access and share information regarding business and industry knowledge and techniques, such as *best practices (benchmarks)*. The demand developed by enterprises to become "learning organizations"[13] supports these benchmarks.

Evolution of Management Information Systems

The evolution of MIS, from data processing through enterprise and global networking took a more mechanical path of development than did total management practice. Although the practice of management is

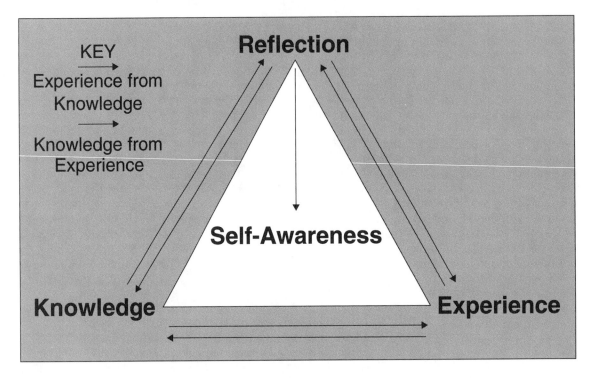

Figure 1.4 Learning Process Model

holistic, technological developments depended mostly on the evolution of electronic (mechanistic) systems. Management reporting processes evolved into *decision support systems (DSSs)* in the 1970s to provide managers with interactive access to critical information, which they manipulated on the basis of specific decision-making criteria. In the 1980s this evolved into *end-user computing,* which provided enhanced interactivity with all the members of the organization. Specialized databases for strategy and policy became available for use as *executive information systems (EISs)* in the later 1980s. Breakthroughs in *artificial intelligence (AI)* and *expert systems (ESs)* in the 1990s resulted in the presence of electronic consultants in areas of *subject matter expertise (SME).* These factors contributed to the role of *strategic information systems (SISs)* and *telecommunications* developments, which have taken us into the enterprise and global internetworking revolution. Currently, we view MIS from the standpoints of operations support systems and management support systems in organizations. Business-related IS activities remain focused on *transaction processing,* which involves interactions among support personnel, end users, and guests of hospitality organizations. Contrary to the older functions of IS, most current systems focus on collaboration networks.

TECH TALK

Advice from the Experts in Hospitality Information Systems
An interview with Jeff Taylor, Technical Manager of XS Orlando

1. **What are your position title and scope of responsibilities?**

   I currently hold the technical manager position, where I am responsible for game and facility maintenance, computer and IS systems, and POS systems, as well as general equipment maintenance.

2. **Has the nature of your work changed over the last couple of years? If yes, how so?**

   Yes, it has. Originally my job responsibilities were strictly game maintenance, computer, and IS systems, but now they have expanded to include the responsibilities listed above.

3. **What are the future prospects in terms of career opportunities for graduates with an interest in IT positions?**

   As technology changes, so will classes and certifications. Those who are studying this field will not stop learning unless they want to. The future will always continue to grow with IT positions, but some of the positions are becoming obsolete because technology has grown to be more automated. Remember, you will have to start at the bottom, but strive hard and you could make it to the top.

4. **In your opinion, should nontechnical managers have a basic knowledge of IT and IS?**

   My opinion is yes on this question. The more knowledge you have about IT and IS, the more efficient you become in your everyday job responsibilities. Learning something about computers will help you excel in your position whether it is in management or general labor.

5. **Any final words of advice or future prophecy for future technologists?**

   Continue to study the field you desire to enter and read materials from educators and writers who are in that field. Learning from those who have experience in that field of study will allow you to grow in your job and future endeavors. Don't give up; you can succeed and become a great success only if you allow it.

   Thank you, Jeff Taylor, for your time and expertise in these areas.

   _____

   A special thanks to Jesse Newton for conducting this interview with Jeff.

REVIEWING INFORMATION SYSTEMS PLANNING, ANALYSIS, AND EVALUATION

The executive-level person in charge of IT and IS for an organization is called the *chief information officer (CIO)*. In large organizations the CIO will have a staff of technology and systems managers and specialists reporting to her. Specialists include programmers, network managers, technicians, database administrators, and others with specific expertise in certain areas of technology and systems. The CIO is directly responsible for the planning, analysis, implementation, and evaluation of all technology and systems used in a hospitality organization.

Two types of planning apply to information system development in organizations. The first is *proactive planning,* which is designed to improve the systems that enhance the productivity of a hospitality corporation. The second is a *reactive planning* approach to solving a situation that is affecting the organization negatively. Whether proactive or reactive, all planning is aimed at solving organizational problems, with proactive planning focusing on future problems and reactive planning attempting to correct current problems. Since productivity components constitute the core of all problem-solving activities, the first consideration in the systems planning phase is to identify where the current or potential problem may exist in terms of inputs, transformation process, or outputs within the organization. Figure 1.5 provides a schematic that can be used to conduct this search.

Problem identification is more difficult than one would expect because organizational systems are complex. Technology managers may view as a problem an irregularity that may not be a real problem but only a symptom of a problem. For instance, one of the outputs for a system at the front desk of a hotel is the ability of the agents to check guests into the hotel. The system outputs are in the form of screens used by the desk agents to perform the check-in process. Customers may have been complaining about the time it takes to check into rooms at the hotel. The IT manager will notice that the complaints started after modifications were made to the front-desk system. Further investigation may reveal that the check-in process now requires the completion of nine screens, versus the four screens that front-desk agents used before the system change. At first glance it seems that there is an output problem that may be the fault of the IT specialists who programmed the system. After further investigation, however, it is discovered that the nine screens were designed at the request of the hotel controller to provide ease of accounting information from guest folios (which are originated at the time of check-in). Therefore, it seems that the output screens were installed intentionally,

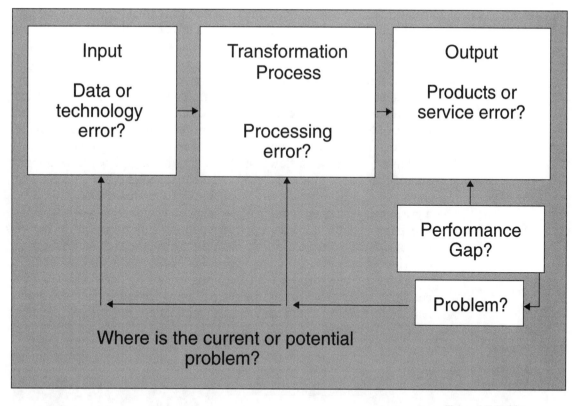

Figure 1.5 Problem Location

as opposed to being the result of a programming glitch. Hence, the outputs are *symptoms* of the real problem, which in this case is a slower check-in speed to accommodate the needs of the back office. What is the solution?

The controller may say that the guests will have to suffer because the corporate office wants the folio information. The front-office manager may say that this is unacceptable because the guests come first. Finally, the IT manager may determine that information conversion files may eliminate the need for nine different screens and still provide the folio information required by the corporate office. In this case the IT manager will assign a programmer to write the conversion files and solve the problem, resulting in faster guest check-in as well as thorough folio information for reporting purposes.

This is an example where the IT manager is faced with a reactive situation called *service recovery*. Could this service glitch have been avoided? Absolutely! If the front-office manager, the controller, and the IT manager had planned the system upgrade together, they would have recognized the conversion file solution before the upgraded system was installed at the front desk. If this had been the case, they would have implemented a proactive problem-solving approach in the first place.

Why, in our scenario, was this not the case? The answer lies in the systems thinking approach to management. There are accounting systems and front-office systems, which are subsystems of the hotel. If all the managers in this case were systems thinkers, they would have realized that the outputs of the check-in process affect the hotel in general, and this would have been cause for collaboration by representatives of all the subsystems (department managers) in the initial planning phase.

Figure 1.6 shows a flowchart for differentiating between symptoms and real problems in the IT decision-making process. All decisions affect the system of the organization. Some decisions are far-reaching and have a great impact. These decisions have a broad scope as opposed to those which have a more limited scope of influence. As managers assume more responsibility in hospitality organizations, the impact of the scope of their decisions increases.

There are two interrelated conditions in making decisions. The first condition is *complexity,* or the number of variables influencing the problem. High levels of complexity create limited amounts of total informa-

Figure 1.6 System
Investigation

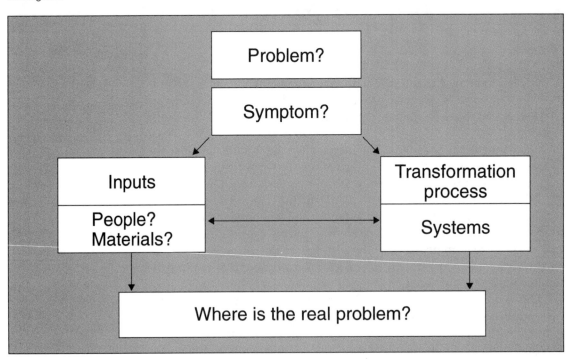

tion, or *uncertainty,* which is the second decision-making condition. Higher levels of uncertainty generate greater levels of *risk* associated with making a decision. In addition, the scope or impact of the decision will add to the level of risk.

Complexity, uncertainty, and risk are additional factors that support systems thinking in all decision-making activities in a hospitality organization. For us to take a systems approach, we must remember that a change on the micro level will affect the macro level. Therefore, as we make each decision, we must ask, "What will be the impact of the solution on the organization as a whole?"

Figure 1.7 describes the process of systems analysis. Once we identify the problem, the rest is easy: Develop *alternative solutions,* analyze the feasibility of each alternative, and select one of those alternatives for implementation. Some problems require large capital investments (computer

Figure 1.7 System Analysis

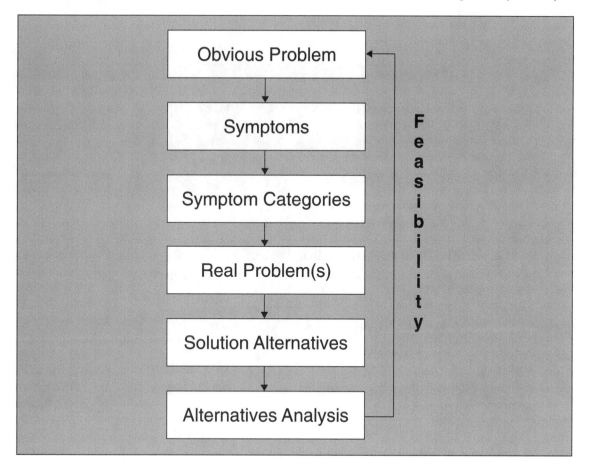

systems, for example). In these cases it may not be feasible to choose the "best" alternative solution because of cost/benefit considerations. The goal of alternative analysis is to choose the most feasible solution for the welfare of the hospitality organization.

Figure 1.8 shows a model that can be used for systems design and implementation. The two key variables are the design and maintenance stages. In computer systems, solutions always consist of a design or development aspect (usually regarding software), and maintaining the solution system is vital (especially in times of rapid technology development). The final step in the design and implementation process is to evaluate the solution in terms of efficiency (cost control) and effectiveness (quality and quantity of outputs).

Feasibility studies are used when a significant investment is required to provide an IS solution. The standard cost/benefit analysis refers to economic/organizational feasibility. Is the solution affordable, and will it help accomplish the objectives of the organization? *Technical feasibility*

Figure 1.8 System Design and Implementation

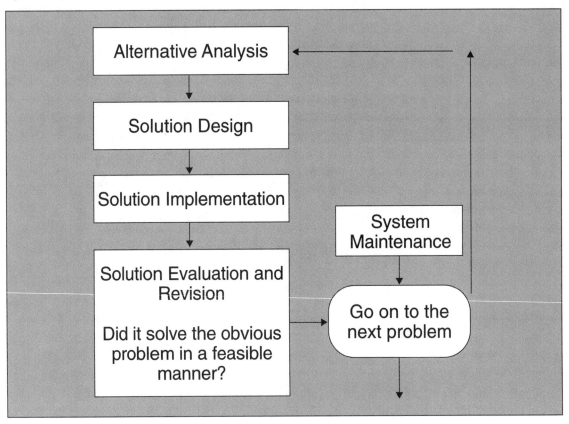

refers to the ability of hardware and software to do the job. *Operational feasibility* considers willingness from the end-user's perspective to use the system in the operations. From a cost perspective, one can calculate tangible costs easily, but it is much more difficult to quantify intangible (indirect) costs.

Systems analysis is nothing more than standard needs analysis applied to computer systems. Categories of analysis include the following:

- Information needs
- System resources
- Products
- Activities
- Capabilities of systems
- End users to get the job done

Functional requirements analysis focuses on interfaces and the processing, storage, and control aspects of the system. Systems analysis results in systems specifications for interfaces, databases, software, hardware, networks, and user skills.

On-the-Job Training . . . Continued

It has been about two weeks since you began your task of collecting information from each restaurant manager about the use of the newly installed interactive system. You started by constructing a questionnaire that you administered to each restaurant manager.

Your survey had three parts. The first part was to determine the internal use of the system for transaction processing such as sales abstracts, menu planning, cashiering functions, cost control, and other administrative functions. The second part asked the managers about the e-business applications that are part of the system. For instance, managers have access to telecommunications systems that provide automated corporate office reporting, electronic purchasing from vendors, Internet reservations from guests, advertising and e-mail capability for repeat guests, and other features used to connect the restaurant with the outside world through the Internet. The final part of your survey focused on the specific functions used by the system. These functions included accounting forms, human resources documents, energy management, and catering planning, among other functions.

You set up your report to reflect the level of use of aspects of part I, part II, and part III of your survey. After tabulating the data, you found that all the restaurants used the part I systems, half of them used the part II systems, and only 10 percent used the part III systems. Out of curiosity, you then compared success factors for each restaurant with use rates of the three-tier system. Not surprisingly, you found a positive correlation between levels of computer systems use and the success level of each restaurant.

The CIO calls you into his office after reading the report and says, "Great job on this study! It never dawned on me to compare successful outcomes with the use of our systems." He concludes; "With this information, I am convinced that we can persuade the executives to fund further computer training for our managers." "Sounds great," you reply. Then the CIO looks at you and says with a smile, "So, what are your full-time job prospects after graduation?"

SUMMARY

This chapter presented a systems view of management and technology. The linear aspect of a system consists of the visible or empirical components. Surrounding the linear system are intangible phenomena that affect the linear system. All things are systems. All systems are interrelated when they operate as subsystems of a larger system. Systems thinking requires managers to consider the impact on one subsystem as it relates to all the other interdependent systems. You should view such systems as open, as opposed to closed, systems that are "segregated." Technology consists mostly of mechanical systems, but organizations are organic systems. Organic systems possess the ability to evolve through adaptive techniques, such as learning processes. This chapter provided a brief timeline of the evolution of both management and technology, taking us to the current state of the practice of and the tools for management.

DISCUSSION QUESTIONS

1. It could be said that technology is a tool that hospitality practitioners can use to provide excellent guest services. Cite examples of how technology systems may be used to produce this outcome.
2. Organizations are systems that consist of people (workers, managers, guests, suppliers, and shareholders). With this in mind, would you say a hospitality organization is a mechanistic or an organic system? Why?
3. Use an example to describe the relationship of a theory, a practice, and tools.
4. Identify a linear model that explains management and technology processes and give examples for inputs, the transformation process, and outputs.

KEY TERMS

Alternative solutions
Artificial intelligence (AI)
Benchmarks
Best practices
Chief information officer (CIO)
Client/server architecture
Closed system

Complexity
Decision support system (DSS)
End-user computing
Executive information system (EIS)
Expert system (ES)
Feasibility studies
Hospitality Information Systems (HIS)
Information system (IS)
Information technology (IT)
Interdependence
Knowledge management system (KMS)
Learning system
Management information system (MIS)
Meaning system
Mechanistic system
Open system
Operational feasibility
Organic systems
Theory
Point-of-sale system (POS)
Practice
Proactive planning
Problem identification
Productivity
Property management system (PMS)
Tools
Reactive planning
Risk
Service recovery
Solution
Strategic information system (SIS)
Subject matter expert (SME)
Systems thinking
Technical feasibility
Telecommunications
Theory
Tools
Transaction processing
Uncertainty
User interface
Value
Value-added manager

REFERENCES

1. G. Hamel. (2002). *Leading the Revolution: How to Thrive in Turbulent Times by Making Innovation a Way of Life.* New York: Plume.
2. Gary Zukav. (1979). *The Dancing Wu Li Masters.* New York: William Morrow.
3. D. V. Tesone. (Winter 2000). Leadership and Motivating Missions: A Model for Organizations from Science Literature. *Journal of Leadership Studies.* 7(1):60–69.
4. P. M. Senge. (1990). *The Fifth Discipline: The Art and Practice of the Learning Organization.* New York: Doubleday.
5. Ibid.
6. F. Capra. (1996). *The Web of Life: A New Scientific Understanding of Living Systems.* New York: Anchor.
7. J. Gleick. (1987). *Chaos: Making a New Science.* New York: Viking.
8. I. Prigogine. (1997). *The End of Certainty: Time, Chaos, and the New Laws of Nature.* New York: Free Press.
9. E. Mitchell. (1996). *The Way of the Explorer: An Apollo Astronaut's Journey through the Material and Mystical Worlds.* New York: Putnam.
10. Capra. (1996).
11. M. J. Wheatley. (1994). *Leadership and the New Science: Learning about Organizations from an Orderly Universe.* Oxford, UK: Berret-Koehler.
12. D. V. Tesone. (2002). *Management and Technology for the Hospitality Industry: Higher Tech for Higher Touch.* Boston: Pearson–Prentice–Hall.
13. M. C. Lohman. (2002). Ten Steps to a Learning Organization. *Human Resource Development Quarterly.* 13(3):243–252.

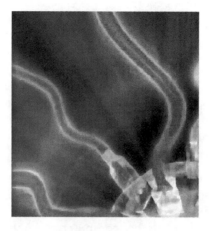

2

Computer Hardware for Hospitality

CHAPTER OBJECTIVES

In this chapter you will learn to:

1. Recognize computer units as self-contained systems.
2. Identify components used for computer input functions.
3. Identify components used for computer output functions.
4. Identify components used for computer storage.
5. Identify components used for computer peripheral connections.

On-the-Job Training

You are working as an intern at a large resort hotel. For the last two weeks you have been assigned to the accounting department to learn various functions. Most of your work assignments have been performed on computers used by accounting clerks. You have noticed that these machines are a bit slower than the ones you used at school, but they still get the job done.

The controller calls you into the office and asks you to input a number of budget revisions. She tells you that she will be in meetings all day and invites you to use the computer in her office. As she leaves the office, you boot up her computer and notice that the screens come up in a flash. You then access the spreadsheet file for budgets and start to work. As you are working, you say to yourself, "This is the fastest machine I have ever used." You wonder why there is such a difference in processing speed between the different computers in the offices.

Later the same day you are having lunch with one of the clerical workers, Kim, and mention your observation about the differences between the machines. Kim smiles and says, "New computers are distributed to individuals based on the level of their positions with the resort." She continues: "The controller is part of upper management and gets the newest machines that are available, while those of us in the clerical ranks use the oldest and slowest machines. By the time a machine gets to our level, it is already five years old and out of date compared with what is currently on the market." She notes: "The speed of the computer is all in the processor. We are using Pentium II processors, while the executives have the newest versions, beyond Pentium IV." She concludes by saying, "The newer the machine, the faster the processor, which means real quick movement among screens and tasks."

Upon hearing this, you think, "Why would the people who use the computers the most have the slowest and oldest machines?"

To be continued . . .

INTRODUCTION

This chapter provides an overview of computer hardware. In some cases, this information is a review of more basic courses, and so the chapter will move quickly through these topics to provide a refresher for readers' memory. For other readers this is a first look at the components used in computing systems. Regardless, all the components discussed here are used in hospitality and tourism organizations to convert data into information. Since all computers are integrated systems, computer hardware components can serve three functions: input, processing, and output (Figure 2.1).

COMPUTER HARDWARE CLASSIFICATIONS

There are three major categories of computers that range in size from largest to smallest:

- Mainframe computers
- Midrange computers
- Microcomputers

People who use computers are referred to as **end users.** Most end users work and play on **microcomputers.** For instance, a personal computer on your desk at home is a desktop microcomputer. A portable

End users Individuals who use computers for work or play.

Microcomputers Small, self-contained computers that include desktops, laptops (notebooks), and personal digital assistants (PDAs).

Figure 2.1 Computer System Model

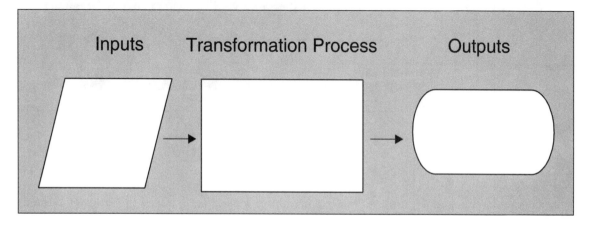

Inputs   Transformation Process   Outputs

A. Laptops are common types
of personal computers.
(Courtesy of PhotoDisc. Inc.)

B. PDAs are common types of
personal computers.
(Courtesy of PhotoDisc, Inc.)

computer is a laptop or notebook microcomputer. Some individuals prefer to use a palmtop machine, which is called a *personal digital assistant* (PDA) and falls within the category of a handheld microcomputer. Thus, most end users use microcomputers as individual machines or as part of a network connected to other computers. With networks, a person may access information that is stored on midrange and mainframe computers through connections with a microcomputer.

Consider a scenario in which you use your microcomputer to access the Internet. In this case you are running through a few servers that use midrange computers to access many databases that reside on mainframe computers. **Mainframe computers** are used mostly for data storage and database transactions. They are the largest machines in the three categories. **Midrange computers** are smaller than mainframes but larger than microcomputers and usually act as servers to some network (including the Internet) or operate as workstations to perform specific functions that require high-powered calculation and artistic functions.

When midrange computers are used as servers, they are linking your computer to a network of other computers. Midrange computers also may be used as stand-alone machines for specialized functions such as computer-aided manufacturing (CAM) and *computer-aided design (CAD)*. These functions are best handled by midrange computers that are called workstations because of the computing power required to perform the tasks related to this type of processing. A **workstation** is a highly specialized midrange computer used for complex high-power functions. Figure 2.2 shows the computers in each category.

Mainframe computer
The largest category of computer; used mostly for data storage and large-volume transactions.

Midrange computers
Midsize computers used as network servers and as workstations to perform specialized high-powered functions.

Workstation Highly specialized midrange computer used for high-power functions such as CAD, CAM, and computer animation applications.

Mainframe computers are the largest type of computer and are used primarily for data storage. (Courtesy Corbis Digital Stock.)

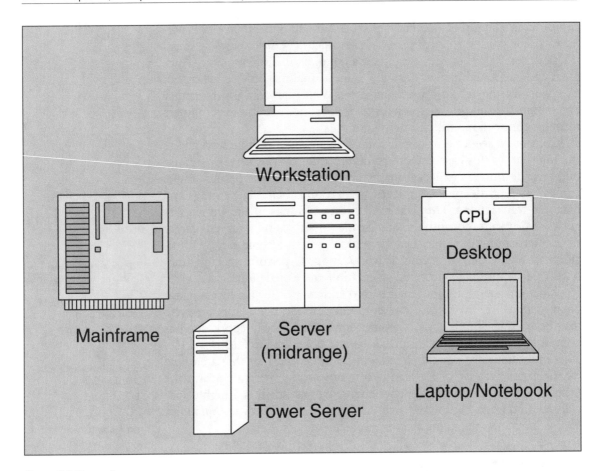

Workstation

CPU

Desktop

Mainframe

Server (midrange)

Tower Server

Laptop/Notebook

Figure 2.2 Types of Computer Hardware

Processor A silicon chip that converts data into information.

Stand-alone machines Computers that are not connected to a network of other computers.

Dumb terminals Monitors used to enter data and read information from a mainframe computer.

Before the late 1980s personal computers were novelty machines that had little real utility in terms of application programs. In business organizations, documents were constructed on specialized word processor machines made by the Wang Corporation in those days. The processors in personal computers before the late 1980s were very slow, resulting in limited calculation and computation capabilities. A **processor** is the silicon chip that converts data into information. It was the development of the 8600 series of processors that caused these **stand-alone machines** to be used in homes and offices as a result of the quicker processing speeds of these chips.

Before the 8600 series processors became popular in personal computers, businesses used mainframe systems with **dumb terminals** (monitors used to enter data and read information) attached to them to process information. Although the mainframes were quite powerful for those times, end users were restricted to using only the functions that were programmed for them by the mainframe operators. The 8600 series processor gave end users the power to manipulate their own data via databases, spreadsheets, and word-processing programs, and this eliminated their reliance on mainframe programmers. Unlike today's generation of computers, personal computer (PC) users in the 1980s needed to be competent in text-based DOS commands and function keys to operate applications on their machines.

Today personal computers are used by most people. As was discussed previously, these computers include desktop, notebook, and palmtop models. Most individuals are familiar with traditional laptop models, which are integrated units that are designed to be portable. Although the laptop originally was used only for traveling, there seems to be a movement toward using these computers as primary machines at home in place of traditional desktop models. This is due to the enhanced computing power and capability contained in these compact models. Some users purchase "docking stations" for home laptop use, which provide connections to a number of peripherals that normally would be hooked into a desktop machine. The typical laptop or notebook weighs an average of six pounds, with a flip-up monitor and a standard-size keyboard. Recent developments have introduced the tablet laptop, which enables the user to write with an electronic pen on the computer screen. These machines appeal to individuals who find handheld keyboards too small for easy use. Tablet laptops also are called digital clipboards and weigh about three pounds, with a thinner and smaller design than that of a typical notebook computer. This machine is intended for users who prefer something between a laptop and a palmtop.

Some individuals engaged in mobile computing and communications use personal digital assistants. The future of the PDA will be phenomenal, especially as it becomes integrated with cell phones. This blend of computing and communications will be our major source of interfacing with each other and with most commercial institutions in the next few years. This wave of technological advancement will be referred to as **telephony,** which is the blending of telephone and computing technology.[1] Figure 2.3 shows the evolution of personal computing technology from the early to the current stages of development. Notice that disks and RAM are measured in units called bytes (a concept discussed in detail later in this chapter) and that processing speeds are measured in *hertz units.*

Old PCs were text-based, using the operating system called Disk Operating System (DOS). In the early 1990s, computers gained popularity with the general public after the development of **graphical user interfaces (GUIs)** such as Windows and Apple, which are now the dominant operating systems. Graphical user interfaces are templates linked to the operating system of the computer that provide "point-and-click" navigation to access the machine's applications and utilities. The

Telephony A blending of telephone and computing technology.

Graphical user interfaces (GUIs) Templates linked to the operating system of the computer that provide point-and-click navigation to access the machine's applications and utilities.

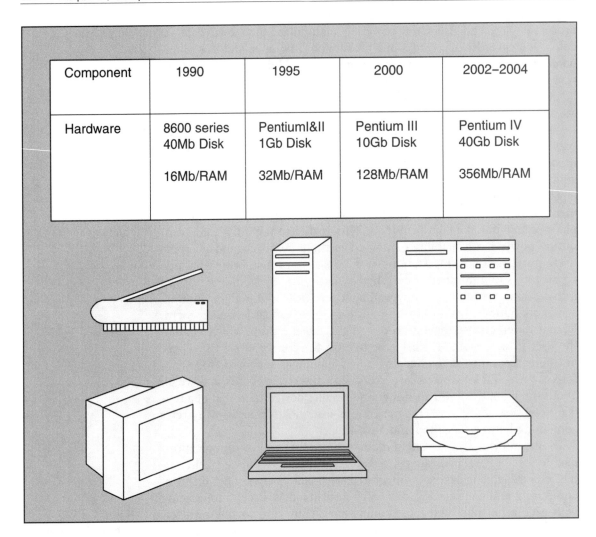

Component	1990	1995	2000	2002–2004
Hardware	8600 series 40Mb Disk 16Mb/RAM	PentiumI&II 1Gb Disk 32Mb/RAM	Pentium III 10Gb Disk 128Mb/RAM	Pentium IV 40Gb Disk 356Mb/RAM

Figure 2.3 The Evolution of Personal Computing Technology

invention of GUIs, along with advance in chip technology and telecommunications, has created demand for multimedia capabilities, which provide for sound, graphics, and animation features that are commonly used on modern personal computers.

Peripherals Hardware components that are attached to computers.

Cameras, video camcorders, DVD /MPEG players, and optical scanners are becoming popular **peripherals,** or hardware components that are attached to computers. Table 2.1 lists hardware components that are part of the regular computer system and those which are considered peripheral hardware units.

A close-up of a RAM memory chip. (Courtesy of PhotoDisc. Inc.)

Some cost-conscious home PC users are opting for low-cost **network computers (NCs)** designed exclusively for use on the Internet. The old dumb terminals hooked to mainframes have been replaced with fully operational personal computers for all end users in business locations.

Network computers (NCs) Personal computers with limited internal components designed exclusively for using the Internet.

Table 2.1 System and Peripheral Hardware Components

Component	System	Peripheral
Keyboard	XX	
Monitor	XX	
Central processing unit	XX	
Microphone	XX	XX
Internal CD/DVD	XX	
External CD/DVD		XX
Internal modem	XX	
External modem		XX
Mouse	XX	
Digital camera with connector		XX
Digital Midi Synthesizer		XX
Printer		XX
Scanner		XX

Although the power of personal computing has advanced tremendously, the real power still lies within the mainframe computer, which is what we access on the Internet. In most business enterprises, end users work on PCs that are networked with midrange and mainframe computers. State-of-the-art mainframes (used in defense, research, and megacorporations) are called supercomputers. They use state-of-art parallel processing architectures and interconnected microprocessors to achieve the phenomenal processing speeds needed to manipulate the huge amounts of data that result in complicated information outcomes. Advances in processor technology are being applied to midrange computers and microcomputers as well. Regardless of the type of machine being used, there are three aspects that concern the user. First, the user requires a means to input data that later will be converted into usable information. Second, the machine performs transformation processes that manipulate the data into formats for later use. Third, the user sends the information to the output area for review and revision.

INPUT DEVICES

Input devices Instruments used to enter data into a computer, such as a keyboard.

Central processing unit (CPU) The collection of boards, chips, and cards that process information.

Input devices are used to put data into the machine. These devices include the keyboard, mouse, touch screen, pen, optical scanner, microphone, and camera. Processing is done by the **central processing unit (CPU),** which performs the transformation of data into information within the computer. Keyboards consist of alphanumeric characters that are converted to binary ASCII code to allow data to enter into the storage areas of the computer for later processing into information. For instance, a person may type a letter in a word processor and send the letter through a network to another digital location. A mouse is a pointing device that is used to identify items on a monitor that are sent to the same storage areas for manipulation. A user may receive an attachment through electronic mail and elect to save it to a disk by using the point-and-click features of a mouse. *Touch screens* provide the same functions as a mouse, except that they permit individuals to press prearranged items on a monitor. A restaurant input machine may use this for servers to enter menu items into the CPU for transmission to the culinary staff. Electronic pens, also known as styluses, are used to write characters on an input pad for processing into printed words, as is commonly done on PDAs to take notes. *Optical scanners* convert printed data into information for storage and later output from a computer. There are various applications for scanner technology, ranging from digitizing printed documents by using *optical character recognition (OCR)* software, to barcode readers that are used to ring up retail items, to magnetic stripe readers for credit card processing, as well as infrared scanners for security applications. Microphones are used as input devices to convert sounds into a digital format. A person may record a message or a song from a tape player into

Electronic pens frequently are used with PDAs and other input pads. (Courtesy of PhotoDisc, Inc.)

Magnetic stripes are used commonly with POS systems. (Courtesy of PhotoDisc, Inc.)

a digital file that may be played as sounds on a computer. Cameras are used to input visual data into a computer for future editing and for distribution from one computer to another.

Other applications provided by input devices include optical scanning using OCR technology with handheld wands or desktop scanners. Forms, invoices, credit cards, airline tickets, and other documents are scanned into databases and billing, sorting, and other functions through the use of these input devices. *Magnetic stripes* are used commonly on point-of-sale (POS) systems and automatic teller machines (ATMs). *Smart cards* contain information embedded on microprocessor chips attached to cards and are read by processing machines. Mobile transponders are used to send and receive information to a central processor from remote locations. Additional input devices include the *magnetic ink character recognition (MIRC)* technology used in banking to convert printed drafts into digital formats. Figure 2.4 shows a number of input and output devices attached to a processing unit.

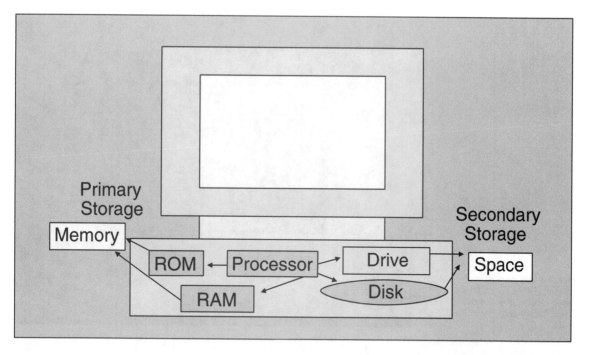

Figure 2.4 Processing Unit Input and Output Devices

OUTPUT DEVICES

Output devices include *video display units (monitors)*, printers, and audio output units, among others. Individuals often confuse computer monitors and other digital *display* panels with input devices, because as soon as they input data, the data are displayed as information. In actuality, the user inputs the data into the CPU for processing, and the output in the form of information appears on the screen. The process is so fast that the user is fooled into thinking the information is being sent directly to the monitor, but this is not the case.

In most cases a display unit such as a monitor, also known as a *liquid crystal display (LCD)* unit in modern screens, is the first level of output for the user and often is followed by forwarding that output to a printer to create a "hard-copy" document. Printer technology has advanced at a somewhat slower rate than have computers, with many users still using *inkjet printers.* An inkjet printer accesses cartridges containing ink to apply characters onto paper to produce printed pages. Before the introduction of the inkjet printer, dot-matrix printers performed the same function by indenting characters through an ink ribbon onto a page, much the way typewriters used to work. A faster form of printing technology is the *laser*

Output device A unit that displays processed information.

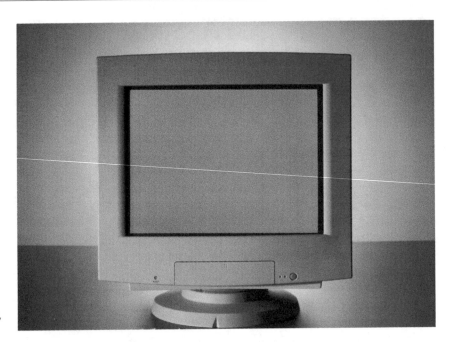

A computer monitor is an output device but often is perceived as an input device. (Courtesy of PhotoDisc, Inc.)

printer, which embeds characters in a fashion similar to that of a copy machine. Although the cost of laser printers has been reduced in recent years, they remain expensive alternatives to inkjet printers, especially if the user requires color printing of hard-copy documents.

There are cases in which portable storage devices also may serve as output units in that the user may distribute copies of the stored files to other users. These devices include *floppy diskettes,* compact disks (CDs), and digital videodisks (DVDs). Floppy electromagnetic disks are 3¼ inches in width and are used to record up to 2 megabytes of data on a drive that is commonly referred to as the A drive. Compact disks and DVDs are used in laser drives, which employ a mechanism different from that in a magnetic drive. Originally, CDs contained read only memory and thus were referred to as CD-ROMs. In those days, a specialized machine called a CD burner was required to write to a compact disk. The advancement of **write once, read many (WORM)** technology has made it possible for all users to place data on compact disks. A further enhancement called the **digital videodisk (DVD)** provides users with digitized video and audio recordings that have replaced videotape technology.

Most computers now come packaged with disk drives that enable compact disk read and write (CD/W/R) capability as well as DVD player functions. As you can see, floppy disks and CD drives may be used to share files with other users, which makes them output units. However,

Write once, read many (WORM) Drives on a personal computer that have the ability to write data onto a compact disk.

Digital videodisks (DVDs) Video and audio compact disks read by lasers; have replaced videotape media.

CDs are both output units
and storage devices.
(Courtesy of PhotoDisc, Inc.)

their primary intended use is to store data for future use, which makes
them storage devices.

STORAGE DEVICES

Storage falls into two categories: primary and secondary.

Primary Storage

Primary storage is called memory and is coded onto chips that are in the
CPU. **Read only memory (ROM)** is coded into a memory chip and runs
the computer. ROM is permanent memory that cannot be changed once
it is coded. **Random access memory (RAM)** operates application programs. RAM is temporary memory; it is used during an application, and
when that application is terminated or when the machine is turned off,
the RAM is cleared. Since RAM runs application programs, more complicated programs require higher levels of RAM. For instance, a word-
processing software program uses little RAM, whereas a presentation
program or a photo editing program requires large amounts of RAM.
When a user is working on a newly installed application and finds that the
computer is freezing up in the middle of a task, the problem is usually an
insufficient amount of RAM. In addition, the key differentiating factor

Primary storage Machine
memory that is coded
onto silicon chips within
the CPU.

**Read only memory
(ROM)** Permanently
stored memory that han-
dles the machine functions
of a computer.

**Random access memory
(RAM)** Temporarily stored
memory that operates ap-
plication programs.

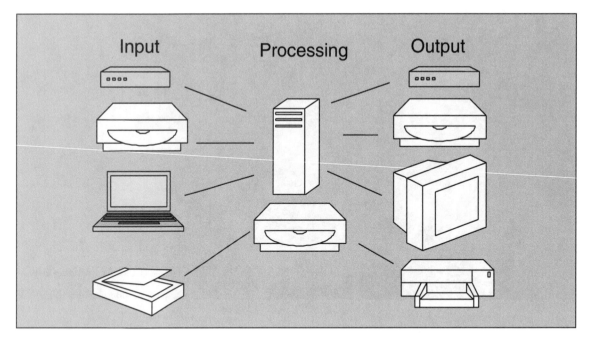

Figure 2.5 Primary and Secondary Storage Locations

between primary and secondary storage consists of the measurement units. "Memory" levels measure primary storage, whereas secondary storage is measured by "space." It would be inappropriate to say, "I am out of memory on my hard disk." Why? A disk does not have memory; it only has space. It would be appropriate to say, "There is not enough memory to run this application," because RAM is memory and does run application software programs. Figure 2.5 shows primary and secondary storage locations in a microcomputer.

Secondary Storage

The most commonly used storage units are referred to as secondary storage devices. These devices include disks and tapes. Before we describe these storage units, we must discuss how the data are categorized within these devices, as well as within primary storage devices. The smallest data element that may be stored is called a *bit* (binary digit). A *byte* contains a group of related data in 7- or 8-bit units. Storage capacities are measured in the following hierarchy: *kilobytes (KB), megabytes (MB) gigabytes (GB), terabytes (TB),* and *petabytes*. A metric KB is equal to 1,024 bits, with a megabyte being equal to about 1 million bytes, a gigabyte equaling 1 billion, a terabyte equating 1 trillion bytes, and a petabyte equaling about 1 quadrillion bytes. Figure 2.6 shows the hierarchy of storage categories.

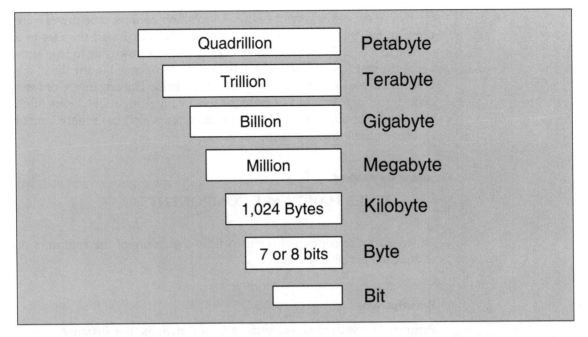

Quadrillion	Petabyte
Trillion	Terabyte
Billion	Gigabyte
Million	Megabyte
1,024 Bytes	Kilobyte
7 or 8 bits	Byte
	Bit

Figure 2.6 Hierarchy of Storage Categories

Direct storage media and magnetic disks are considered direct access storage devices (DASDs); once the data are stored, they may be accessed individually from their assigned location. Other storage media, such as tape, are limited to sequential access, which means the data may be accessed only in the order in which they were stored. Hence, *magnetic tape* is known as a sequential access device.

The most popular type of magnetic storage is on the main disk of the computer, which is referred to as the hard drive or C drive. Users access this drive to such an extent that it is considered a primary storage unit, although it is secondary storage in reality. The hard drive disk is indexed into sectors of storage; this is why users may use the hard drive as a DASD. Modern personal computers usually possess hard drive space that is measured in gigabytes. Most machines possess at least 40 gigabytes of hard drive storage space. When a computer "crashes," it usually means that the hard drive has become incapacitated. The computer will no longer function once a crash has occurred because the program that runs the computer, the operating system, is stored on the hard drive. Other programs, such as utilities and applications, also reside on the hard drive. Additionally, users may choose to save data files created through applications to folders that exist on the hard drive, such as "My Documents" in a Windows-based system.

Before the development of drives with laser readers, tape drives were popular. For instance, a computer user would back up all the files in a system to a tape drive. As has been mentioned, the downside to tape storage is the restriction of sequential file access, as opposed to the direct access made available by magnetic and laser disks. The advantage of laser disks is the large amount of storage capacity on a single CD. Users often save smaller groups of files to floppy diskettes, which have more limited storage capacity than do compact disks.

OTHER HARDWARE COMPONENTS

Other hardware components exist within the casing of the computer or as attached peripherals.

Peripherals

Modem (modulator/de-modulator) Used to convert communication signals from digital to analog and back to digital.

Peripherals are used to perform various functions. For instance, a user may want to use a computer to go onto the Internet. To do this, the computer must be linked with the outside world. One way to do this is through a telephone line. The problem with telephone lines is that they communicate via analog signals, which are sound waves. Computers are digital, meaning that they communicate via electronic impulses. Thus, for a computer to communicate on the Internet through a phone line, it is necessary to convert the digital computer signal to an analog signal and then reconvert it to a digital signal when it reaches another computer. The hardware device that accomplishes this task is called a **modem,** which stands for *modulator/dem*odulator. A modem is usually located within the casing of a computer.

However, external modems may be connected to computers as peripherals to accomplish the same task. Other types of modems may be used to access the Internet through cable and dedicated digital phone lines, providing communications at greater speeds than those achieved through ordinary phone lines. A cable modem is used for communications over a television cable line, whereas a digital subscriber line (DSL) modem is used for dedicated digital lines owned by the phone company.

Internal Components

If we look at the components that reside inside the computer casing, we will see boards, chips, and cards. The main board that runs the computer is the motherboard, which contains the electronic components that are essential for computer processing. There are smaller boards called cards in the casing to perform various functions. For instance, a person who uses wireless communication devices will find an Ethernet card inside the computer. Cards also are inserted for peripherals such as scanners. Cards are inserted into the computer and connect to a slot on the exterior of the machine; these slots are called ports.

External Components

The tip of the cable designed to fit a port is called a connector. For instance, a port may exist on the outside of the computer to connect it to a printer. There are two types of ports used for this purpose. One has 26 holes and is designed for a printer cable with a connector that has the same number of pins (a parallel connection). If the slot contains a wide space for a connector with an equally wide protrusion, this is referred to as a serial connection. Each type is a different standard for accomplishing the same task: to connect the computer to a peripheral such as a printer. If we went to a computer store to buy a printer cable, we would tell the salesperson that we are looking for cable with a 26-pin parallel connector.

Other ports of various sizes exist on the exterior of the computer for connections to peripherals such as scanners, microphones, and monitors. The most advanced form of connection is the universal serial bus (USB) port. This is a thin slot designed to be connected by an equally thin and narrow serial connector. The advantage of these ports is the instant recognition of the attached peripheral by the computer. This type of connection is so advanced that users may connect a peripheral while the computer is turned on and begin to use that device without having to turn the computer off and on again in a process called rebooting. The process of adding an item to the computer while it is turned on is called hot linking.

On-the-Job Training . . . Continued

After working in the accounting office for one month you were assigned to the human resources office, where you are working as part of your internship. Having worked alongside most of the clerks, you notice that their computers seem much faster and more modern than those used by the accounting clerks.

This morning the human resources director asks you into his office for a briefing on a new project. He says, "This is great opportunity for you to learn how we do succession planning strategies." He advises: "All you have to do is enter the projections from our forecast into these templates, and the computer will do the rest of the work." As he is briefing you, you wonder, "If the clerks' machines are fast, I'll bet this machine is state of the art." The director leaves you in his office to complete your project on his computer.

When the director returns, he takes you to lunch in the employee cafeteria. After some chitchat you mention to him, "You know, I did a project on the controller's computer, and it was really a fast machine. When I worked on your computer, I noticed it was slower than the ones the accounting clerks use." You conclude: "I thought new computers were allocated by organizational rank. Don't you rank very high?" The director laughs at your conclusion and responds, "Well, they do give me the newest machines, but I pass them along to my clerical staff, since they do all the data-processing work. I just use my computer for e-mail and such, and an old machine suits me just fine." "Don't get me wrong," he continues. "I would love a new machine, but my workers can be more productive with the ones we have, so I will wait for the next new one to be allocated." As the director is telling you this, you think to yourself, "Wow, this guy must be a really good leader."

SUMMARY

This chapter identified the hardware components that constitute a computer. A computer is a self-contained system of parts that provide for inputs, transformation processes, and outputs. The purpose of the system is to convert data into information. The three categories of computers are used primarily for different functions. The largest category is the main-frame computer, which is used for data storage and database transaction processes. Midrange computers are used as network servers and work-stations, which produce highly complex and specialized functions. Most people use microcomputers, the smallest type, which include desktop, laptop, and handheld computers. The common term used for microcomputers is personal computers, since individuals use them in homes and offices.

The most common input component is the keyboard, although there are other means of inputting data, including microphones, cameras, and scanners. Output devices include monitors and printers. Certain components serve primarily as storage devices but also may be used for output. These components include floppy diskettes and compact disks.

Floppy diskettes are considered storage devices since they are used to save information on electromagnetic disks via the A drive in the machine. The same is true with compact disks, except that storage device is written and read by lasers. The hard drive is the primary form of secondary storage in that all programs and utilities and many files exist on this electromagnetic disk, which is a permanent part of the computer. Primary storage resides on silicon chips in the form of read only memory, which contains the code for machine operation, and random access memory, which is temporary memory used to run application programs. The chips and the hard disk are located within the casing of the computer.

Other components inside the computer include boards containing electronic chips and conductors, with the motherboard containing the "brain" of the machine. Cards are electronic circuits that connect to ports, which are visible on the outside of the computer casing. Cards drive peripheral components through cables that connect to the ports.

All the tangible items that constitute a computer are referred to as hardware. Intangible code constitutes computer software, which is the topic of Chapter 3.

DISCUSSION QUESTIONS

1. If a computer is a system, it must consist of more than one part. How many parts are there in a computer system? What are they called? Give examples of the components used for each part of the system.
2. The specifications for a given computer reads as follows:

   - 2.00-GHz processor with a 40GB hard drive
   - 512 MB of RAM
   - 15-inch diagonal display
   - DVD/CD-RW multifunction drive

   Name the component identified by each specification and the meaning of each specification pertaining to the respective component.

3. You decide to add a printer as a peripheral for your home computer. You notice that you do not have a cable to connect the printer to the computer. How would you determine the right specification for your cable, and how would you describe it to the salesperson at the computer store?

KEY TERMS

Arithmetic-logic unit
Bits
Bytes
CAD
CD-RW
Central processing unit (CPU)
Computer hardware
Computer terminals
Digital cameras
Digital videodisk (DVD)
Display
Dumb terminals
End user
Floppy
Graphical user interface (GUI)
Hertz
Inkjet printers
Input devices
Kilobytes, megabytes, gigabytes, terabytes, petabytes
Laser printers
Liquid crystal display (LCD)
Magnetic disks
Magnetic ink character recognition (MIRC)
Magnetic stripe
Magnetic tape
Mainframe computers
Main microprocessor
Microcomputers
Midrange computers
Modem (modulator/demodulator)
Network computers (NCs)
Network servers
Network terminals
Optical character recognition (OCR)
Optical scanning

Output device
Pen-based computing
Peripherals
Personal digital assistant (PDA)
Pointing devices
Primary storage processor
Processor
Random access memory (RAM)
Read only memory (ROM)
Smart cards
Speech recognition
Stand-alone machines
Storage
Telephony
Touch pad
Touch screens
Trackball
Transaction terminals
Very Large Scale Integration (VLSI secondary storage on chips)
Video displays
Video monitors
Wands
Workstations
Write once, read many (WORM)

REFERENCES

1. G. Gilder. (2000). *Telecosm: How Infinite Bandwidth Will Revolutionize Our World.* New York: Simon & Schuster.

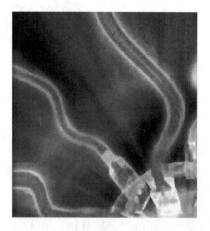

C H A P T E R

3

Computer Software for Hospitality

CHAPTER OBJECTIVES

In this chapter you will learn to:

1. Identify the basic functions of various application programs.

2. Understand the basic structure and hierarchy in database programs.

3. Become familiar with the basic functions of computer operating systems.

4. Comprehend the functions of business application software.

On-the-Job Training

You are working as a supervisor in the reservations office of a large cruise line. The director calls you into her office to discuss a pending project. When you arrive at the office, the director offers you a seat and begins to describe what she has in mind. "We have an opportunity before us," she begins. "If we can convince the executive managers that a new reservation system will enhance our productivity, they will give us the capital funds to acquire state-of-the-art hardware and software." "Sounds interesting," you reply. "But how can I help with this?"

"Well," she says, "you are one of our new 'stars,' and since you are fresh out of college, I figure you have the computer skills to put together a really dynamic report and presentation." She continues: "I'll provide you with all the information you need. All you have to do is create the documents and slides for us to present to the big bosses. It has to be a real WOW type of presentation." She concludes: "I'll work along with you every step of the way and get someone to handle your usual duties while we work on the project. I would do the whole thing myself, but I just don't know how to use this newfangled computer stuff. I have seen your reports, and I know you can handle this presentation. But this is a voluntary project; it's up to you if you want to do this."

After considering the offer for a few minutes, you look at the director and say, "Count me in. I'll even show you how to use the latest software as we work through the project." She gives you a look of relief and responds, "Great! I'll make the arrangements, and we can start on this first thing tomorrow."

To be continued . . .

INTRODUCTION

Computer software The term used to describe the code that permits a computer to perform a number of functions as required by the end user.

While computer hardware consists of tangible components—things that can be seen and felt—**computer software** provides for the intangible workings of a computer. *Computer software* is the term used to describe the code that permits a computer to perform a number of functions as required by the end user.

Code consists of programmed instructions for performing computer functions. The code for primary storage devices such as ROM and RAM is integrated by the manufacturer into the development of the chips that reside in the computer. For all other functions, **computer programmers** write software instructions by using programming languages to establish the codes that reside on magnetic or compact disks.

Most users are familiar with one set of computer programs called **application programs.** These programs are software packages designed to perform functions required by end users. There are two major categories of application programs.

Most packages for personal computers are referred to as **general-purpose application programs** because they perform generic functions that can be used for a number of different outcomes. For instance, a word-processing program is designed to permit users to create documents. It may be used to write letters, memorandums, and reports; make certificates; create forms; or generate any other type of document. Hence, the application results in the creation of documents, whereas the specific type of document created is up to the computer user, and this makes the purpose of the program general in nature.

Although most commonly used application programs are for general purposes, there is a second category known as **application-specific programs.** These programs are specialized for single-purpose use, such as computer animation and computer-aided design (CAD). Although these programs are used extensively on midrange computers designed to function as workstations, certain application-specific programs are designed for use on personal computers as well. For instance, all computers require specialized software to manage the operations of the system.

Some software manufacturers bundle a number of software applications into packages that are referred to as **software suites.** For instance, Microsoft Corporation sells a suite called Windows Office, which consists of Word, Excel, Access, and PowerPoint general-purpose application programs. Although most users would not use all of these programs, they purchase the suite of programs, which is less costly than buying two or more application packages separately. Some users, especially those in commercial enterprises, prefer to customize the bundling of application programs, which is not an option when one is purchasing a software suite. Those users often opt for **integrated software packages,** which facilitate the inclusion of specific application programs in a single purchase. An example of this practice would be a hotel that bundles Lotus 1-2-3 spreadsheet (numerical applications) with Lotus Notes (communications software) for users at the property. Table 3.1 lists popular general-purpose application programs.

Code Programmed instructions for performing computer functions.

Computer programmers Individuals who write code for computer instructions, using program languages.

Application programs Software packages designed to perform functions required by end users.

General-purpose application program An application program that performs generic functions that may be used for a number of different outcomes by the end user.

Application-specific programs Software programs designed for single-purpose use.

Software suites Bundled packages consisting of various software applications.

Integrated software packages Customized bundling of compatible software applications.

Table 3.1 Popular Application Programs	
Application	*Products*
Word processors	Microsoft Word, WordPerfect
Spreadsheets	Lotus 123, Microsoft Excel
Databases	FoxPro, D-Base, Microsoft Access
Presentation	Microsoft PowerPoint and Publisher
Electronic mail	Outlook, Yahoo!, Hotmail, ISPs
Web page design	Dreamweaver, FrontPage
Multimedia	Macromedia Director and Flash

WORD-PROCESSING PROGRAMS

Perhaps the most commonly used general-purpose application program is the word processor. The two most popular personal computer versions of *word-processing* packages are Word for Windows by Microsoft and WordPerfect by Corel Corporation. The evolution of electronic word processing began with the typewriter, which was used to imprint letters directly onto a page of paper. Although typewriters produced printed documents, each one was created from scratch as there was no storage component on those machines. In addition, typewriters required proficient keyboarding skills because typing errors were printed directly onto the paper page, requiring backspacing with corrective tape and reprinting over the error.

The first electronic/disk processing machine was the Wang word processor that was introduced in the late 1970s. Those exclusive-use machines provided individuals with the ability to produce digital versions of documents on magnetic diskettes prior to printing them on paper. The machines were expensive and were limited in that they produced only certain types of printed documents, such as letters and memos.

As processing power for personal computers increased, software companies began to produce word-processing programs that could be used on those machines. The first popular versions of PC-based word-processing applications were WordStar and WordPerfect. This development eliminated the need to purchase specialized machines for only one purpose. In addition, as new application programs were developed, individuals could perform multiple administrative tasks on a single personal computer. As new and improved versions of the word-processing software were created, they could be loaded onto the same machine that previously held the earlier version. Hence, users did not need to purchase new hardware to run new programs.

Modern versions of word-processing application programs have been improved dramatically and now include numerous functions that were not available in their earlier counterparts. Virtually any type of document manipulation is available to users with a click of the mouse. In addition, features permit the inclusion of outputs from other software packages into word-processing documents. For instance, a grid of budget items can be taken from a spreadsheet program and placed into a memorandum.

SPREADSHEET APPLICATION PROGRAMS

Spreadsheet application software is designed to manipulate numbers in an electronic format. The first popular spreadsheet program was Lotus 1-2-3, which is still in use today; however, Microsoft's Excel appears to

Spreadsheet applications are used frequently for maintaining financial records. (Courtesy of PhotoDisc, Inc.)

be the more prominently used program at the current time. Other than toolbar functions, current spreadsheets do not differ dramatically from earlier versions.

Spreadsheet screens are arranged in a gridlike pattern. Each small square is called a **cell,** which is a separate field of information that relates to the other cells only when the user instructs the program to create a connection. The value of this design is that the user can easily input-view-replace numeric information in the spreadsheet to create hypothetical outcomes. This is called what-if analysis, and it has implications for any decision-making process. To do what-if analysis, the user places formulas in each cell that is being used and then enters the numerical data for analysis.

Cell An individual field in a spreadsheet that may contain data or formulas.

Let's say a manager is working on a project to produce a financial budget for her department. The manager will arrange the spreadsheet cells to represent revenues and expenses. Next, she will place formulas into the cells to tally and compare those numbers. Once this is done, she may plug in the numbers to compare expense items and revenues to determine financial profits or losses. She may rework the figures continuously, using the same cells on the worksheet (spreadsheet page) until she determines the right mix of revenues and expenses for each month during the fiscal year. Once these decisions are made, the manager may place the information into a graph to provide a visual depiction of the highs and lows of the proposed budget. She saves the information and sends the proposed budget to the corporate controller for review. If the controller needs revisions to the proposed budget, the figures may be entered into the cells, and the formulas will handle the calculations automatically. In addition, the chart representing the annual figures will change to reflect the new revenues and expenses. Budget development was a process that used up countless labor hours in the past. However, with today's spreadsheet programs this work can be accomplished in just a fraction of the time, permitting managers to do more important things, such as running their operations.

In keeping with the budget scenario, the manager can enter actual expense and revenue figures on a daily, weekly, monthly, or quarterly basis to track the performance of her department. Preset formulas automatically calculate the difference between actual and budgeted financial performance, giving the manager a "report card" of departmental status (called a variance report). The information in this report will permit the manager to adjust monthly projections to ensure that she meets the goals of the annual budget at the end of the year.

Of course, accounting functions are only one application of spreadsheet programs. Today's software packages are able to handle more complex data, including statistical analyses. In addition, spreadsheets often are incorporated into databases used to store large amounts of numerical data.

DATABASE PROGRAMS

The general-purpose application software that provides for the storage, manipulation, and retrieval of information is called a database program. Although end users may choose to develop their own databases, programmers design the majority of these applications. However, newer database packages using higher-level programming approaches such as **object-oriented programming (OOP)** make database development much less complicated than were the earlier languages used for database design.

OOP universally recognizes all data fields, lessening the need for the use of complicated definition codes in the programs. A microcomputer software program called Access, which is made by the Microsoft Corporation, provides easily recognized definitions in the categories of tables, queries, forms, and reports. Tables provide data storage by data types. Queries are designed to interrogate the tables for usable information, frequently using a language called **Standard Query Language (SQL).**

Forms are data categories used for data input and output; reports are output objects used to display information from the data. Earlier databases were programmed using complicated languages, such as COBOL, whereas object-oriented programming permits entire databases to be developed using simpler languages such as Visual Basic (VB). For instance, an individual who chooses to be a full-fledged database programmer using Microsoft Access would need to know only VB to create complex databases. The difference between COBOL and VB is that COBOL is procedurally based, whereas VB is more naturally oriented and thus is like speaking languages.

All computer users access databases frequently. For instance, a person surfing the Internet is accessing information continually from databases all over the world. In organizations, users typically access information that resides on internal databases, although this scenario is changing because of the proliferation of electronic commerce in current hospitality organizations.

Hierarchy of Data

Since users get information from a number of databases, it is important to be aware of the **hierarchy of data** residing in these storage units. Figure 3.1 shows this hierarchy in terms of size.

The smallest data item that is visible to the human eye is called a character, a single alphanumeric symbol. A group of related characters constitutes a data "field," and a group of related fields constitutes a data

Object-oriented programming (OOP) A high-level programming language that universally recognizes all data fields.

Standard Query Language (SQL) A program for users to interrogate a database to extract useful information.

Hierarchy of data The range of data items from the smallest to the largest visible unit.

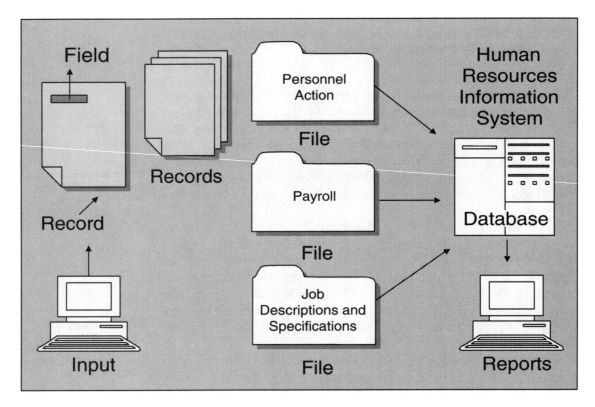

Figure 3.1 Hierarchy of Data

"record." The related records result in a data "file," and the combined related files result in a database.

Database management system (DBMS) A group of individual databases that are linked together.

Database administrator (DBA) The individual responsible for overall database management system performance, including development, interrogation, maintenance, and applications.

Chief information officer (CIO) The executive-level individual responsible for information technology and information systems in an organization.

Database Management

In commercial enterprises, there are usually several individual databases that are linked together into a **database management system (DBMS).** The individual who is responsible for the administrative functions of a DBMS is called a **database administrator (DBA).** A typical DBA is responsible for the development, interrogation, maintenance, and applications that reside in a database. Usually this person reports to the **chief information officer (CIO),** who is the executive-level person in charge of information systems and information technology for an organization. Figure 3.2 shows the configuration of a DBMS.

The first task of the database administrator is development, which includes the planning, design, and building of each database that ultimately will be linked into a centralized system. Next, the administrator performs daily maintenance activities that ensure the effective operation of the

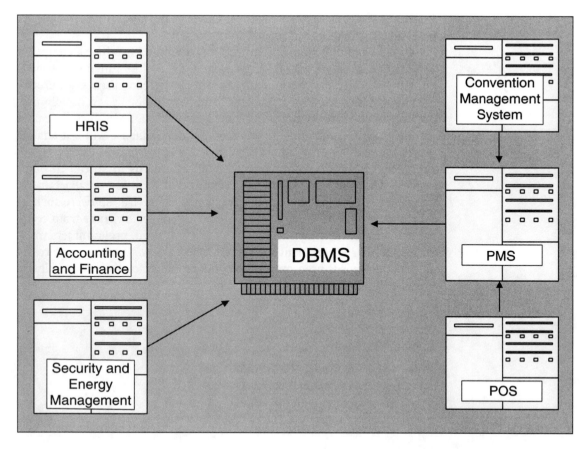

Figure 3.2 DBMS Configuration

DBMS, including updates, archiving, security, and disk reallocations. Concurrent with the function of maintenance is the process of writing query programs for interrogation and designing applications that serve the needs of the end users. Since organizations require more information and applications over time, the DBMS is a dynamic system that changes and grows on a continuous basis.

Database Security

Since the database management system is the hub of a hospitality organization, continuous upgrades are made to the security systems that are in place. One of the downsides to the technological revolution is the existence of **computer hackers,** individuals who practice unauthorized entry into the databases owned by others, often for destructive purposes. The primary protections against unauthorized database entry are devices

Computer hackers
Individuals who attempt to gain unauthorized entry into databases, often for destructive purposes.

known as *firewalls,* which consist of codes that grant entry permissions and flag the trails of entry by different users.

One form of destructive action by hackers is to introduce a computer virus into a database that disables one or more of its functions. A virus consists of coded instructions that the database recognizes as an execution program designed to replicate itself continuously, eventually disabling the computers that are networked to the DBMS. Viruses called *worms* attempt to burrow into the memory of a database without attaching themselves to programs. Users unknowingly "spawn" some viruses onto other networked computers, causing the virus to spread through e-mail address books over the Internet and affect other database management systems. Database administrators use antivirus software such as Norton and McAfee programs to detect and eradicate viruses from computers. When a new version of a virus is introduced, programmers must write a new virus elimination program called a *patch.* Patches later are included in antivirus program updates that are downloaded periodically by DBAs and other savvy computer users.

OTHER GENERAL-PURPOSE APPLICATION PROGRAMS

Presentation Software

Most people who provide professional presentations use computer-generated slides to provide visual reinforcement of the topics under discussion. Usually the presenter places the slides on a floppy or compact disk, which is inserted into a laptop computer at the site of the presentation. The images are projected onto an auditorium screen through a liquid crystal display (LCD) projector connected to the laptop computer. The software used to prepare and display the slides is called presentation software. Perhaps the most common presentation software on the market is Microsoft Corporation's PowerPoint, which is one of the packages bundled into the Office software suite. Presentation software is similar to word-processing software, with the addition of a few multimedia enhancements. The screens are formatted into templates that permit the user to create text, art, and photo boxes on each screen. Presentation software also allows the user to add limited multimedia enhancements such as sound and animation. In addition to using the software to generate presentation slides, users may import miniature versions of the templates onto printed documents for publication.

Desktop Publishing Software

Desktop publishing software uses templates to provide professionally designed print materials. The most prominent PC-based desktop publishing software is called Adobe Acrobat, which creates files in portable document format (.pdf). This versatile design enables the publication of professionally produced print materials, such as articles, in a digital form that is both printer- and database-friendly as long as the user has a copy of Acrobat Reader installed on the computer.

Acrobat Reader is an example of software that is available to the public at no charge, a category called **freeware.** For instance, a user may be conducting research through a library database. The user may find a full-text article available in the .pdf (usually noted with a camera icon) format. For users to read the file containing the article, they must have a copy of the Reader software on the computer. An icon for downloading of the software is usually available on the site that hosts the database for users to attain a free copy of the software. Once the user has downloaded the software, she may read the article and will have options that include sending the article to a printer or e-mailing the article.

Freeware Software that is available to the public at no charge.

E-Mail Software

Electronic mail (e-mail) software provides the capability for users to send text messages to other users over networks, including the Internet. In some cases, e-mail software is provided by Internet Service Providers (ISPs) to users who subscribe to their services, such as the America Online (AOL), Yahoo!, and Hotmail mailer services. Separate e-mail packages sometimes are purchased by organizations for use on their networks as well as on the Internet. The default e-mail program for users of the Internet Explorer browser is called Outlook, which is produced by the Microsoft Corporation. This e-mail program is called a "shared application" because it combines with the copy of Microsoft Word residing on the user's computer. Owing to its popularity, many organizations have converted networked e-mail systems from packages such as GroupWise to the Outlook program. Individuals may use e-mail to send individualized electronic messages as well as file transfers containing photos, slides, documents, and Web pages to other networked users.

Web Software

A Web page is an electronic document that is designed for viewing on the Internet. These documents are called Web pages because they reside in files on Internet servers called websites. "Web" refers to the World Wide

Web (WWW), which is the portion of the Internet that is commonly accessed by users. The programming language used to create Web pages is called *Hypertext Markup Language (HTML)*, which consists of code used to create templates for the electronic viewing of pages. A more developed version of HTML called *Extensible Markup Language (XML)* adds electronic "*tags*" to Web page items that expedite the coding process. A person who creates and maintains pages on a website is referred to as a webmaster. Most webmasters are familiar with the software options used to generate Web pages, including "Web-editing" programs. These programs create templates for Web designers to enter text and other objects and automatically provide conversion into the HTML format. The most popular Web-editing programs at the current time include Microsoft's FrontPage and Dreamweaver. Professional webmasters are also proficient in the use of programming languages that create miniature applications attached to Web pages called *applets*. The commonly used languages for this purpose and other applications are *Java* and *C++*. Individuals with knowledge of these programs have the ability to develop professional *multimedia* publications that include sound, animation, graphics, photos, and video. Many multimedia producers use sophisticated authoring system software packages such as Macromedia's Flash.

OPERATING SYSTEM SOFTWARE

Operating system
Software that manages computer resources, files, applications, and tasks.

The most commonly used type of application-specific program is called an **operating system.** Operating systems are software packages that manage all the functions of mainframe computers, midrange computers, and microcomputers. They handle tasks such as computer start-up/shutdown, utilities, peripheral recognition, disk allocation, and all the other tasks that make the computer perform the functions required by the user. As opposed to application programs that are loaded onto the computer by the user, operating systems are written to the computer's hard disk by the manufacturer. For this reason, the market is dominated by just a few versions of operating systems. This works to the user's advantage as there is no need to learn new operating systems when using different brands of computers.

The dominant system that runs mainframe and midrange computers is called the *Unix* operating system, and the system that runs most microcomputers is called the Disk Operating System (DOS). Other operating systems that can be used in personal computers include the Linux and OS/2 versions; however, these systems are used in only a small percentage of manufactured computers. Early computer users were required to learn text-based commands in both DOS and Unix in order to use large and small computer systems.

The underlying operating system on a computer today is invisible to the user because of the development of the *graphical user interface*. The GUI is a system overlay that appears in the form of windows on the user's monitor and permits navigation of the computer's operating system with the point-and-click features of a mouse. The best known graphical user interface is appropriately called Windows, which is produced by the Microsoft Corporation. The Windows operating system runs virtually all commonly used personal computers, with the exception of palmtop models that use varieties of *personal information manager (PIM)* operating software. Most individuals upload information from their palmtop computers into larger personal computers through a process of hot synchronization (hot-synch), permitting the files to be recognized by applications that are driven by the Windows operating system.

Three Main Functions of Operating Systems

Three functions are performed by operating systems: resource management, file management, and task management. Resource management involves the hardware and software in the computer system. The operating system manages the interfaces of input devices such as keyboards and output devices such as the monitor. Peripherals such as printers are other resources that the operating system manages. When it comes to resource management, the practices include device/software recognition, interfaces, and updates. Small programs contained in the operating system called *utilities* assist the user in managing the resources (hardware and software) that are part of the computer.

Certain computer resources are used to write information files, which is the function of each application software program. The operating system enables file storage, maintenance, and retrieval from the hard drive as well as other drives connected to the computer. When application software is loaded onto a computer disk, the operating system places it in a category called program files. One of the program files is designated to execute or launch each application, which is appropriately noted as an execution file. Once the execution file is activated, it will run the application by accessing other files within the software with the help of the operating system. The operating system is also responsible for application program exit, file save function, and disk allocation of newly created application files in designated folders such as "My Documents" on a Windows system. The operating system keeps track of file locations on disks as well as remaining disk space for future use through a task called a disk scan.

Other Operating System Maintenance Tasks

A number of other maintenance tasks are performed by the operating system. The Windows operating system permits more than one task to be performed at the same time; this is referred to as multitasking. Other tasks include starting up the computer on demand (booting), restarting when necessary (rebooting), and executing the procedure to turn the computer off safely (shutdown). When a user boots the computer, it automatically runs through a program of diagnostics used to locate programs, file locations, and other functions. While the computer is running, it will notify the user of any irregularities in the operation through "error messages." If there is an unexpected shutdown, such as a power loss, the operating system will perform additional diagnostics such as reboot that will check for irregularities in the disk allocations or file maintenance. Also, the operating system may save interrupted application program files, permitting the user to recover lost work.

In essence, the computer operating system coordinates all the resources, files, and tasks from start-up through shutdown in a manner that is mostly unobtrusive to the user. The first version (3.1) of the Windows operating system was created in the early 1990s, and the most recent version used in new computers is called *Windows XP*, an intuitive and sophisticated operating system. The system is intuitive in the sense that it uses a form of logic to predict the needs of users based on their activities while using the computer. Also, the XP program contains a few breakthroughs that permit users to create multimedia projects with specialized application programs such as Microsoft Producer. These developments provide evidence that computer software is entering a new stage of program language development.

Programming Language Development

There has been an evolution of software trends over the last 40 years of computing. In earlier times, users wrote their own programs for computers by using *machine languages* such as binary code, which some consider the first generation of computer programming.[1] The tedious task of programming in machine language was eliminated with the creation of *assembler translators,* which converted code into machine symbols, marking the second generation of programming languages. In the third generation, generic operating systems and *high-level codes* that used languages such as Pascal, Fortran, Basic, and COBOL resulted in packaged programs. Today we may be reaching the *fourth generation of program language* development with the proliferation of object-oriented languages and natural language programming, such as Visual Basic, SQL, and Oracle, used to program databases. Future language assistance may be made available to programmers through technologies such as fuzzy logic, neural networks, and artificial intelligence.

BUSINESS SOFTWARE FOR HOSPITALITY ORGANIZATIONS

The rapid development of computer programming languages has had a direct effect on the business aspects of hospitality management. The business aspects of our business are the interactions and interfaces that are similar to functions contained within other business enterprises. Business systems include transaction processing, information communications, and decision-making support.

Proprietary Systems and Open Platforms

The specifics of transaction processing are discussed in other chapters of this text. However, from a generic perspective, it should be noted that privately owned packages called **proprietary systems** were the transaction-processing formats of the past. The strategic problem with this thinking is that proprietary packages do not interface with other computerized functions. The result within a hotel, for instance, could be the acquisition of property management systems, point-of-sale systems, catering systems, and accounting systems that do not communicate with each other. The purpose of using technology in business is to create holistically interfaced systems for all business-related functions. Today's technology provides the means to accomplish this objective through the use of generic foundations of business application programs called **open platforms.**

The platform is the architecture that supports the hardware and application software through its operating systems within a business enterprise. An open platform is one that permits these systems to interface with each other. An example would be an open platform used to support the business systems of a hotel. In this case the hub may be the property management system, which is interfaced with the point-of-sale system that supports retail outlets other than the front-office area. The hub (property management system) also interfaces with the accounting systems on the back end (accounting office functions). Proprietary systems are designed to be freestanding processors in that they are not intended to communicate with any other system. The goal of business application systems is to provide connectivity among all subsystems to enhance organizational communication flows and managerial decision-making

Proprietary systems
Hardware and software that are owned by a specific vendor that do not permit interfaces with commonly used operating systems.

Open platforms
Operating systems that support commonly used hardware and application software packages.

support. An example of enhanced communication flows is provided by software applications that are shared among users in an organization to work collaboratively on projects.

Rent or Buy?

With the rapid rate of software program development, many hospitality organizations are making strategic choices to lease or rent computer software through outside companies known as application software providers (ASPs) to handle business functions. The advantage of this strategy is that the hospitality organization does not purchase the soft-

Software management systems such as Restaurant Manager are used commonly in foodservice operations. (©Action Systems Inc.)

ware and the ASP provides new versions as they become available. This allows the organization to avoid investing in technology that will become outdated rapidly and require new investments for upgraded software. However, some organizations prefer to own the software used in their business systems. Regardless of preference, the strategic choice to own or lease these applications should be considered part of the technology planning process.

Decision Support Systems

When it comes to strategic planning for all areas of an organization, decision support systems (DSSs) provide statistical support to justify or nullify what managers intuitively apply to making decisions. It is important to note that the key word here is *support*. Some managers confuse the recommendations of these systems with the final decisions. If this were true, there would be little need for thinking managers. It is important to remember that technology is intended not to replace people or thinking but to be used as a tool by people in organizations. Before the development of sophisticated DSS systems, spreadsheet application programs were touted as a manager's greatest tool for what-if analysis. With DSS systems, the what-if aspects go way beyond the figures plugged into a spreadsheet.

Other DSS applications include data mining, executive information systems, and enterprise information portals. These functions require data warehousing interfaces to access both internal and external sources of information. Data-mining software analyzes huge volumes of historical data to identify trends and patterns for current and future use.

Executive information systems formerly were used to help top-level managers make long-range strategic decisions. Today most managers involved in the strategic planning process use these systems. Enterprise information portals link internal and off-site data warehouses with employees of the organization to access and analyze data within and outside the company. When linked with hypermedia databases, the information is converted into business knowledge for current and future use; this is known as a knowledge management system.

ARTIFICIAL INTELLIGENCE SOFTWARE

Artificial intelligence (AI) comes from the disciplines of computer science, biology, psychology, linguistics, mathematics, and engineering. The goal of AI is to create machines with human physical and mental abilities (reasoning, learning, and problem solving). AI is not a new technology application; however, it was not used widely until recently, as cost and machine power limitations prevented the development of its application for practical uses. Some of the aspects of AI are listed below:

- *Neural networks:* The closest electrical simulation of an organic system; consist of networked processors that interact as transponders and have the capacity for learning based on identification of patterns and relationships.
- *Fuzzy logic:* Processors that can perform reasoning based on inferences and incomplete data (the opposite of crisp data) in response to SQL inquiries.
- *Virtual reality:* Computer-simulated reality based on multisensory input and output devices to create undetected simulated environments through telepresence illusions.
- *Intelligent agents:* Applets that perform tasks for end users by using a built-in knowledge base about processes. Application wizards are good examples.
- *Expert systems:* Knowledge-based systems that possess expertise in a single discipline. Users pose questions and problems, and the expert system provides solutions.
- *Knowledge base:* The information contained by the system in factual and heuristic form.
- *Inference engine:* Provides analysis tools for if/then reasoning and adds experiences to the knowledge base through repetition.
- The *expert shell:* Programmed by a knowledge engineer and a logic programmer.

All these applications have been available since the early 1990s. Although chips have been built into commonly used machines and appliances that use some of these technologies (automobiles, for instance), the more powerful applications have been prevented from reaching marketplaces by hardware constraints. Today, however, with more powerful microprocessors and lower hardware costs, researchers are considering broad applications of these technologies. The implications for the hospitality/tourism industry over the next 10 years will be limited only by decision makers' imaginations. This is a wonderful time for technology because these technologies permit hospitality managers to use their creative talents to envision and develop applications in conjunction with technical experts.

On-the-Job Training . . . Continued

It has been about a week since you began the project with the reservations department director. Since the computers in the office use the Windows operating system, you chose to create your report documents using Microsoft Word's word-processing program. However, to demonstrate the enhanced productivity associated with the new reservation system, you needed to crunch some numbers. To do this you used the Excel spreadsheet program to perform the calculations and produce visual graphics based on the numbers. Those reports were added as addenda to the back of your written report. However, you also chose to import into the narrative sections some of the spreadsheet highlights as figures to support the content of the report.

Today is the day for the big presentation to all the members of the senior management team. You have prepared a complete set of slides, using PowerPoint presentation software for this occasion. Finally, the moment of truth arrives. The executives are seated in the boardroom. The reservations director stands at a podium as she presents the argument for the new system while you work the slides from a laptop computer. The executives are impressed with your clever inclusion of sound and animation in conjunction with the projected slides. The executives applaud heartily at the conclusion of the presentation. Then they ask you and the director to leave the boardroom while they discuss the merits of your system request.

After what seems like an eternity of waiting outside the room, you are both invited in to join the executives. The chief executive officer addresses you on behalf of the group. He begins by saying, "I want to thank you and compliment you both on your presentation. You have stated the case clearly for an investment in a new reservation system, and we have unanimously agreed to fund your project." He continues: "We are particularly impressed with your written report and presentation slides." Then he concludes: "We would like to share your documents with all the managers in the organization as a benchmark for all future professional presentations, with your permission."

You both readily agree, delighted with the recognition you have received in addition to the approval for your new system.

SUMMARY

The chapter began with a discussion that differentiated computer software from hardware. Computer chips are "hard-coded" with instructions and data; program language code or software consists of instructions placed onto a computer disk or a secondary storage device. Most software programs perform functions for computer users and are classified as application software packages. General-purpose application software is used for many different outcomes. Examples of this software include word processors, spreadsheets, and databases.

Other software applications are written for specific uses, which means they are used for specialized functions. Design programs such as computer animation and computer-aided design are single-use applications. Business applications also are designed for specialized purposes such as transaction processing, communication, and decision-making activities. Other software programs are intended to perform nonapplication processes such as managing the functions of a computer.

Operating system software manages computer resources, files, and tasks as well as the application programs used by individuals. The dominant operating system for midrange and mainframe computers is called Unix, and the underlying operating system for microcomputers is called the Disk Operating System. Most computer users are unaware of the underlying operating system since the development of graphical user interfaces. For instance, Microsoft Windows is a GUI that most individuals use to run personal computers. Palmtop machines called personal digital assistants use some version of personal information manager software as operating systems. Operating systems have become quite sophisticated as a result of developments in program language evolution.

Whereas early adopters of computer programming used machine language, translator programs, and symbolic codes, current programs write computer instructions in "high-level" languages. Examples are the COBOL, Fortran, Pascal, and Basic programming languages. More recent developments are generating a shift from procedural to natural language programming code. Visual Basic and object-oriented programming are examples.

Toward the end of the chapter there was a discussion of business software applications for hospitality organizations, which are considered as application-specific programs. Business functions include transaction processing, information communication, and decision support systems. Some hospitality organizations rent or lease business application programs from outside vendors known as application service providers, and others choose to purchase programs. The key strategic feature for business applications is the acquisition of open platforms, which are operating systems that recognize and manage various application programs, as opposed to systems owned by a single company, which are proprietary in nature.

DISCUSSION QUESTIONS

Answer the following questions with true/false responses.

1. An application program and an operating system are the same.
2. Design programs used on workstations are included with other general-purpose application programs.
3. A software suite consists of a customized bundling of application software packages.
4. Object-oriented programming is the same as machine language programming.
5. Standard Query Language is used to interrogate a database to extract useful information.
6. A file is the largest item in the hierarchy of data contained within a DBMS.
7. The CIO is the executive who is responsible for the IT and IS functions in an organization.
8. Groupware is software that is available to the public at no charge.
9. An operating system consists of software that manages computer resources, files, applications, and tasks.
10. A proprietary system is open to interfaces with most software packages.

KEY TERMS

Application programs
Application-specific program
Assembler language
Business software page
Cell
Chief information officer (CIO)
Code
Computer hackers
Computer programmers
Computer software
Database administrator (DBA)
Database management system (DBMS)
Electronic mail
Firewall
Fourth generation languages—nonprocedural and natural

Freeware
General-purpose application program
Groupware
GUI
Hierarchy of data
High-level codes
Hypertext Markup Language (HTML)
Integrated software packages
Java—C++—Applets
Language translator programs
Linux page
Machine language
Multimedia
Object-oriented programming (OOP)
Open platforms
Operating system
Personal Information Manager (PIM) used on PDAs
Programming language
Proprietary systems
Security monitors
Software suites
Spreadsheets
Standard Query Language (SQL)
System management programs
Unix
Utilities
Windows XP
Word processing
XML-Extensible Markup Language tags

REFERENCES

1. J. A. O'Brien. (2002). *Management Information Systems: Managing Information Technology in the E-Business Enterprise,* 5th ed. Boston: McGraw-Hill Irwin.

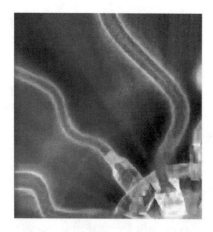

CHAPTER

4

Computer Networks and Telecommunications for Hospitality

CHAPTER OBJECTIVES

In this chapter you will learn to:

1. Identify the basic functions of different networks.
2. Understand the basic methods of sharing data resources through networks.
3. Be familiar with the basic functions of network architecture topologies.
4. Comprehend the functions of business and individual Internet connections.

On-the-Job Training

You are a marketing intern for a property that is part of a widely recognized hotel chain, working on a project to identify guest profiles. The philosophy behind the project is that information about the backgrounds, preferences, and demographics of current guests will help the property produce more effective marketing strategies to attract new guests.

The marketing manager is an older person who has always relied on the guest history files contained in the property management system at the hotel for such information. He is known to complain about the lack of good marketing information in these files. Although the guest history files are thorough in terms of the likes and dislikes of current hotel guests, they provide very little information that could be used for developing marketing plans aimed at new guests.

As you work with the marketing manager, you begin to identify with his level of frustration. However, you can't help thinking that in this day and age that vital information must be available somewhere.

To be continued . . .

INTRODUCTION

Although individual computers are systems within themselves, consisting of input, processing, and output devices and software, the real power of the computer for hospitality management enterprises and individual users lies in networking and telecommunications.

A **computer network** consists of several terminals that are linked together for a common computing purpose. **Computer telecommunications** is a general category that includes computer communications from remote locations.

In most commercial enterprises, individuals work on computers that function as stand-alone machines used for general-purpose applications such as word processing and spreadsheets. These computers are also part of a computer network consisting of other computers within the organi-

Computer network Several terminals that are linked together for a common purpose.

Computer telecommunications A general category that includes computer communications from remote locations.

zation. Individuals who are able to access the Internet from their work computers are linked via *telecommunications* to the outside world. Hence, the user works on a computer that is a system within itself and also connects with other computers within and outside the organization, which are larger systems. When a computer is used as part of a system it becomes a subsystem of that system. The key advantage of networked computers is the ability to share resources.

NETWORKING DATA RESOURCES

The software application for managing data resources is called a database. Multiple interconnected databases constitute a database management system, which is managed by a person known as the database administrator. When databases become part of a network, the data resources within them are distributed to multiple users. Hence, a networked database is referred to as a **distributed database.**

Most distributed databases work within a network structure, which permits many people within the organization to access most of the available data. For instance, a luxury resort may use a networked database to identify multiple factors influencing guest services that may be accessed by a number of operating departments, such as engineering, housekeeping, and the front office. In essence, a network structure database is one that provides "many-to-many" interfaces. In most cases, network structure databases are located at the property, whereas other distributed databases exist in remote locations.

Large hospitality chains are likely to have centralized databases that contain all the information generated by operational databases at the property level. This type of large database is known as a **data warehouse.**

Because a data warehouse is very large, the information contained in it is divided into topical units called *data marts*. This permits users to access data by topic, such as guest service standards, marketing analysis, and guest history trends. Since the data warehouse is in a remote location, access from the property level is accomplished through telecommunication networks such as the Internet. The advantage of this type of network lies in the ability to access data mart information from a remote site by using search criteria, a process called **data mining,** and analyze the data immediately, a process known as **online analytical processing (OLAP).** Data mining and OLAP are useful tools for market analysis and operational strategic planning.

Because there is so much additional information available at Internet sites, which exist in hypertext format, many organizations also use

Distributed database A database that is accessed over a network to more than one user.

Data warehouse A centralized group of databases.

Data mining The process of drilling through information contained in a data warehouse to access specific information.

Online analytical processing (OLAP) The ability to process information online as opposed to downloading it to a computer.

Hypermedia databases
Databases containing hypertext formatted information from the Internet.

networked **hypermedia databases** to add information to their marketing and other strategic initiatives.

Data warehouses permit remote access and manipulation of data resources from central locations through the OLAP process. Material resources also are shared through networks. The most common application is the use of remote peripherals connected to each computer terminal in a network. Let's say a person has a small printer in her office for most print jobs. When she wants to print a report with many pages, she will access the shared printer that is behind the front office. If she wants a laser printer to provide a full-color version of the report, she will route the print job to the printer in the computer office upstairs. In this case, one user has access to three printers, which are output peripherals. Although networks permit multiple users to access the same material resources, additional hardware is required to establish network systems.

COMPUTER NETWORKS

As long as the need for digital-analog-digital conversion exists, networks will require the use of *telecommunication processors* (switches, routers, and modems) to link host, server, and user computers. The *host* computer contains the information that the end user is seeking. For instance, the database mainframe computer is the host computer that is linked to a user who is engaged in a marketing research project. The server is the computer that links the user to the host. A network server is the machine that manages the tasks, files, nodes, and resources contained in the network.

The computer transmits to a *modem,* which is a *modulator/demodula-tor* unit that follows a channel (wire or satellite) to a router (a backbone transmission carrier) and a switch (a computer that controls message switching among nodes in a network) for servers and host computers that receive and transmit requested data back to the user. For instance, a person working on a corporate local area network computer will connect to the Internet through the corporate router from the network hub (interfacing of nodes to the network server). Subsequently, that person will be taken through a switch at the Internet Service Provider site and then be forwarded through the Internet backbone (main trunk) routers and switches to the host access device and back. This is the telecommunications process through which a user at a commercial enterprise accesses information sources found on the Internet.

Local area networks (LANs) may be small enough to be contained in one room. Wide and metropolitan area networks (WANs and MANs) are

A server links the user to the host. (Courtesy Corbis Digital Stock.)

used for distances ranging from a few miles (WAN) to huge expanses (MAN). Figure 4.1 demonstrates the relationships of LANs, WANs, and MANs.

Each network requires a network server, which is a dedicated machine (usually a midrange computer) for managing the network operations. The network server must be connected to all the computers on the network, which are referred to as **network nodes.**

Network nodes
Terminals connected to a network.

Topologies

The configuration of the nodes is determined by the network's **architecture topology** or structure.

For instance, one topology calls for the nodes to be strung in a circle around the network server. This is called a *ring topology* and represents a central reliance on the server to process network requests in order of their receipt. Figure 4.2 shows the ring architecture topology.

Architecture topology
Configuration of network nodes.

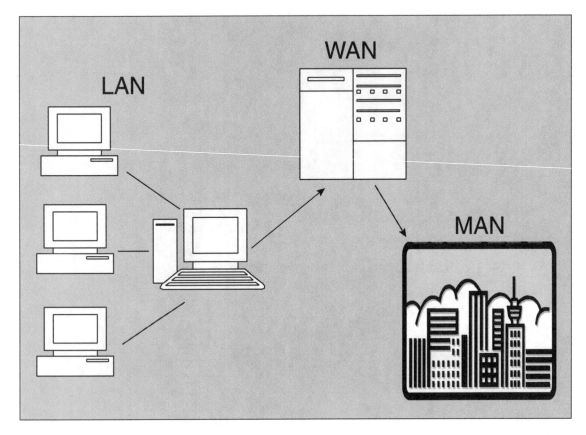

Figure 4.1 The Relationship between LANs, WANs, and MANs

A scheme similar to the ring topology is called a *bus topology,* in which the nodes are stretched outward from the server, with the farthest node representing the end of the network connection, as is shown in Figure 4.3.

Both ring and bus topologies continue to be used for networking computers. However, they focus on the server as the determiner of network services. A more centralized approach is called the *star topology* (Figure 4.4).

Star topology is consistent with the *client/server* model of network computing. In this scheme the nodes are considered "clients" of the network server. The server provides network services directly upon demand from each node in the network. This is a centralized form of network service and a decentralized type of node relationship to the server. Both ring and bus architectures also provide client/server interactions, but in a more decentralized manner. Of course, the centralized nature of the star configuration has a downside because it relies on a single server. In the event of a server *crash,* the entire network will go down. This is not the

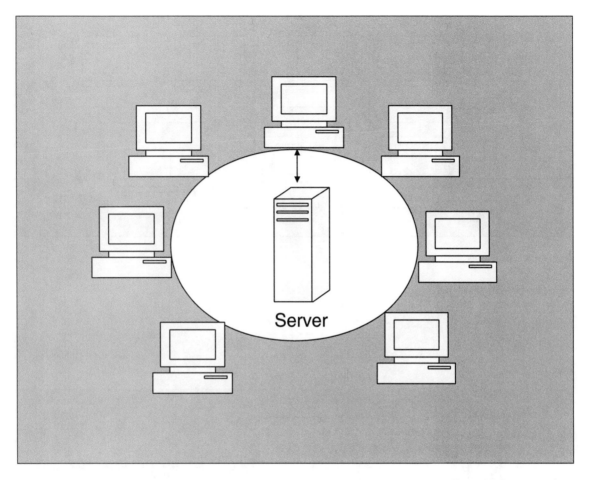

Figure 4.2 Ring Network Topology

case with ring and star topologies, as the nodes continue to support each other while the server is not working.

Network Connections

Regardless of the chosen topology, connections must be established among the all nodes and servers in every network. Most small networks use hard wires for connectivity. The most commonly used type of copper wire is *twisted-pair* wiring, which is used for electrical connections and phone wires. The wire that connects to your telephone is an example of twisted-pair wiring. Another copper wiring alternative is *coaxial cable* wire, which is commonly used for cable television hookups. Coaxial cable is designed for video and audio transmission, which means it has a larger **bandwidth** than the twisted-pair wiring that is designed for analog voice

Bandwidth The range of frequency for the transmission of data.

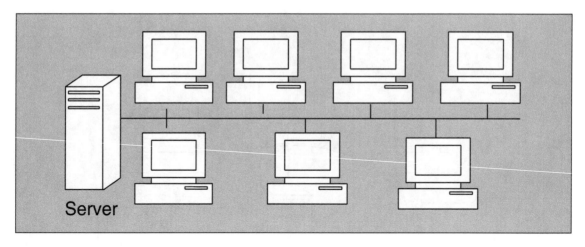

Figure 4.3 Bus Network
Topology

Figure 4.4 Star Network
Topology

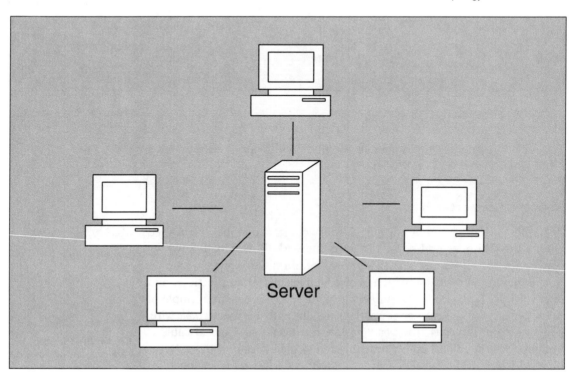

transmission. Bandwidth is the range of frequency for transmission and thus determines the maximum transmission speed of data.

Transmission speed is measured in **bits per second (BPS).** Finally, there is wiring consisting of glass fiber filaments that are thinner than a human hair. A single cable will consist of millions of these fibers, which can move data at almost the speed of light. These are known as *fiber-optic wires,* which exist on a practically global level thanks to the wiring initiatives sponsored by telecommunications and entertainment corporations over the last 10 years. The goal of these initiatives is to provide **broadband** telecommunications among all the nations around the world. *Broadband* is a term used to describe very high levels of bandwidth with transmission speeds in excess of 256,000 BPS to billions of BPS.[1]

Bits per second (BPS)
Volume of data transmitted through a telecommunication channel to determine the speed of the medium.

Broadband A channel with transmission speeds in excess of 256,000 BPS.

Telecommunications Media

Telecommunications channels consist of satellite media in addition to wired connections. Satellites transmit microwave beams for wireless transmission. Antennas on buildings, towers, and mountains carry terrestrial microwaves. Traditional *geosynchronous satellites* operate as relay stations as they orbit the equator at speeds that synchronize their locations with specific geographic areas. Large enterprises use *very small aperture technology (VSAT)* satellites mounted on buildings to bypass commercial communication channels. *Low Earth Orbit satellites (LEOs)* are much smaller than traditional space orbit satellites, and that permits them to function at lower altitudes to perform channel relay functions for VSAT as well as traditionally wired locations.

Cellular phones use radio technologies to communicate between cells located on towers. *Personal communications services (PCS)* systems are providing digital transmission with greater efficiency and security for cell phone users. Integration of phone and radio technologies is providing multiuse "packet radios" through cell phone carriers. The cost of wiring buildings for LANs is often prohibitive, and this has caused enterprises to consider wireless LANs that use high-frequency, low-frequency, and infrared beams. *Wi-Fi* technology uses wireless microwaves and has been implemented on a large scale in buildings designed for public accommodations, such as airports and arenas. *Modems* convert digital to analog to digital to provide communications between computers over nondigital channels. *Multiplexers* provide many terminals with the ability to communicate at the same time over a single channel. *Bandwidth* refers to the speed of transmission over telecommunications channels as measured in bits per second. High-speed digital channels are referred to as broadband use combinations of microwave, fiber optics, or satellites to transmit at speeds up to several billion BPS. An agreement among Web providers of a standard called *Wireless Application Protocol (WAP)* shows promise for

Seasons 52, a new restaurant concept being tested by Darden Restaurants, is completely wireless. (Courtesy Darden Restaurants, Inc.)

combining cell phone and personal digital assistant technology to produce a new generation of telephony.[2]

NETWORK OPERATING SYSTEMS

Home-based individuals as well as business enterprises use networks and telecommunication channels on a regular basis. Business networks use this medium for collaboration, communication, and coordination of activities within an organization and among the shareholder groups that do business with an organization. Network servers are used to manage all aspects of computer connections, and the individuals who are responsible for this operation are called *network managers*. The servers are run by network operating systems in the same way that Windows and DOS run a stand-alone computer. The most popular network operating systems are called Novell and *Windows NT*. These operating systems handle the resources, files, and tasks of the network and its telecommunication to remote sites.

Intranets

The Internet, intranets, and extranets support e-mail, videoconferencing, chat/discussion groups, and multimedia Web pages among different locations. **Intranets** are communication channels that are privately owned by commercial enterprises that permit employees to access information from inside the organization or from remote locations. Intranets resemble the Internet in that they use *browsers* and *search engines* to help employees navigate the system. For instance, cast members (employees) with Walt Disney World in Orlando, Florida, access *portals,* or intranet sites, to access human resources requests and sign up for company benefits and services.

Intranet A private communication channel for employees to access an organization's networks; resembles the Internet.

Extranets

Extranets are the same as intranets except that they are provided to outside individuals who do business with the organization, such as vendors, guests, and other customers. Most extranets provide only limited access to a company's information to assist in the communications processes with the commercial enterprises that provide products or services to an organization.

Extranet A private communication channel for corporate outsiders such as guests, vendors, and other customers to access an organization's limited network areas; has a configuration that resembles the Internet.

In today's economy networks and telecommunications are used to link customers electronically with organizations to view product catalogs and order products or services from inventory and distribution databases. This is called electronic commerce (e-commerce), which uses the Internet to link the customer or guest with the hospitality enterprise. Seamless and rapid telecommunication networks make this form of customer interaction possible.

Among people who follow the stock market, it is common knowledge that technology stocks were "hot" in the 1990s. Part of the reason for that was the deregulation of telecommunication organizations. Major and smaller firms are still competing fiercely for market share in wired and wireless telecommunications in the fields of information, communications, entertainment, commerce, and education. Exorbitant investments in e-coms during those years resulted in a number of failed projects and bankrupt organizations. The financial analysts at that time downgraded investment opportunities in e-commerce firms. However, the competition is still very strong in the e-commerce field, and many practitioners consider themselves e-commerce specialists. The e-commerce aspects of hospitality and tourism organizations as competitive strategies are discussed in Part II of this text.

Connectivity and the E-Business Environment

What is the reason for the competitive nature of the e-business environment? The answer, in a word, is connectivity. Everyone is racing to be the first and best in the field of connectivity. Thanks to the popularity of the Internet, an open systems approach to telecommunications is driving the competition. Open systems are facilitated by standards of compliance for hardware, software, applications, and networks. These standards permit connectivity and interoperability among networks on a global level. Examples of standardization include *open systems interconnection (OSI)* models established by the International Standards Organization (ISO) and the Internet's TCP/IP file transfer protocol standard. Ask any CIO for a hospitality/tourism organization and she will tell you that these standards are affecting the industry. Figure 4.5 shows the seven layers of standards contained within OSI, which is adhered to by all network managers.

Developing Technologies

A major influence in telecommunications has been the shift from analog transmission to digital network technologies. Digital transmits in discrete binary impulses (as computers do) to provide higher transmission speeds, larger amounts of information movement, greater efficiency, and much lower error rates. Billions of dollars have been spent by communications and entertainment organizations to replace copper wire media with fiber optics that transmit data via laser light impulses. Land-based microwave

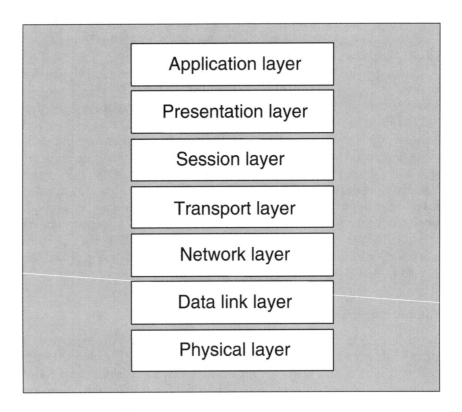

Figure 4.5 Open Systems Interconnection Model

wireless services are being replaced with low orbit and regular satellite transmitters. Finally, developments in PDA and PCS technologies are bringing consumers closer to telephony. Managers must be aware of these core technologies when making investment decisions concerning telecommunications to enhance the strategic positioning of their organizations.

Using the Internet

People who use the Internet are attaching their home or office computers to a telecommunications network that consists of billions of computers. When people surf the Net, what they are really accessing is just one portion of the Internet known as the *World Wide Web (WWW),* where most commercial applications reside. Addresses on the Web take users to *domains,* or websites owned by individuals, commercial profit and non-profit enterprises, and government and educational institutions. Domain addresses are governed by the standard called the *Universal Resource Locator (URL)* and end in suffixes that indicate the type of domain ownership. For instance, commercial sites end in .com, not-for-profit entities use the .org suffix, and government agencies and educational institutions use the suffixes .gov and .edu, respectively. A number of steps occur before one can reach an intended URL server.

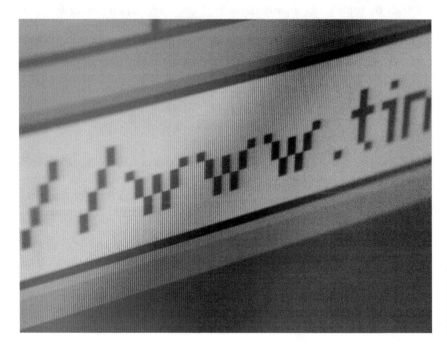

The Internet has become an integral part of today's society and a key component of today's hospitality businesses. (Courtesy of PhotoDisc, Inc.)

Internet Service Providers

An Internet user must load software onto the computer to link it to an *Internet Service Provider (ISP)*. The ISP may be a company such as America Online (AOL) or may be the provider of a modem, such as a telephone or cable company. A modem is a medium channel that converts signals from digital to analog to digital. The word *modem* stands for *mod*ulator (analog) *dem*odulator (digitizer). The three types of modems are telephone, digital subscriber line (DSL), and cable modems. Telephone modems operate at about 56.6 kbps, whereas DSL and cable modem channel information at speeds of almost 200 kbps. DSL modems usually are provided by communication companies (telephone companies, for instance), and cable modems often are offered through a television cable provider. Modem units may be built into computers or used as peripheral connections.

When a user intends to enter the Internet, he or she will click on the icon of the ISP, which instructs the modem to connect the computer with the ISP server. Next, the user will launch a browser, an Internet connection software package such as Netscape or Internet Explorer (IE). Once the browser is launched, the user is taken to a browser or ISP *home page*, which is a screen demonstrating various Internet utilities, such as e-mail, with a URL window displayed at the top of the page. If the user is familiar with the specific URL address of a website, she or he may simply type that address into the URL window. However, a user who wants to look for sites by topic or company name will use a search engine to find the URL address. Commonly used search engines include Yahoo!, Google, and AltaVista. When the user clicks on the correct URL address, she or he is taken from the ISP server to the server owned by the intended website. Figure 4.6 provides an illustration of the steps that take the user from a home computer to a website.

Network Connections

Some individuals use laptop computers to connect to LANs and WANs in schools and organizations as well as to the Internet through wireless connections. The most commonly used method is the Ethernet card that is inserted into a slot on the laptop and uses terrestrial microwaves to communicate with various networks.

Users who connect from commercial enterprises to the Internet go through the same steps, with a few complex modifications. First, an office user runs through the company network to a hub, which connects the user to a router, taking that user to the Internet switch that is managed by the corporate network. From that point on the steps for connection are the same as those for the home user: running through an ISP and

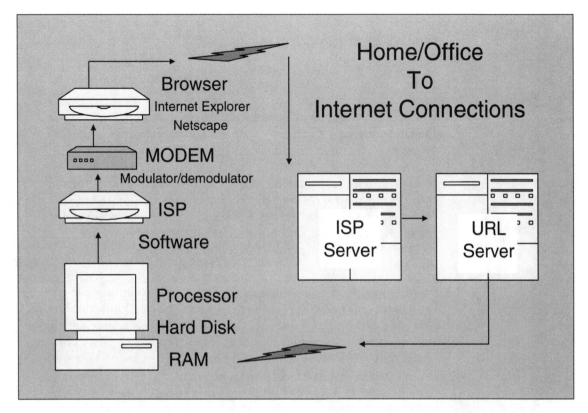

Figure 4.6 Connecting from Home to the Internet

browser and connecting directly with the Internet site by typing in a URL address (http://wiley.com, for instance), or using a search engine to find the site ("Wiley books," for example). The prefix used for entering a direct URL address is known as the hypertext transfer protocol (http://), which is the standard used to identify universal resource locators.

On-the-Job Training . . . Continued

Later that evening you are discussing the project with your roommate, who is also a student at the hospitality school. "Wait a minute," the roommate says. "Isn't your property part of a chain? I wonder if there is any information on the distributed databases at the corporate offices that can help with a marketing strategy." "Hmmm," you think as you access the corporate intranet from your apartment. As you search the databases, you notice that 80 percent of the reservations placed by guests at your property were booked through the central reservations systems at the corporate office. However, these records do not contain any information other than the names, addresses, and business affiliations of the guests. "Not much marketing information here," you think to yourself as you download the last 90 days of reservation activity.

After looking at the data for a while, you decide to import the reservations records into a spreadsheet and sort the guest information by ZIP Code. Next, you go onto the Internet and go to a search engine to find a site that provides ZIP Code indexes. You go to that site and notice that most of the guests come from three metropolitan areas in the northeastern part of the United States. Further, you notice that these areas have large corporate offices for the same technology organizations. Next, you search for a geographic map site to identify the international airports that are points of departure for the majority of the guests.

First thing the next morning you meet with the marketing manager to discuss the project. You tell him, "I noticed that the majority of our reservations come through the central rez system and that these guests work in the technology industry and are traveling out of these three airports." The manager looks at you and asks, "How did you get this information?" You reply modestly, "Well, the reservation info is readily available from the shared corporate databases, and I found the locations of the homes and offices of these guests through a Zip Code site and MapQuest." You conclude: "It took me only about a half-hour."

A week later the manager congratulates you in front of the general manager for providing the marketing information that resulted in a successful marketing campaign targeting trade publications in the northeast and an airport campaign in your local metropolitan area. Everyone thinks you are a hero, but you think to yourself, "Anyone could have found this information."

SUMMARY

This chapter discussed the connection of computers through the use of networks and telecommunications for the purpose of local and global communications. LANS are local networks, usually contained within a building, that provide for the sharing of information and computer resources. WANs and MANs perform the same functions over much broader ranges. The public domain access for telecommunications is the Internet, more specifically the World Wide Web portion of the Internet. Hospitality and tourism organizations configure networks to connect internally within the organization and externally to the world through the Internet. Figure 4.7 shows a picture of these connections.

Figure 4.7 Connecting to Internal and External Systems

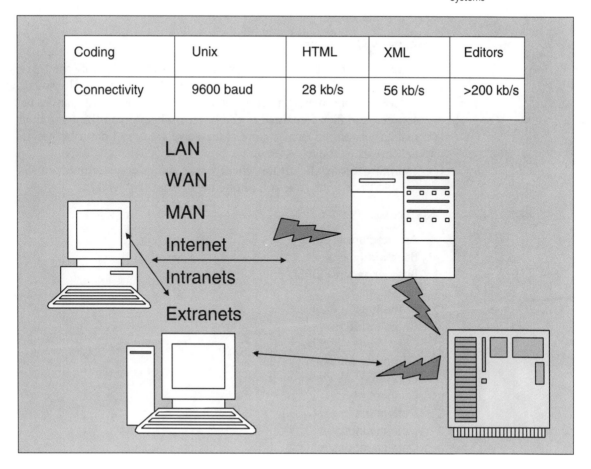

Coding	Unix	HTML	XML	Editors
Connectivity	9600 baud	28 kb/s	56 kb/s	>200 kb/s

LAN

WAN

MAN

Internet

Intranets

Extranets

Intranets and extranets use the same configuration as the Internet (browsers and search engines) but are private networks that are owned by an organization. Intranets permit access to information, such as employee portals, for employees in the organization's properties as well as those working from remote sites. Extranets are used to link outside parties to limited information sources within an organization.

The corporate network manager is the individual responsible for the development, maintenance, and resource management of an organization's networks. The software that performs these functions is called the network operating system. There are various network architecture topologies, with no specific format being appropriate to every situation. However, the current philosophy is to employ topologies designed within the client/server model, which permits end users to use networks to their full advantage.

The prominence of the Internet has brought the hospitality and tourism industry into the e-business age. Managers must become aware of recent developments in telecommunication technologies to serve the needs of customers and guests and maintain competitive strategies for their organizations.

DISCUSSION QUESTIONS

1. When using computers at work and school, can you identify the LAN, WAN, and MAN that are parts your network? Describe how they work.
2. Since network managers are responsible for the maintenance, resources, and files contained in the system, what do you think are their main areas of concern? Name at least five areas and describe potential threats to those systems.
3. Thinking toward the future, what types of things do you think you will be able to do with your cell phone in the next few years?

KEY TERMS

Architecture topology
Bandwidth
Bits per second (BPS)
Broadband
Browser
Cable modem
Client/server architecture
Computer network
Computer telecommunications
Connectivity
Data marts
Data mining
Data warehouses
DB structures—network

Distributed database
DSL
Extranet
Fiber-optic wires
Host
Hypermedia database
Intranet
Interoperability
Internet Service Provider (ISP)
Intranet
Modems
Multiplexers
Network architecture
Network managers
Network nodes
Network operating systems
Networks
Object Oriented DBMS—on the Web
Online analytical processing (OLAP)
Open systems
Open systems interconnection (OSI)
Processors
Protocols
Search engine
Switching
Telecommunication channels—media, wiring
Telecommunications
Telecommunications control software
Telecommunications processors (modems, switches, routers, hubs)
Terminals
Topologies
Twisted pair, coaxial, fiber optic
Universal Resource Locator (URL)
WAN, LAN, MAN, Intranets, Extranets
Windows NT
Wireless—Terrestrial microwave, communications satellites
    (geosynch, LEOS, VSAT), Cellular and PCS, Wireless Application
    Protocol (WAP) for PDAs
World Wide Web (WWW)

REFERENCES

1. J. A. O'Brien. (2000). *Management Information Systems: Managing Information Technology in the E-Business Enterprise, 5th ed.* Boston: McGraw-Hill Irwin.
2. G. Gilder. (2000). *Telecosm: How Infinite Bandwidths Revolutionize Our World.* New York: Simon & Schuster.

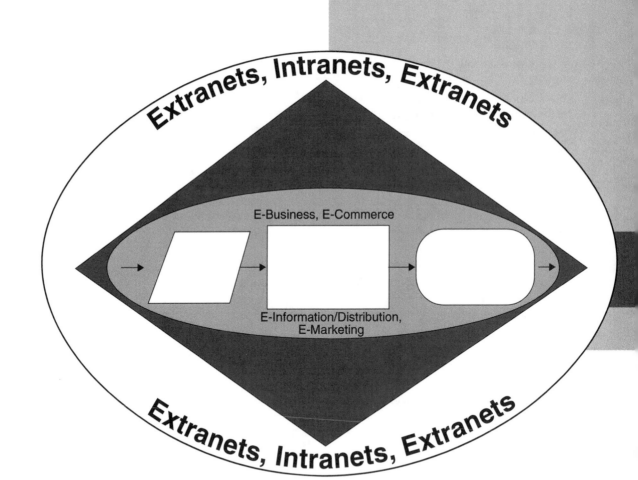

Hospitality Management and the Internet

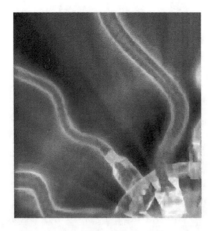

Electronic Commerce (E-Commerce)

CHAPTER OBJECTIVES

In this chapter you will learn to:

1. Apply e-commerce architecture to hospitality networks.

2. Identify e-commerce functions for hospitality organizations.

3. Identify the technical components of e-commerce networks used by hospitality organizations.

On-the-Job Training

You are working as an intern for a large meeting planning company. One of the clients of the company is planning a professional conference that will take place in Orlando. The conference attendees will book their own rooms on a transient basis. Your manager assigns you to help with the account. She asks you to identify suitable hotels around the perimeter of the meeting site and list the posted transient room rates for each of those hotels. In the next step of the project you will contact each hotel and solicit a discount room rate for conference attendees who book in advance. Your report is due to go to the manager in five days. As you review the requirements for this report, you ponder the quickest and easiest way to get the information.

To be continued . . .

INTRODUCTION

What pictures come into your mind when you think about the hospitality industry? Most people have visions of hotels, airlines, cruise ships, restaurants, health spas, and the like, based on their personal experiences. All aspects of the industry are involved in business processes at the operations level. Business processes consist of transactions and interactions with guests or customers, employees, and even other businesses. A transaction is an activity, such as checking in to a hotel or placing an order in a restaurant. Interactions include the relationships that take place during each transaction. A desk agent at a hotel takes the opportunity to create a positive first impression with a guest during the check-in process. An experienced restaurant server provides information about the preparation of menu items to enhance the dining experience. Hospitality differs from most other industries in that interactions create memorable customer experiences, whereas transactions merely satisfy basic customer expectations.

The business of the hospitality business consists primarily of interactions (guest relations) that occur during the flawless processing of transactions. Since we are involved in conducting a business, we are engaged in the practice of commerce. *Commerce* is a broad term that is used to describe the activities of businesses or commercial enterprises. **Electronic commerce** involves transactions and interactions that occur through computer telecommunications media, such as the Internet. **E-commerce** is the shorthand term used to describe electronic commerce. Before the popularity of the Internet, most business transactions and interactions took place in person in a commercial building made of "bricks and mortar." Beginning in the late 1990s, some retail establishments started to offer customers the option of transacting online or in person. These businesses usually are referred to as "clicks 'n bricks" today. There are other businesses that engage in commerce exclusively over the Internet, such as amazon.com; those businesses formerly were referred to as dot-coms. Today e-commerce professionals call them "clicks-without-bricks" enterprises.

Electronic commerce Transactions and interactions that occur through computer telecommunications networks.

E-commerce The shorthand term used to describe electronic commerce, which consists of transactions and interactions over computer telecommunications networks.

E-COMMERCE TRANSACTIONS

Electronic commerce includes all business functions that may be processed over telecommunications networks in any industry. For this reason the term *e-business* is used interchangeably with *e-commerce*. General e-business or e-commerce transactions may occur at four levels of interaction.

The Four Levels of E-Commerce Transactions

B2C transactions involve business-to-consumer interactions. A person who goes online to book an airline reservation (consumer) is engaged in that transaction with the reservations department for an airline (business).

B2C Transactions involving business-to-consumer interactions.

B2B transactions occur between two business entities. Let us say you book a hotel room through Orbitz, an online broker of travel and lodging arrangements. Orbitz is a business that prepurchases blocks of rooms from a given hotel (another business) for sale to you at discount prices. The arrangement between Orbitz and the hotel is a B2B transaction, whereas your interaction as an online customer of Orbitz is a B2C transaction.

B2B Transactions involving business-to-business interactions.

B2E consists of transactions that occur between a business and its employees. Delta Air, for example, provides an electronic system for flight mechanics to order replacement parts for aircraft called INIRN, which stands for "I Need It Right Now." In this case the business is providing an electronic service for its employees.

B2E Transactions involving business-to-employee interactions.

C2C transactions occur between two or more consumers (consumer-to-consumer). eBay is an example of a business that exists to bring

C2C Transactions involving consumer-to-consumer interactions.

together consumers who wish to sell merchandise with consumers who are looking to buy items over the Internet. Figure 5.1 shows the e-commerce transaction categories.

Intranets and Extranets

Do all e-commerce transactions occur over the Internet? Those transactions look as though they occurred over the Internet, but some of them really use private networks that only appear to be the Internet. There are three points of access to an e-commerce site: the Internet, intranets, and extranets. The Internet is a public domain that consists of an unknown number of servers around the world. An Internet user surfs the Internet via a browser: software such as Netscape or Internet Explorer. The same scheme is true for users of both intranets and extranets, leading to the appearance of Internet use for those users.

Figure 5.1 E-Commerce
Transaction Categories

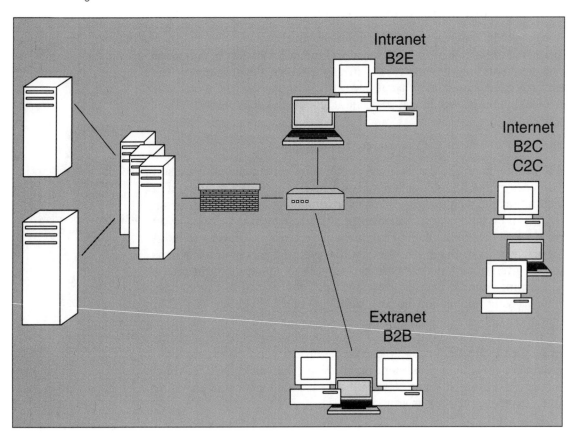

An **intranet** permits access to private network areas by individuals who are employed or otherwise affiliated with a hospitality organization. Individuals who have permission to enter the company intranet will access it directly from the Ethernet network while they are at the workplace. Individuals may gain access from remote locations through the Internet website for that organization. Once they enter the company's intranet, they are surfing on a private network that is owned by that hospitality company. Some employees use intranets to perform their jobs from their homes or other remote locations, a process known as **telecommuting.** For instance, a hotel reservations agent could forward a phone extension to her home and book guest reservations through an intranet that interfaces with the central reservations system.

Intranet Permits access to private network areas by individuals who are employed or otherwise affiliated with a hospitality organization.

Individuals or companies that are not employees or "insiders" of a hospitality organization may be permitted access to private areas of a network through an extranet. These connections almost always are made from remote locations; thus, **extranet** users enter through the hospitality company's Internet website. Extranet users include vendors, consultants, and service providers who do business with the hospitality organization. In some cases, special customers, such as airline frequent fliers, may be given extranet access to review their accounts and take advantage of certain privileges.

Telecommuting Employees using intranets to perform their jobs from their homes or other remote locations.

Extranet Permits access to private areas of a hospitality organization's network for individuals who are not employees or company affiliates.

Users of intranets and extranets may think they are using the Internet because the access points to private networks are "seamless." That is, it appears to the user that he or she is using the Internet even though he or she has accessed areas of a private network. This is the case because intranets and extranets use the same types of browsers and search engines that are available on the Internet.

SPAN AND SCOPE OF E-COMMERCE

What specific business functions are provided through e-commerce? It is the nature of some industries to provide all their functions and services to others via electronic networks. However, this is not the case with hospitality and tourism organizations, in which the core business involves the creation of memorable F2F (face-to-face) experiences. Many hospitality functions, though, are available through electronic means for the convenience of customers, employees, and commercial enterprises that do business with our industry. Figure 5.2 depicts e-commerce business functions for the hospitality industry.

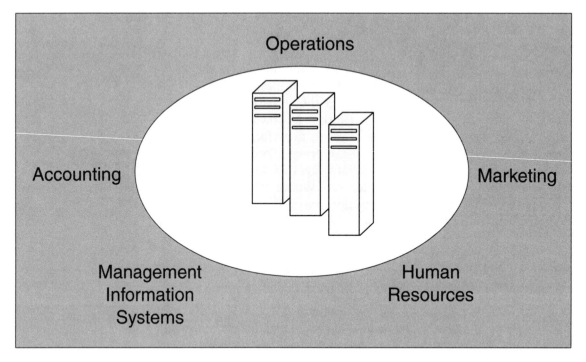

Figure 5.2 Hospitality E-Commerce Business Functionalities

Management Information Systems

Management Information Systems (MISs) Link information technologies with information systems to support enterprise transactions and interactions.

Electronic information systems provide the foundation for all e-commerce transactions. This function falls within the domain of **management information systems (MISs),** which link information technologies with information systems to support enterprise transactions and interactions. MIS technologies include hardware, software, databases, and application programs that are used to convert data into usable information. Information systems use telecommunication tools to create networks that provide connectivity within the hospitality organization and beyond through the Internet. There is thorough discussion of electronic information systems in Chapter 6.

Marketing The management of the pricing, placement, and promotion of products and services provided by a specific hospitality enterprise.

Marketing

The majority of hospitality e-commerce systems are focused on the marketing business function. **Marketing** involves the management of the pricing, placement, and promotion of products and services provided by a specific hospitality enterprise. **E-marketing** uses electronic networks for the promotion and placement of products and services. For instance, W Hotels, a portfolio of luxury-boutique properties owned by the

E-marketing Electronic networks used for the promotion and placement of products and services.

Business travelers expect electronic conveniences provided by airports, airlines, and other hospitality businesses. (Courtesy Corbis Digital Stock.)

Starwood Hotel Group, was one of the first to offer online "virtual tours" of its properties. This enables a prospective client to conduct site visits without having to travel to each property. Most branded hotels provide this promotion feature today. If a client makes the decision to book a group with one of the properties, the arrangements also may be made on-line; this is an example of electronic placement of the hotel product.

Accounting

Accounting Financial transactions, including accounts payable, accounts receivable, payroll, journal entries, ledgers, banking, and cashiering.

Suppose the online client books her group with a specific W Hotel and wants to establish a master folio with billing arrangements at the time of booking. The sales agent will have to make these arrangements through the accounting office for the hotel. The **accounting** function is responsible for all financial transactions, including accounts payable, accounts receivable, payroll, journal entries, ledgers, banking, and cashiering. In this case, the client will establish a credit account (ledger) with the hotel that will translate into a master folio that places all the charges incurred at the hotel to that ledger account. At the time of group departure from the hotel, the ledger account is transmitted to accounts receivable for billing and payment by the client in accordance with the instructions made available on the ledger. Once the payment is received by the hotel, the ledger will be cleared, with the account being marked as "paid in full." If the reservation requires a cash deposit, the client can provide payment with her corporate credit card through a **secure electronic payment system,** which provides for encrypted payment transactions to protect the credit card information from access by unauthorized individuals referred to as "network sniffers." The majority of accounting transactions are handled electronically through private computer networks that link operating departments as well as corporate offices. Interfaces for client transactions usually are located on Web pages that may be accessed through the Internet.

Secure electronic payment systems Encrypted payment transactions that protect credit card information from access by unauthorized individuals.

Operations

Vendors Organizations that provide materials, equipment, and supplies to a hospitality company.

Electronic data interchange (EDI) Permits the electronic exchange of inventory information, purchase orders, invoices, and funds transfers to settle accounts.

Some hospitality organizations establish electronic connections with **vendors,** which are companies that provide materials, equipment, and supplies to a hospitality organization. This type of connection, which is called an **electronic data interchange (EDI),** permits the electronic exchange of inventory information, purchase orders, invoices, and funds transfers to settle accounts.

Human Resources

Human resources (HR) Recruitment, selection, development, and retention of employees.

Portal A location on a telecommunications network for access by all the members of a special-interest group.

The **human resources (HR)** function of a hospitality organization is responsible for the recruitment, selection, development, and retention of employees. Human resources departments use e-commerce over the Internet to announce job openings. In some cases the HR office will provide online applications for employment to be filled out by interested job candidates. Some HR offices also use B2E networks to communicate with existing company employees. This is done by setting up a **portal** for employees to view benefit plans, file insurance claims, access other benefits, and even take advantage of employee discounts on products and services offered by outside organizations. A portal is a location on a telecommunications network for access by all the members of a special-interest group. In this case an employee portal provides a single location for all the workers in a hospitality organization to view information, complete online forms, and access perquisites and other benefits associated with their employment.

E-COMMERCE APPLICATIONS FOR HOSPITALITY ORGANIZATIONS

The hospitality industry is composed of many service-oriented businesses. Those businesses include lodging facilities such as hotels, resorts, motels, and bed and breakfasts and hostels run by innkeepers. The public foodservice domain includes upscale and midrange full-service, theme, casual dining, and quick service restaurants. The travel sector is composed of airline, cruise line, ground transportation, and tour organizations. Golf, tennis, and city and yacht clubs as well as health spas, casinos, theme parks/attractions, showrooms, and nightclubs fall within the recreation/entertainment sector. Finally, there are the convention, conference, retreat, and banquet facilities that constitute the meetings and events segment of the industry. All these businesses may implement e-commerce systems and strategies at the B2C level. Some of them also may include B2B, B2E, and even C2C applications. Figure 5.3 shows the different sectors of the hospitality and tourism industry.

Lodging

Most B2C e-commerce in the lodging sector focuses on product and/or service awareness as well as the placement of reservations. Hotel websites are listed with major search engines on the World Wide Web to enhance the chances of discovery by consumers who are seeking lodging facilities at desired destinations. Hotel websites are designed with plentiful photo graphics that allow visitors to inspect the facility, grounds, guestrooms, and amenities visually. Many hotel websites provide enhanced multimedia presentations designed to give virtual tours of the facilities to prospective guests, using streaming videos and 360-degree viewing platforms of lobby areas, guestrooms, meeting facilities, and other full-service amenities.

Visitors to the sites may click on pricing information as well as package deals and other special booking incentives. Many larger hotel chains

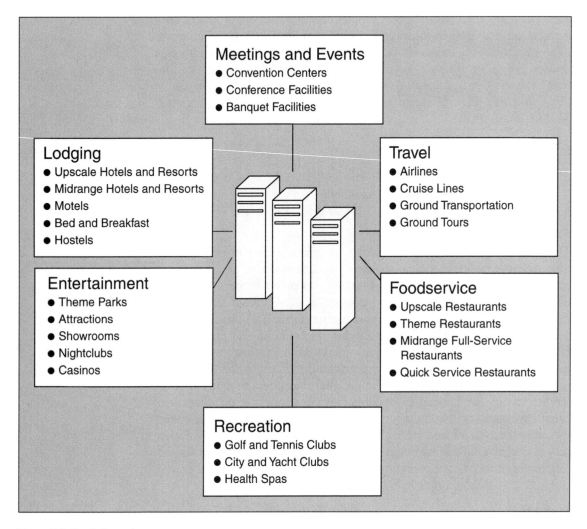

Figure 5.3 Hospitality and Tourism Sectors

provide a link to a reservations system portal, permitting clients to book reservations online. In these cases the hotel will provide a secure billing feature for potential guests to secure the reservation with a major credit card. Others will take room reservations via e-mail or provide a phone number to connect to the central reservations office. From a general e-commerce perspective, the purpose of most hotel websites is for shoppers to discover and evaluate the products being offered by a specific lodging facility to encourage the placement of a reservation.

In many cases, search engines take Web surfers to the sites of lodging brokers such as Hotels.com and Orbitz. These companies are known as **intermediaries,** organizations that purchase blocks of hotel rooms for

Intermediaries
Organizations that purchase blocks of hotel rooms for resale to travelers, often at discounted rates.

resale to travelers, often at discounted rates. Travelers who use these services actually are booking guestrooms through third-party entities that perform services similar to those formerly provided by travel agents. Hotels contract with these intermediaries to fill guestrooms during non-peak occupancy periods.

Travel and Foodservice

Restaurant and travel companies employ B2C e-commerce strategies that are similar to those used by the lodging sector. In the case of restaurants, the purpose of the website is to use graphics and multimedia to entice customers to reserve a table either online or by phone. The same thing is true for cruise vacations and ground tours. Travel organizations, in contrast, focus on ticket pricing and availability through their websites. Airline websites, for instance, have tables and limited graphics for visitors to view. The visitor enters destination information into windows that launch tables that display available flights and pricing information. A link to the central reservation system is available for those who decide to book a specific flight. Similar to the case in the lodging industry, many individuals book their flights through intermediaries such as cheap-tickets.com and priceline.com.

Meetings and Events

E-commerce strategies for the meetings and events sector of the hospitality industry closely mirror those for the lodging sector, with one exception. This sector is focused solely on group bookings, which means the client is the host of a group. The hotel market consists of both group and transient (individual) bookings. The website for a meetings and events facility is designed to entice a host to book the facility for a group of individuals.

Recreation and Entertainment

Recreation and entertainment sector e-commerce strategies are perhaps the narrowest in scope among the hospitality niches. Most of these sites exist to provide product discovery, awareness, and evaluation. They do not for the most part seek a booking transaction from website visitors. In the case of recreation and social clubs, some are private, which means individuals must purchase memberships to use the facility. These transactions still occur mostly on a face-to-face basis. Public clubs encourage nonmember visitation; however, most clubs arrange tee and court times by phone. Yacht clubs are in the business of renting dockage to boaters, and these arrangements usually are made by phone, by mail, or in person. Show venues commonly assign ticket purchases to centralized global systems such as Ticketron, whereas nightclubs and theme parks are mostly in the business of selling tickets "at the door."

All sectors of the hospitality industry embrace the use of B2C e-commerce, although with certain limitations arising from the intimate nature of the services that are provided to guests and clients. It is feasible for hospitality organizations to offer e-commerce solutions for customers to research core products, learn about those products, and be stimulated to engage in booking transactions in most cases. However, product distribution and customer support functions take place in person, which is not the case with the alternatives available to retail operations.

Many sectors of the hospitality industry provide retail outlets such as gift shops that sell specialized products, including packaged food items and logo merchandise, to the public. These items may be marketed, ordered, and distributed to customers through e-commerce interfaces within hospitality organizations. Although the sales of such items are often lucrative, the retail aspect is ancillary to the core products and services provided by hospitality companies.

TECHNICAL COMPONENTS OF E-COMMERCE

All computer networks consist of two major areas: the front end and the back end.

Front and Back Ends

Front end Points of access for e-commerce end users, including customers, employees, and business affiliates.

Back end Contains interfaced components designed to provide e-commerce services to end users.

Firewall Computer communications processor that filters all network traffic to provide a safe transfer point for access into a network and transmission to other networks.

The **front end** of an e-commerce network consists of points of access for end users, which include customers, employees, and business affiliates. The **back end** of the network contains interfaced components designed to provide e-commerce services to the end users. Both ends of the system include computer hardware, software, and telecommunication interfaces. A pictorial representation of a typical e-commerce network is given in Figure 5.4.

The front-end computers are those to the right side of the **firewall:** a computer communications processor that filters all network traffic to provide a safe transfer point for access to a network and transmission to other networks. The Internet exists at the farthest point from the e-commerce network that lies to the left of the firewall. Authorized Web users may access various servers within the network, including intranets and extranets, from remote locations. Conversely, individuals at the

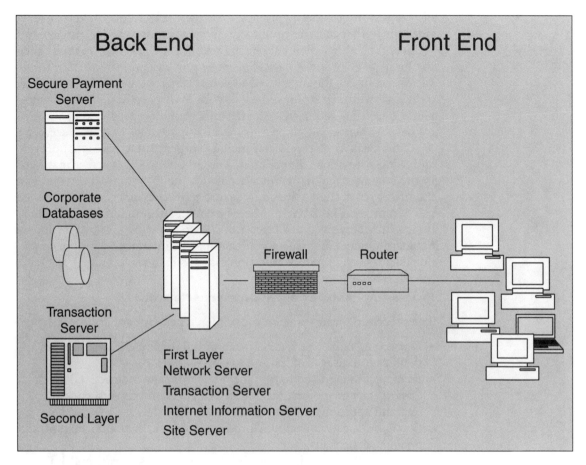

Back End   Front End

Secure Payment
Server

Corporate
Databases

Firewall   Router

Transaction
Server

First Layer
Network Server
Transaction Server
Internet Information Server
Second Layer   Site Server

Figure 5.4 Typical
E-Commerce Network

worksite can use the network to launch out to the Internet. Hence, there is a two-way exchange between the e-commerce network of servers and the Internet.

The back-end network architecture consists of two layers of servers. The first layer is just behind the firewall, where the local network server, transaction server, and Internet information servers may be accessed directly by end users. This layer is interfaced with a number of core servers that may include corporate databases and transaction-processing servers in the second layer. The intermediary between end users and the firewall is an electronic component called a router. Users access the firewall through the router and pass the security clearance process to enter the Internet information server.

The site server holds an index of files written in **Hypertext Markup Language (HTML),** a code used to generate Web pages. Web pages

Hypertext Markup Language (HTML) A code used to generate Web pages.

display text information, graphics, and hyperlinks to other Web directories. They often include multimedia presentations that are run by Java script applets. When a user accesses a site, the first page to pop up is called the home page or index page. This page provides an introduction to the site and contains the links used to access different areas of the site. The individual with primary responsibility for Web page design and maintenance is called a webmaster. The server is connected to the company's local network server, which provides a gateway to other back-end servers.

Other back-end servers may include corporate databases that provide all business functions. In addition, a second transaction server may exist in the second layer that is interfaced with the first transaction server in the first layer of the back end. A secure payment server also may be located in the second layer to process payments through financial institutions. Other servers in this layer (not shown in Figure 5.4) may include a Standard Query Language server that may be interfaced with the corporate database and credit verification and profiling servers.

Processing Features of E-Commerce Networks

The processing features of an e-commerce network are listed below:

- *Security* and *access control* takes place within the firewall and includes authentication, user profiles, and log-on records.
- *Search applets* are used to find locations from the index of server files.
- *Content maintenance* ensures that information on the Web pages is current and appropriate for users to view.
- *Catalog management* includes product and/or service information and pricing calculations.
- *Payment management* involves the maintenance, security, and linkages with payment servers.
- *Workflow management* consists of logical configurations for user interaction and transaction processing.
- *Event notification* includes transaction messaging and advertisement notices sent to profiled end users.

Access Process for Web Users

A Web user will begin by logging on to an Internet Service Provider. Next, the user will launch a Web browser such as Netscape or Internet Explorer to reach the default home page established by the user. If the user is unsure of the Universal Resource Locator (URL) address of an e-commerce site, he will invoke a search engine such as Google or Yahoo! The user enters key words to start the search for the e-commerce site. The user then clicks on the URL address provided by the search engine, which takes him to the home page for the e-commerce site. Figure 5.5 shows this process.

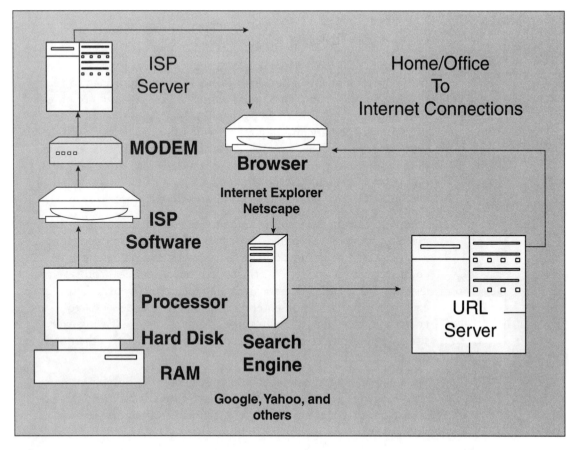

Figure 5.5 Connecting to an E-Commerce Site

The home page contains links to various servers that support the site from the back end *(content maintenance)*. Let's say the user has visited the site for an airline and wants to view the availability and pricing of flights for a specific range of dates *(catalog management)*. The user clicks on a link to view flights *(search applets)*. He may be asked for profile information such as frequent flier identification to gain entry through the firewall into the flight availability database *(security and access)*. When the user finds a suitable flight, he is linked to the airline's central reservation system (CRS) to book a reservation *(workflow management)*. Once the flight is selected, the user is transferred to a secure payment server to enter credit card information *(payment management)*. When the payment is verified, a confirmation number appears on the user's screen and a receipt is sent to the user's e-mail account *(event notification)*. This completes the booking transaction for the user. The profile of the user is entered into the marketing database of the airline for future e-mail advertisement notifications *(future event notification)*.

On-the-Job Training . . . Continued

While pondering your steps in producing the report for the meeting planning company, you decide to take a strategic approach to getting hotel information. First, you conduct a Google search of hotel intermediaries and find three companies. Next, you enter the website of each intermediary and request a listing of hotels in the targeted area. The result of this search is a list of 20 suitable hotels. You then plug in your occupancy dates and request daily rates for each hotel on the list. The result of this activity is a listing of 20 hotels, types of accommodations, and posted room rates for each hotel.

Next, you compose a letter that identifies you as representing the meeting planning company. The letter includes dates of occupancy and projected room blocks. The letter serves as a request for discounted guestroom rates for the conference attendees. You save the letter in your word processor. You then locate the website URLs for each of the hotels. Upon entering each site, you review posted guestroom rates for your dates of occupancy. Before leaving each site, you click on the e-mail icon and paste your letter to the hotel e-mail account.

You open your spreadsheet software and enter the hotel information, room rates from each of the three intermediaries, and posted rates from each hotel website. As you finish entering the information, you realize it is time to go home.

When you return to the office the next morning, you find a number of e-mails waiting for you from many of the hotel reservation managers. By lunchtime all the hotels have responded to you with their best discounted rates. As soon as you return from lunch, you enter this information on your spreadsheet.

You glance at the spreadsheet, which now reveals the following: a listing of 20 suitable hotels, posted rates from three intermediaries, posted rates from each hotel website, and discounted rates from each hotel. It is just 24 hours since the manager gave you this assignment. You hand a copy of the spreadsheet to the manager, and she is shocked that you found so much information in such a short period. She asks, "How were you able to get so much information so quickly?" You reply, "Oh, it is just a little trick I learned in school about working smarter, not harder." You both chuckle, and you leave the office knowing that the boss is very impressed with your efficiency.

SUMMARY

This chapter provided a snapshot of the e-commerce systems that are used in the hospitality and tourism industry. We learned that hospitality customer service consists of transactions and interactions. The core transactions of our business involve intimate face-to-face interactions, which have certain limitations in regard to the use of e-commerce in the hospitality industry compared with other enterprises, such as retail. However, certain electronic applications are appropriate for the convenience of guests and clients.

Although the main telecommunications link for e-commerce is the Internet, private networks such as extranets and intranets are also part of the e-commerce landscape. The major functions of B2C, B2B, and B2E e-business include management information systems and the marketing, accounting, human resources, and operations departments. The chapter gave examples of these functions as they are applied to various hospitality business sectors.

Next, there was a discussion of the technical aspects of hospitality e-commerce from the perspectives of the front end used by customers, businesses, and employees and the back end of the system, where transaction processing takes place. The chapter described the processing features of hospitality e-commerce systems and concluded with a discussion of the processes in action from a Web user's perspective.

DISCUSSION QUESTIONS

1. What are your thoughts on e-commerce applications to the hospitality industry? Do you see areas where new applications may be developed, or do you think the current applications are sufficient?
2. What are the advantages and disadvantages of implementing intranets for hospitality workers to use? Do you think intranets can enhance productivity? Why or why not?
3. If you were a webmaster for a hospitality e-commerce site, what actions might you take to improve the site's Web pages?
4. Toward the end of the chapter we discussed a Web user's access to an airline site. See if you can replicate these activities for booking a hotel guestroom.

KEY TERMS

Accounting
B2B
B2C

B2E
Back end
C2C
E-commerce
Electronic commerce
Electronic data interchange (EDI)
E-marketing
Extranet
Firewall
Front end
Human resources
Hypertext Markup Language (HTML)
Intermediaries
Intranet
Management information systems (MIS)
Marketing
Portal
Secure electronic payment systems
Telecommuting
Vendors

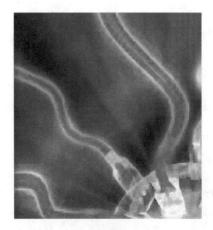

E-Information and Distribution Systems

CHAPTER OBJECTIVES

In this chapter you will learn to:

1. Apply the components of interactive IT to e-information systems.

2. Identify the business functions that constitute an integrated system.

3. Identify the components included in enterprise resource planning systems.

On-the-Job Training

For the last year you have been working part-time in the reservations office of a hotel in a popular beach resort town. The hotel is one of three similar properties within a four-block radius along the beach. All three hotels are owned by the same company, yet each property operates as an individual entity.

It is the practice at your hotel to overbook reservations by 10 percent, resulting in 110 percent bookings when the hotel is fully booked. Guests who arrive after the hotel is sold out are "walked" to one of the sister hotels and given rooms at a discounted rate. If the sister hotels are sold out, the guests are walked to a competitor, which charges the hotel the full "rack" rate for each walk.

You meet with the front-desk manager, Ken, for lunch to find out that he is very distressed. "What's bothering you, Ken?" you ask. He starts going off on how all he does is deal with dissatisfied guests who get walked to other properties. You ask, "Why do we overbook the way we do?" He responds, "As long as I have been here, it has been company policy to fill rooms at the sister properties." He mutters in apparent disgust, "There has to be a better way."

To be continued . . .

INTRODUCTION

Hospitality e-commerce consists of transactions and interactions between the business and customers (guests), employees, and other businesses. People in the industry recognize that our business-to-customer transactions are personal and intimate, which somewhat limits this aspect of e-commerce in the hospitality industry. These limitations, however, do not apply to the e-information and distribution systems that help us enhance productivity in our businesses.

This chapter focuses on applications of information and distribution systems that provide interfaces to each of the hospitality business functions. The transaction processes that occur in the hospitality industry, such as order placement and payment, are pretty much the same in all industries. The face-to-face interactions between hospitality staff members and guests and clients constitute the core product of our business. E-information and distribution systems use technology to provide communication among interdependent operating units; this permits the staff members to focus on the core competencies of creating memorable experiences for the guests of our hotels, restaurants, recreation facilities, entertainment venues, and travel companies.

HOSPITALITY BUSINESS FUNCTIONS

Hospitality operations are quite complex because of the need to manage every moment that constitutes the guest experience. E-information and distribution bring together all the business functions that contribute to the operation of successful hospitality organizations. For this reason, a functional approach is taken in this chapter. The **business functions** of hospitality organizations include marketing, human resources management, accounting, and operations. Figure 6.1 provides a sample organization chart based on the business functions of a hospitality company.

Business functions
Include marketing, human resources management, accounting, and operations.

The Productivity Process

The **productivity model** for hospitality organizations consists of inputs, transformation processes, and outputs. Another term for *inputs* is *resources,* since inputs include material, financial, and human resources. **Resources** are the people and things that are required to produce a product or service. The hospitality industry falls within the mixed-use classification, since all our organizations primarily provide intimate services but also produce their own products. Note that technology is included in the list of resources in Figure 6.2. Today technology is a resource that serves as an important input for hospitality organizations to enhance productivity, competitive posture, and service quality. Hospitality organizations now include information systems and technology as part of the strategic corporate direction for each firm. The emergence of **chief information officers (CIOs)** as members of senior management teams demonstrates the importance of technology in enhancing productivity processes.

The shareholders of the organization provide financing to purchase resources that are used to generate products and services in hospitality organizations. These shareholders expect a return on investment (ROI) from the profits that are created through organizational outputs. The **transformation process** includes all systems that are used to convert

Productivity model
Consists of inputs, transformation processes, and outputs.

Resources The people and things that are required to produce a product or service.

Chief information officers (CIOs) Members of senior management teams responsible for information technology and information systems in organizations.

Transformation process
All the systems that are used to convert resources into outputs (products and services).

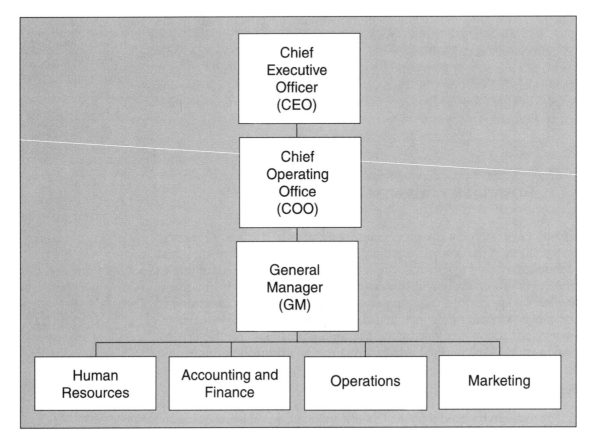

Figure 6.1 Hospitality Organization Chart by Business Functions

Figure 6.2 Productivity Process

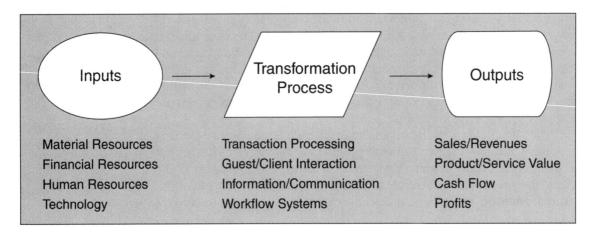

resources into outputs (products and services). **Outputs** are measured in terms of quantity and quality. Quantity measures focus on sales volumes, which equate to revenues. The difference between revenues and expenses (resource and transformation costs) is profit. The profits that are generated from outputs are used to reimburse the shareholders for their initial investments in resource acquisition.

Quality measures equate to the value of the products and services that are produced. The value perception lies solely with the customers, clients, and guests of the hospitality organization. As the value perception increases, the sales price per unit also increases, and this in turn increases both revenues and profits. An example of value perception is the case of the Ritz-Carlton hotel chain, which has twice earned the prestigious Malcolm Baldrige Award for Quality Excellence. Company executives provide the primary source of transient guestroom business for Ritz-Carlton hotels. These individuals recognize the value of the Baldrige Award, which makes them willing to pay higher room rates for each visit to a Ritz-Carlton property. The average daily rate (ADR) for guestrooms increased significantly after Ritz-Carlton won the award. Higher ADR generates increased revenues. If costs remain constant, a higher ADR also will result in more profits, which will increase the ROI for shareholders.

Historically, we have managed the productivity model in hospitality organizations manually. Today, however, newer technologies permit hospitality managers to improve and automate the interfaces among resource allocation, transformation systems, and output generation. Figure 6.3 depicts productivity model interfaces from a stakeholder perspective.

Outputs Products and services that are measured in terms of quantity and quality.

Figure 6.3 Productivity Stakeholders

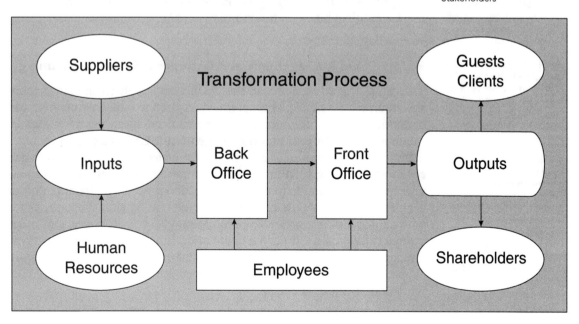

Stakeholder Groups

There are four basic **stakeholder groups** in a typical hospitality organization: guests (customers/clients), employees, shareholders, and the community (suppliers, neighbors, industry colleagues, society, etc.). The shareholders invest capital finances to fund the acquisition of resources used to produce products and services. The expectation of this group is to recover the initial investment plus additional remuneration based on the profits of the company. Employees are human resources that convert material and information resources into outputs through the transformation process of the productivity model. Suppliers are part of the community stakeholder group that provides resources such as equipment, supplies, and raw materials for employees to convert into hospitality-related products and services. The guests or clients are the recipients of the outputs produced by the company's employees. The expectation of this group is to enjoy quality hospitality experiences. The perceived guest value of the services rendered by a hospitality enterprise drives the pricing of that firm's outputs.

E-BUSINESS PROCESSES

There is a new model for the information distribution process that supports hospitality and tourism organizations. The key feature of this business process is the design of cross-functional information systems that handle multiple business functions.

Supply Chain Management and Enterprise Resource Planning

The two processes presented in this chapter are supply chain management and enterprise resource planning, which are used to facilitate front-end and back-end electronic commerce (e-commerce) and internal employee application interfaces. **Supply chain management (SCM)** is a system of information interfaces with sources of supply for material resources. **Enterprise resource planning (ERP)** is the overall information system used to maximize resource utilization in the transformation process and manage output generation. Hospitality **e-commerce** is the use of electronic media for transactions and interactions among guests/clients, employees, and other business enterprises. **Employee application interfaces (EAIs)** are B2E information systems that are used to maximize employee productivity. Figure 6.4 provides an overview of the hospitality e-commerce model from an information distribution perspective.

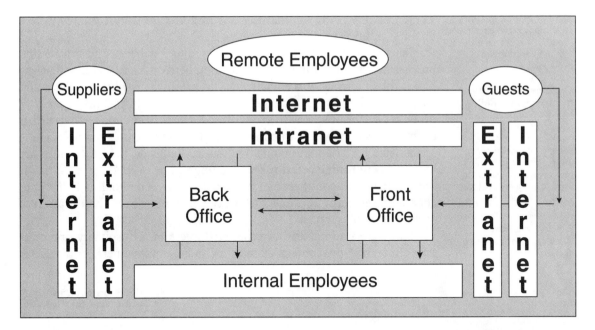

Figure 6.4 Hospitality E-Commerce Model

Marketing Support Technologies

The business function of **marketing** is concerned with the planning, promotion, and sales of existing or new products in new or current markets. Figure 6.4 shows the information systems and technologies used to support the marketing function. Mass marketing is intended to create a market from the masses of potential consumers. Direct marketing is aimed at a specific niche of consumers. Interactive marketing involves interdependent communications with consumers and ultimately customers about a product or service. The Internet makes interactive marketing a common feature in business enterprises, including the manufacturing and service sectors.

Hospitality operations fall within the service industry classification. However, these organizations also are in the business of manufacturing products. For example, a full-service hotel includes a food and beverage department that is responsible for the management of restaurants and other related outlets. The culinary staff in a restaurant is in the business of creating menu items from raw ingredients. In this sense, the culinary staff is producing manufactured products that are distributed to the guests of the restaurant outlet by the service staff. This feature is unique compared with general business models that place commercial enterprises in one of two categories: manufacturing or service. Most sectors of the hospitality industry are both manufacturers and service providers.

Marketing A business function that is concerned with the planning, promotion, and sales of existing or new products in new or current markets.

Mixed-function industry
Hospitality business sectors that are both manufacturers and service providers.

Customer relationship management (CRM) A holistic system of advertising, promotion, and target marketing; market research; and forecasting using electronic data mining and analysis to generate long-term guest/customer loyalty.

External customers
Guests, passengers, and clients.

Therefore, one could say that this is a **mixed-function industry** from a business administration perspective.

Sales force automation provides access to databases and transaction processing from remote locations by members of the sales force that enhance the efficiency and effectiveness of product distribution. Sales and customer relationship management provides analyses and reports of product distribution. The Internet provides enhancements to advertising, promotion, and target marketing efforts. Market research and forecasting are assisted by data mining and analysis. Collectively, these functions are known as **customer relationship management (CRM)** systems; this is the essence of e-commerce in its current state. The goal of CRM is to generate long-term guest/client loyalty that will last for the duration of each guest's life span.

There are internal and external customers in a hospitality organization. **External customers** consist of guests, passengers, and clients.

Customers, both internal and external, are integral to the hospitality industry. (Courtesy Corbis Digital Stock.)

Internal customers are employees who serve those people; hence, they are the customers of the support staff. In turn, the support staff members use information systems to do their jobs, which makes them internal customers of the information technology staff. Thus, everyone is a customer.

Internal customers
Employees who serve other employees who serve external customers; otherwise referred to as support staff.

Holistic E-Commerce Approach

Figure 6.5 depicts a holistic e-commerce approach for hospitality constituencies.

The holistic e-commerce model provides for business-to-business functions on the supply chain side of the organization (inputs). Business-to-customer functions occur at the front end of the organization through outputs. In addition, business-to-employee functions enhance productivity by using technology to support workers in the transformation process. Figure 6.5 shows the interactive services that occur throughout the productivity process of inputs, transformation processes, and outputs.

All the information presented in Figure 6.5 was mentioned earlier in this text. Guests and suppliers now interface with the hospitality organization through the Internet, which leads them to the company's extranet and takes them into the back- and front-office operations, respectively.

Figure 6.5 Constituency E-Commerce Approach

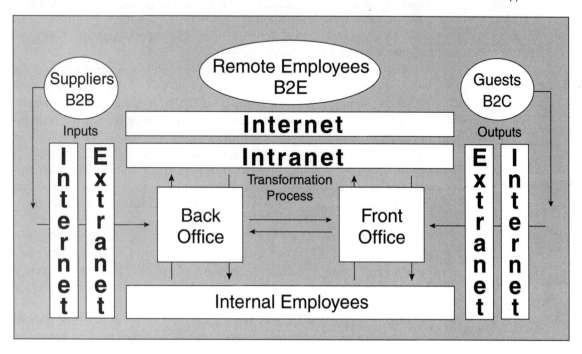

Remote employees also use the Internet to access the company's intranet to gain access to front- and back-office operations. Internal employees are those at the work site who use the intranet (direct Ethernet connection) to access databases and groupware.

ENTERPRISE RESOURCE PLANNING SYSTEMS

Electronic data interchange (EDI) Systems with suppliers that facilitate automated purchasing, inventory process control, just-in-time inventories, and electronic billing and payment processes; part of the SCM system.

The Enterprise resource planning model typifies the open systems model by allowing electronic access to the hospitality organization by all the stakeholder groups. B2C interfaces enhance customer relationships by providing direct access to sales and marketing information and parts of the property management system, such as reservations. B2B functions include **electronic data interchange (EDI)** systems with suppliers that facilitate automated purchasing, inventory process control, just-in-time (JIT) inventories, and electronic billing and payment processes. EDI is part of the supply chain management network. B2E is the newest focus of ERP systems; it enhances worker productivity by streamlining the transformation process and providing automated external services (such as dry cleaning pickup and delivery) to enhance the quality of life of employees and reduce outside distractions. Figure 6.6 shows these applications within a single organizational system. A small number of hospitality organizations have implemented ERP architecture throughout their operations on a global level. This form of operational centralization soon will become the norm for companies.

The next wave for MIS is to contribute to the strategic positioning of the hospitality/tourism organization. We saw this in the 1980s when the personnel department was elevated to the human resources function. The cause of the increased status was the strategic approach to HR management, recognizing that employees are human capital. The key force in MIS becoming a strategic business unit has been the opportunity for global networking via the Internet, intranets, and extranets. There are numerous opportunities to expand the open systems aspect of hospitality corporations. The only limitation for current and future hospitality managers is their imaginations.

Networking capability has eliminated geographic and time barriers to doing business. Information technology is playing a major role in business reengineering for the improvement of effectiveness and efficiency. Changes in workflow, job requirements, and organizational structures are attributable to IT.

Quality processes are enhanced greatly by IT. Continuous improvement processes, mass customization, service levels, costs, and customer

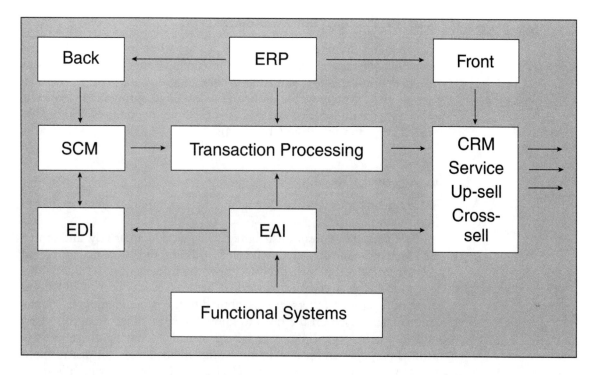

Figure 6.6 E-Business Systems

responsiveness are enhanced by IT applications. The statistical measurement process is tedious and time-consuming when it is done manually. Computer computation removes this burden and permits work units to focus on products and services.

Hospitality organizations that use IT capabilities enhance their competitive edge. Customized solutions, business collaboration, and flexible organization structures all provide what the customer is looking for when doing business with a firm.

As a customer, you may not realize that other organizations are participating in the development of your product or service, as you may be dealing with a virtual company that consists of many firms acting in collaboration. An example of this in our industry is the proliferation of online intermediaries that provide cruises, airline flights, and hotel rooms by working as brokers in collaboration with hospitality firms. In the near future hospitality organizations will establish their own intersector collaborative initiatives, which will eliminate the role of the independent hospitality broker. An example of this trend in the present is the near elimination of travel agents as third-party contractors of hospitality and tourism services.

Managers' Use of Information Systems

Information systems are efficient and effective when it comes to the management information used to make decisions. Managers have access to automated information that used to take long hours of tedious manual operations to compile. This is one of the intended outputs that drove the developments in the areas of database development and networking (discussed at greater length in Chapter 4).

Management Reports

Table 6.1 lists four types of management reports that are generated from information systems.

The periodic reports (distributed daily, weekly, quarterly, and annually) are automatically generated and distributed to lists of managers and executives based on their need to know the information. Additional reports such as schedules, hours worked, banquet event orders (BEOs), and occupancy, among others, are distributed to the general employee population, again based on the need to know the specific information. Many individuals in organizations are accustomed to having these reports printed on paper and placed in intracompany mailboxes for distribution. More progressive companies use electronic distribution, which is more effective and efficient than printed reports.

The other three examples listed in the table include reports that indicate an occurrence that is out of the ordinary scenario of business as usual. The reports are intended for notification that usually requires some action on the part of the manager.

Table 6.1 Management Standard Reports	
Periodic scheduled reports	Standard reports generated on periodic bases. Examples include night audit reports on a daily basis, month-to-date budget reports on a weekly basis, and variance reports on a monthly basis.
Exception reports	Produced and distributed when something out of the ordinary occurs. Flash and pop-up reports are examples.
Demand reports	Sorted and specialized reports available to managers through database report generators and SQL.
Push reports	Exceptional information "pushed" through the network to the workstations of all managers with a need to know. Similar to exception reports but distribution to a more specific group of managers.

Table 6.2 Online Analytical Processing	
Automated environment analysis	Data warehouses linked through a database management system with data-mining features.
Consolidation	Chain of regional offices to provide information by property, city, geographic region, district, or nation.
Drill-down	The opposite of consolidation. The chain home office can identify top producers at specific properties in ranking order and compare them with regional, district, or national performance benchmarks.
Slicing and dicing	Breaking information into customized segments, sectors, or niches.

Remember that reports are generated by queries that order the sorting and combining of various records in the database used to provide specific information and analysis. Marketing and project managers are particularly fond of the power associated with online analytical processing procedures available in progressive hospitality organizations. **Online analytical processing (OLAP)** uses electronic media to provide data collection and analysis from remote locations in real time. Table 6.2 provides a list of these activities.

The information presented in the table is particularly useful in marketing analysis to generate timely and accurate marketing plans. Note that the data may be arranged from broad volumes to very narrow areas for analysis. This feature provides information for specific analysis used in trend forecasting and single "snapshots" of individual operations as they relate to the entire organization. This type of analysis usually is performed by chain operations in lodging, restaurant, and travel-related organizations. For instance, an airline would use this procedure to view specific flight routes in terms of passenger load and profitability and use the information to redirect, add, or cancel segments. So far, we have examined the powerful ability of OLAP query, sort, distinction, and manipulation functions. This is the data collection, differentiation, and cross-categorization phase of OLAP. Once the data are placed in desired categories, managers may perform analyses by using decision support systems. Table 6.3 provides an overview of DSS functions.

Online analytical processing (OLAP) Uses electronic media to provide data collection and analysis from remote locations in real time.

Decision Support Systems

When it comes to strategic planning for all areas of the organization, **decision support systems (DSSs)** provide statistical support to justify or nullify what managers intuitively apply to making decisions. The table

Decision support systems (DSSs) Provide electronically generated statistical support to justify or nullify what managers intuitively apply to making decisions.

Table 6.3 Decision Support Systems	
Statistical software	Used to perform complex analysis of multiple variables to enhance revenue management.
What-if analysis	Considers hypothetical scenarios. For instance, what if a disaster were to occur in two major cities that would cause the immediate business interruption of leisure destination travel (the 9/11 tragedy of 2001)?
Sensitivity analysis	Specialized what-if analysis. For instance, how would different group profiles affect hotel retail sales in a given geographic location?
Goal-seeking analysis	Referred to as "how-can" analysis. For example, how can we increase sales by 10 percent over the same period as last year for a given number of hotels?
Optimization analysis	Provides templates for decisions to maximize profit and/or revenues. Yield management is a perfect example.

provides a listing of the most commonly used statistical analyses for the hospitality industry. It is important to note that the key word here is *support*. Some managers confuse the recommendations of these systems with final decisions. If this were true, there would be little need for thinking managers. Remember that technology is not here to replace people or thinking but to be used as a tool by people in organizations. Before the development of sophisticated DSS systems, spreadsheet application programs were touted as a manager's best tool for what-if analysis. With DSS systems, the what-if aspects go way beyond the figures plugged into a spreadsheet.

Other DSS applications include data mining (used for both data collection and decision support), executive information systems, and enterprise information portals. These functions require data-warehousing interfaces to access both internal and external sources of information. More information is provided for these functions in advanced technology courses covering e-commerce design and development. A brief description of each of these tools is provided in the following list:

- *Data-mining software:* Analyzes huge volumes of historical data to identify trends and patterns for current and future use.
- *Executive information systems:* Formerly used to help top-level managers make long-range strategic decisions. Today most managers in the strategic planning process use these systems.
- *Enterprise information portals:* Link internal and off-site data warehouses with extranets and intranets to access and analyze data within and outside an organization. When linked with hypermedia databases, the information is converted into business knowledge for current and future use; this is known as a knowledge management system.

ARTIFICIAL INTELLIGENCE

Artificial intelligence (AI) comes from the disciplines of computer science, biology, psychology, linguistics, mathematics, and engineering. The goal of AI is to create machines with human physical and mental abilities (reasoning, learning, and problem solving). AI is not a new technology application; however, it has not been used widely until recently, as cost and machine power limitations once prevented the development of its application for practical uses. Some of the aspects of AI are listed below[1]:

- *Neural networks:* The closest electrical simulation of an organic system. Composed of networked processors that interact as transponders and have the capacity for learning based on the identification of patterns and relationships.
- *Fuzzy logic:* Processors that can perform reasoning based on inferences and incomplete data (the opposite of "crisp data") in response to SQL inquiries.
- *Virtual reality:* Computer-simulated reality based on multisensory input and output devices to create undetected simulated environments through telepresence illusions.
- *Intelligent agents:* Applets that perform tasks for end users by using a built-in knowledge base about processes. Application wizards are good examples.
- *Expert systems (ESs):* Knowledge-based system that has expertise in a single discipline. Users pose questions and problems, and the ES provides solutions. The three components of all expert systems are as follows:
  —The knowledge base (KB) is the information contained by the system in factual and heuristic form.
  —The inference engine provides analysis tools for if/then reasoning and adds experiences to the KB through repetition.
  —A knowledge engineer and a logic programmer program the expert shell.

All these applications have been available from technology R&D laboratories since the early 1990s. Although smart chips have been built into commonly used machines and appliances that use some of these technologies (automobiles, for instance), the more powerful applications have been precluded from reaching marketplaces because of hardware constraints. Today, however, with more powerful microprocessors and lower hardware costs, researchers are considering broad applications of these technologies. The implications for the hospitality and tourism industry over the next 10 years will be limited only by the imaginations of decision makers. This is a wonderful time for hospitality practitioners, as these technologies permit hospitality managers to use their creative talents to envision and develop applications in conjunction with technical experts.

Artificial intelligence (AI)
The blended disciplines of computer science, biology, psychology, linguistics, mathematics, and engineering.

On-the-Job Training . . . Continued

After consoling Ken during lunch, you return to the department and share his concerns with the reservations manager. It so happens that one of the technology guys is fixing a computer in the area and overhears your conversation about overbooking. He says to you both, "Did you guys know that you can view the availability screens for the other hotels?" Marsha, the reservations manager, looks surprised. "How can that be?" she asks. The computer guy responds, "Well, when we did the installation of the new system, we went with a single server that is located at this property but also serves the other two." He continues: "A couple of years ago the owners were told that they could save a lot of money by purchasing one server, as opposed to individual servers for each property."

The computer guy then sits at a vacant monitor to display the availability screen from a sister property. "See," he says. "This screen will update every few minutes or so to show availability at the sister property." Marsha asks, "Do the GMs know they are all on the same system?" The computer guy responds, "I doubt it. They are left out of the loop when it comes to property technology."

As you are getting ready to end your shift, Marsha comes to you and invites you to a meeting with the general manager and Ken. The meeting takes place in the reservations office. Marsha sits at a monitor and says to all of you, "Watch this." She brings up the availability screen for the property, showing that it is fully booked. She then minimizes that screen and pulls up the availability for a sister property that shows 90 percent occupancy. She announces, "We could place reservations directly into the sister property inventories." The GM is shocked.

Early the next day, the GM brings the managers from the two sister properties into the reservation office. Marsha is not available, and so they ask you to demonstrate the split screens that show availability at the other two properties. The property managers are amazed at what they see.

The GM announces, "From now on, we book our own properties first." He continues: "When we reach 100 percent at one property, we book the others. It will be our policy never to overbook." The managers agree and thank you for showing them this way to make the guests happy, maximize revenues, and avoid paying high rates to competitors. You say to them, "Don't thank me, thank the computer guy."

SUMMARY

This chapter discussed many of the advances in technology and information telecommunications that have allowed the establishment of fully functional e-commerce systems. These systems infiltrate the interior aspects of the organization and link them to outside sources via the Internet, intranets, and extranets. The key driver for these applications is the overall advance of telecommunications technologies. As discussed in the chapter, technology is facilitating new forms of open systems within, between, and among the variables in the external environment.

DISCUSSION QUESTIONS

1. Consider the productivity model presented early in this chapter. Identify the four classifications of resources and give examples of how they contribute to the transformation processes intended to yield outcomes for hospitality organizations.
2. There are back-office and front-office areas in all hospitality enterprises. Give examples of these areas as they apply to internal and external customers for specific hospitality operations (hotels, restaurants, airlines, etc.).
3. Quite a few "alphabet soup" acronyms are discussed in this chapter. Can you identify and give examples of ERP, EAI, SCM, EDI, and CRM? ·
4. We identified fours specific business functions in this chapter. Can you recall their names and provide descriptions of what each function does?

KEY TERMS

Artificial intelligence (AI)
Business functions
Chief information officers (CIOs)
Customer relationship management (CRM)
Decision support systems (DSS)
E-commerce
Electronic data interchange (EDI)
Employee application interfaces (EAIs)
Enterprise resource planning
External customers
Internal customers
Marketing

Mixed-function industry
Online analytical processing (OLAP)
Outputs
Productivity model
Resources
Stakeholder groups
Supply chain management
Transformation process

REFERENCES

1. J. A. O'Brien. (2000). *Management Information Systems: Managing Information Technology in the E-Business Enterprise,* 5th ed. Boston: McGraw-Hill Irwin.

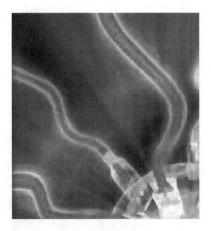

C H A P T E R
7

E-Business Strategies and Solutions

CHAPTER OBJECTIVES

In this chapter you will learn to:

1. Apply the strategic planning model to e-business system development.

2. Identify the steps in providing e-business solutions to solve problems.

3. Identify the processes of needs analysis, systems analysis, and feasibility analysis.

On-the-Job Training

As part of your management training program you have been assigned to work in the purchasing office for a large convention hotel. It has been about six months, and you really like the purchasing director, who seems to be a knowledgeable and efficient person in addition to being a nice guy. Fred, the purchasing director, seems to be well liked by everyone at the hotel with the exception of the executive chef. Fred and the chef, Pierre, have nothing nice to say about each other. Each thinks the other is incompetent. Everyone at the hotel thinks there is a personality conflict between them.

One day you enter the office to hear Fred screaming at the top of his lungs on the telephone. You are not surprised when you learn that the person on the other end of the line is Chef Pierre. Fred's face is beet-red as he shouts a few final obscenities before slamming down the phone. You watch as he storms out of his office toward the loading dock to calm himself down.

After a few minutes you decide to step out to the loading dock to see if you can help Fred get over his tantrum.

To be continued . . .

INTRODUCTION

This chapter provides techniques for developing strategic plans to enact e-business systems and solutions to enhance the value of hospitality organizations. Competitive hospitality managers realize that specific methods must be employed to create **organizational value** within hospitality enterprises. Organizational value is the perception on the part of stakeholders (guests, employees, shareholders, and the community) of the viable success of a hospitality enterprise as a marketplace competitor. The single measurement of value creation for a hospitality organization is the continuous enhancement of productivity. **Productivity** is outputs (products and services) divided by inputs (resources). E-business systems (B2B, B2E, and B2C) contribute to enhanced productivity by streamlining the transformation processes used to convert resources into hospi-

Organizational value The perception on the part of stakeholders (guests, employees, shareholders, and the community) of the viable success of a hospitality enterprise as a marketplace competitor.

Productivity Outputs (products and services) divided by inputs (resources).

tality products and services; this results in higher levels of outputs in relation to allocated resources.

Let's look at an example of productivity enhancement in action. Let's say there are two hotels in a particular city. The first hotel has an informational website, but potential guests may book hotel rooms only by calling the reservation center. The second hotel offers two options to potential guests: They can call the reservations center or book directly online from the website. Suppose there are two individuals trying to book guestrooms at each hotel. They both call the first hotel at the same time. One person speaks to a reservations agent, and the other is placed on hold for the "next available agent" to assist him. From the second hotel's website, one person calls the reservation center, while the other places a reservation to an automated system online. Both reservations are booked at the same time.

Which hotel is being more productive, the first or the second? At the first hotel, a person must speak with a reservations agent to book a room. Therefore, even though two calls came in at the same time, one was placed on hold while the other was handled. At the second hotel, two individuals booked their reservations at the same time even though only one reservations agent was available. Therefore, at that point in time there was one reservations agent booking one hotel room at the first hotel, whereas at the second hotel two reservations were booked even though only one reservations agent was available. The second hotel has double the productivity level of the first hotel (outputs = two reservations, resources = one agent). Further, it is likely that the caller placed on hold at the first hotel hung up and placed an online reservation at the second hotel, which would triple the productivity level for that hotel (three reservations, one agent). This is an example of a B2C system that enhances productivity for a hotel.

It can be seen that e-business systems provide solutions for enhancing the productivity levels of hospitality organizations. There are two approaches to developing e-business initiatives. A **proactive approach** involves strategic planning aimed at preventing problems from arising in the future. A **reactive approach** involves organizational interventions to fix problems that exist in the present.

Proactive approach
Involves strategic planning aimed at preventing problems from arising in the future.

Reactive approach
Involves organizational interventions to fix problems that exist in the present.

STRATEGIC PLANNING PROCESS

The strategic planning process provides a model for practicing the proactive aspects of management and technology.

Examination of External and Internal Environments

External environment
Factors that are outside a hospitality organization that influence the performance of that enterprise.

Internal environment
The inside operations and business functions of an organization.

External scan The process used to collect and analyze data from outside an organization.

Internal audit The process used to examine and analyze the business functions of an organization.

Consistent with systems thinking, the first phase of the strategic planning model requires an examination of both the outside and inside environments of the hospitality business enterprise. The **external environment** consists of factors outside the hospitality organization that influence the performance of that enterprise. The inside operations and business functions of the organization consist of the **internal environment** of the organization. The process used to collect and analyze data from outside the organization is called an **external scan.** An **internal audit** is used to examine and analyze the business functions of the organization. The external scan and internal audit are the first two steps in the strategic planning process described in Figure 7.1.

Figure 7.1 Strategic Planning Process

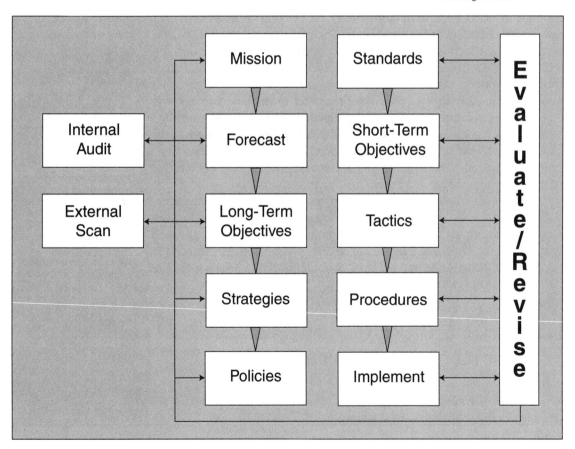

Analysis of Strengths and Weaknesses

When both environments are viewed, managers analyze the internal environment in terms of **strengths and weaknesses** (things they do well and things they could do better) and the external environment from the viewpoint of **opportunities and threats** (things that can have positive or negative outcomes). This is a type of situational analysis known as **SWOT** (strengths, weaknesses, opportunities, threats) analysis. Strengths are the functions the organization does well. Weaknesses are the internal things it could do better. Opportunities are situations in the external environment that could provide benefit to the organization. Threats are things in the external environment that could cause harm to the organization. The organization has control over strengths and weaknesses; it has no control over opportunities and threats.

Strengths and weaknesses Things a company does well and things it could do better within the internal environment of an organization.

Opportunities and threats Things from the external environment of the organization that can have either positive or negative outcomes.

SWOT Situational analysis of strengths and weaknesses within an organization as well as opportunities and threats from outside the organization.

Articulation of Mission Statement

The **mission** of an organization describes its current purpose and philosophy; it is why the organization exists. The mission should be audited on an annual basis. The mission or purpose of an organization deals with the present, whereas the **vision** is concerned with the future direction of the firm. The mission is articulated in the **mission statement:** a printed paragraph or so depicting the purpose of the organization. It is appropriate for an organization to be mission-driven. This means that every decision should involve the question, "Will this activity help fulfill the mission?" If the answer is yes, it is an important decision.

Mission The current purpose and philosophy of a hospitality organization.

Vision The future direction of a hospitality organization.

Mission statement A printed paragraph or so depicting the purpose of a hospitality organization.

The goal of planning is to develop objectives (goals) and strategies (action steps) for the organization to achieve. It focuses on future performance. Top-level managers should spend most of their time in a planning mode. Objectives are established on the basis of the functions of management. Thus, there are goals for organizing, influencing, and controlling performance. All objectives are aimed at improving productivity. Therefore, the productivity model serves as the guide for establishing objectives. Premises are derived from an analysis of alternative objectives. These objectives result in the final goals for performance.

Development of Action Plans

Once objectives are established, action plans are developed to achieve stated standards for performance. Action plans for long-term objectives are called strategies; action plans for short-term objectives are called tactics. The systems approach is the means by which large organizational objectives are converted to smaller departmental and individual objectives. Each individual and department is a subsystem of the larger system.

Some organizations have separate planning departments that are isolated from the operations. Many managers believe that planning should be an integrated activity throughout the organization. General Electric's former chief executive officer (CEO), Jack Welch, fired the strategic planning department as one of his first official acts.[1] It was his opinion that every manager should be a planner, and that is probably good advice for managers in the hospitality industry.

Setting Objectives

Management The process of accomplishing the objectives of an organization through the activities of others.

This is a good time to focus on the definition of **management,** which is that management is the process of accomplishing the objectives of an organization through the activities of others. **Organizational objectives** are defined as targets for performance. There are two things to remember about objectives: They should flow from the mission/vision or purpose of the organization, and they are passive. They just sit there and require an action plan (strategy or tactic) to bring them to fruition.

Organizational objectives Targets for performance in a hospitality organization.

Objectives, or targets for performance, support the mission of the organization. They become the guidelines for decision making, effectiveness, efficiency, consistency, and evaluation of individual and team performance. Goals (objectives) are integrated with individual, group, and overall organizational performance. Short-term objectives are goals for less than one year; long-term objectives are goals for more than one year. In the past managers used the term *intermediate objectives*. The concept of intermediate goals has been rendered outdated by the complex nature of the external environment. All objectives should contribute to the mission. All decisions should contribute to the accomplishment of objectives.

Suboptimization Conflicts between smaller goals and larger goals.

Objectives are established for various aspects of the operation. Financial objectives address fiscal performance. Product–market mix objectives identify service and product goals. Functional objectives are based on individual departments or divisions and feed into overall financial and product–market mix goals. All these objectives are supported by e-business strategies and solutions. There is a hierarchy of objectives from overall goals to individual goals. **Suboptimization** occurs when there are conflicts between smaller goals and larger goals. Information systems and technology managers play a prominent role in the overall strategic direction of hospitality organizations to prevent the occurrence of suboptimization. Figure 7.2 shows the flow from objectives through evaluation in the systems management process.

Management by objectives (MBO) A process of top-down shared goal setting.

The establishment of both long-term and short-term goals is driven by two criteria. The first criterion is called the guidelines for setting objectives. The second process is called **management by objectives (MBO),** which is particularly important for the development of e-business strategies and solutions.

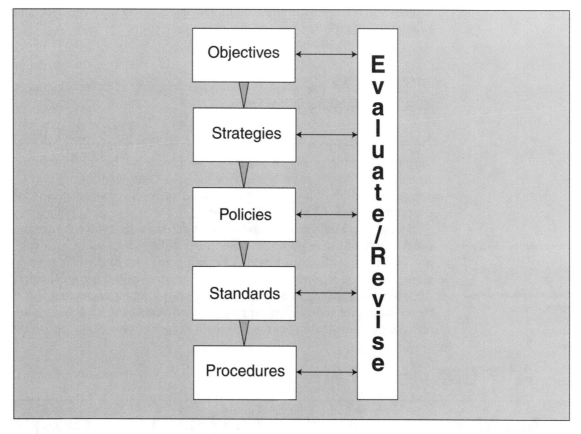

Figure 7.2 Objectives and Strategies

Guidelines for Setting Objectives

- Individuals should participate in determining objectives. In addition, the personal objectives of workers should be considered in the context of organization objectives.
- Objectives should be stated simply and specifically with established due dates for accomplishment.
- Objectives should be challenging yet attainable. A common characteristic of new managers is that they tend to set lofty goals with unrealistic due dates.
- All objectives should feed into the mission of the organization.

Management by Objectives (MBO)

Management by objectives is a process of top-down shared goal setting. The boss sets her objectives and shares them with those below her. Those employees set objectives to feed into the boss's objectives. They discuss and revise them. They send their objectives to the next layer, and the process is repeated throughout the organization.

E-BUSINESS SOLUTIONS

Once objectives have been established, actual performance should be monitored continuously in regard to standards set by the objectives. Revision should occur on a frequent basis, as contingencies are part of organizational life. Things will go wrong in the course of organizational processes. Figure 7.3 shows this process.

Hospitality managers are paid to make decisions that will enhance the productivity of the organization. System planning, organizing, influencing, and control all require skills in making effective and efficient decisions. Some decisions are routine; they are called **programmed decisions** and are highly structured. One-of-a-kind decisions that lack a formal structure are called **nonprogrammed decisions.** All decisions affect the business system of the hospitality organization. Some decisions

Programmed decisions Decisions that are routine and highly structured.

Nonprogrammed decisions One-of-a-kind decisions that lack a formal structure.

Figure 7.3 Something Went Wrong

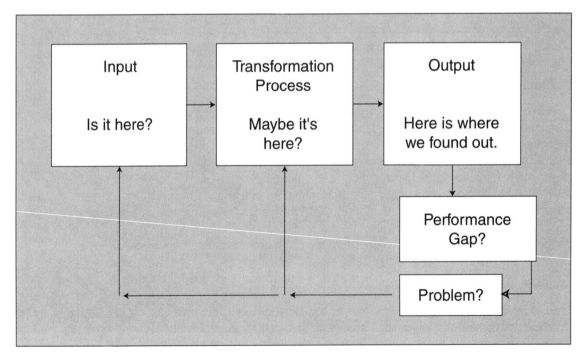

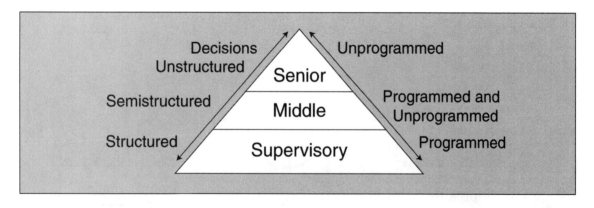

Figure 7.4 Management Hierarchy

are far-reaching and have a great impact. These decisions have a broad scope, as opposed to those which have a more limited scope of influence. When managers are promoted to higher-level organizational positions, they assume more responsibility and their scope of decision making increases. Figure 7.4 shows this scenario.

Most decision making is aimed at solving problems. A problem is defined as an adverse situation concerning actual performance in relation to standards for performance. The toughest part of decision making is identifying the problem. Often managers will see symptoms and assume that they are problems. Evaluation of symptoms is performed to identify the actual problem. Next, the manager identifies alternatives for solving the problem. At least three alternatives should be generated in most situations. Then the manager analyzes each of the alternatives in terms of efficiency and effectiveness. In many cases, the optimum alternative is not the best selection because it is cost-prohibitive. Thus, the manager will select the next best alternative. The manager implements the alternative and monitors for effectiveness and efficiency. This last part is the feedback loop that belongs in every model in the field of management. Figure 7.5 shows the system investigation process of problem identification.

There are two interrelated conditions in making decisions: **complexity** and **risk.** Complexity is the number of variables influencing the problem; risk is the probability of a negative consequence associated with a decision. High levels of complexity create limited amounts of total information, or uncertainty. Higher levels of uncertainty equate to higher levels of risk in making a single decision. In addition, the scope or impact of the decision will add to the level of risk in terms of the **utility** associated with the overall effect. Utility is a measurement of the consequences associated with an action.

Complexity The number of variables influencing a problem.

Risk The probability of a negative consequence associated with a decision.

Utility A measurement of the consequences associated with an action.

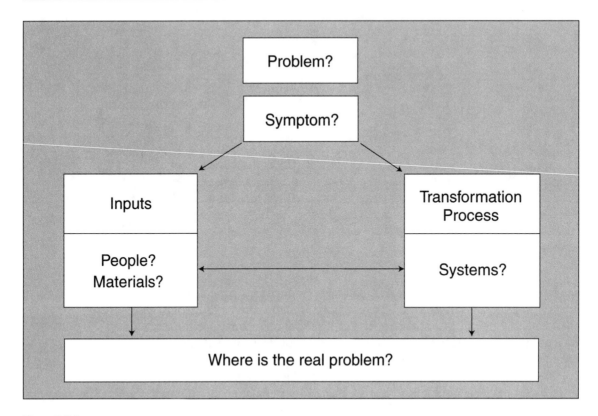

Figure 7.5 System Investigation

Brainstorming A group activity used to generate creative ideas to solve problems.

Nominal group technique (NGT) Assures all participants equal participation in decision making by consensus measurements.

Delphi technique The distribution of questionnaires that are recycled until a consensus is reached.

Brainstorming is a group activity that is used to generate creative ideas to solve problems. In this activity participants are encouraged to share any idea that comes to mind. All ideas are accepted without criticism and listed for further analysis. The result will be a number of generated alternatives based on group consensus. This is a creative but time-consuming activity. **Nominal group technique (NGT)** assures all participants equal participation in decision making by consensus measurements. A recently developed technique hooks laptop computers to a server, and each person types ideas that are shown on an overhead projector. The **Delphi technique** uses the distribution of questionnaires that are recycled until a consensus is reached.

Some managers label various formats as systems approaches to problem solving when in actuality they present the standard problem-solving paradigm. For us to take a systems approach, we must remember that a change on the micro level will affect the macro level. Therefore, we must ask the question, "What will be the impact of the solution on the organization as a whole?"

Steps for Solving Systems Problems

A sequential order of steps is used to solve problems in a systems environment. Figure 7.6 shows the systems analysis process.

The figure shows six steps toward problem solution. The first step is the most difficult. Often we are presented with one or more symptoms of a problem, and an inexperienced manager assumes that the symptom is the problem. This is a big mistake, as the outcome will result in the expenditure of resources to fix something that may not be a real problem. One must remember the definition of a **problem.** A problem is a negative (adverse) gap between actual organizational performance and standards for performance. If performance is not being affected, there is not

Problem An adverse situation concerning actual performance in relation to standards for performance.

Figure 7.6 System Analysis

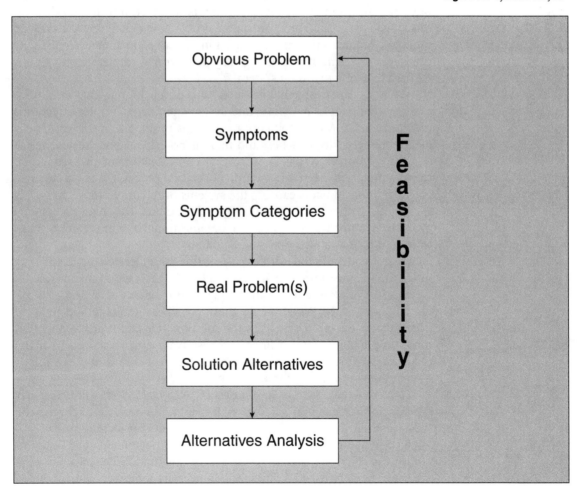

a problem by this organizational definition. If we suspect that a problem exists, we collect data via observable criteria that may or may not be symptoms of the problem. We then analyze the data to determine the actual problem.

For instance, we may witness conflicts arising among staff members in different departments at a hotel (symptom). Analysis determines that these individuals are sequentially dependent on each other's functions (a chain of events), such as the purchasing, receiving, storeroom, and operating departments. The cause of the conflict appears to be blame for missed due dates being placed on individuals in the sequential chain. Further analysis determines that production forecasts are being established by each individual department without consultation with the other departments. What is the problem?

The problem is that department managers are setting standards without communicating with the departments that feed into the production line. Thus, there is a communication problem, which is really a systems problem. All problems may be placed in one, two, or three categories. By the way, a problem of this nature may be solved by implementing an enterprise resource planning system.

What are the problem categories? All problems may fall within the categories of people, materials, and systems problems. Which category is most prevalent? Most problems are systems problems. In this case, people are trying to do their best and there is no evidence of the absence of material resources. What is lacking is consideration of the sequential steps in the production system (transformation process). Thus, a system's problem exists. What is causing the systems problem? In most cases, it is a lack of accurate and timely information. Thus, this type of systems problem is concerned with effective organizational communication, a key feature of B2B and B2E e-business systems.

Once we identify the problem, the rest is easy: Develop alternative solutions (ERP, meetings, e-mail, and reports in the case of this problem). Next, select an alternative solution. Then implement it (if design is required, as in an ERP system, do that first). Then evaluate and revise if necessary based on the results of the solution. It is important to note that the example above cites a linear process (very easy to solve). In many cases we must look at interrelationships, as many are nonlinear; this is where systems thinking comes into play.

Some problems require large amounts of capital investment (computer systems, for example). In these cases it may not be feasible to choose the "best" alternative solution because of cost/benefit considerations.

A modified model of problem solving can be applied specifically to e-business solutions. Figure 7.7 describes this model. The two key variables are the design and maintenance stages. In computer systems, solutions always consist of a design or development aspect (usually regarding

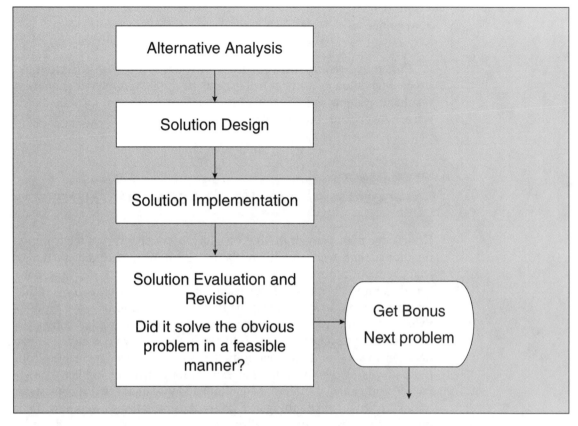

Figure 7.7 System Design, Implementation, and Evaluation

software) and maintaining the solution system is vital (especially in times of rapid technology development).

Feasibility studies are used when a significant investment is required to provide an IS solution. Many aspects of feasibility should be considered during this process. **Cost/benefit analysis** determines economic/organizational feasibility. Is the solution affordable, and will it help accomplish the objectives of the organization? **Technical feasibility** refers to the ability of hardware and software to do the job. **Operational feasibility** considers willingness from the end user's perspective to use the system in the operations. From a cost perspective, tangible costs are easy to calculate, whereas intangible (indirect) costs are more difficult to quantify.

Systems analysis is nothing more than standard needs analysis applied to computer systems. Categories of analysis include the following:

- Information needs
- System resources

Cost/benefit analysis Determines economic/organizational feasibility.

Technical feasibility The ability of hardware and software to provide a business solution.

Operational feasibility The willingness on the part of end users to use the system in operations.

- Products
- Activities
- Ability of systems and end users to get the job done

Functional requirements analysis provides a focus on the interface, processing, storage, and control aspects of the system. Systems analysis results in systems specifications for interfaces, databases, software, hardware, networks, and user skills.

COLLABORATIVE KNOWLEDGE MANAGEMENT

Knowledge management (KM) evolved from earlier forms of telecommunications that were made available through networked systems.[2] Management information systems use multiple network nodes to convert data into information. Knowledge management systems convert that information into usable knowledge that can be used to improve productivity and gain a competitive advantage. Implicit knowledge comes directly from bytes of knowledge information that may be used for future decision making and strategic initiatives. Tacit knowledge evolves from the patterns of relationships that exist among bytes of implicit knowledge. Another way to describe tacit knowledge is to say that it consists of metaknowledge, or the things we know about the things we know. Tacit knowledge helps us conceptualize the "big picture" of things and events concerning the intelligence of our business.

Business intelligence (BI) is a process that critiques the information surrounding various strategies within a hospitality enterprise, such as B2B, B2C, e-market analysis, demand and supply chains, customer relationship management, and outsourcing, among other tactical issues. If we share these types of information among a number of hospitality enterprises, the accumulated information will create silos of knowledge broken down into topical areas like those mentioned above. That practice is known as business analytics (BA), which exists in industries such as agriculture, manufacturing, construction, education, and health care. BA is not used commonly by practitioners of hospitality management. However, potential versions of this model are evident in best practices research that is sponsored by academic institutions such as the hotel school at Cornell University. Similar knowledge repositories in the field of tourism exist at the Travel Industry Management School at the University of Hawaii and the University of Central Florida's Rosen College of Hospitality Management in Orlando through collaborative arrangements with the World Tourism Organization (WTO).

Hospitality and tourism industry practitioners may choose to assess these types of knowledge repositories through the implementation of virtual communities of practice (VCOPs) in the near future. This is already the case with certain engineering and health-care organizations that have attempted to establish electronically networked intelligent communities (ENICs) to facilitate global strategic initiatives.[3] Sophisticated test-mining software tools are required to generate useful knowledge from information repositories such as those made available through the WTO. These tools are designed to find, access, analyze, link, and use text-based information that may be synthesized into useful knowledge at the practitioner level.[4]

Beyond the scope of business practices, individual participation in virtual communities has become a social trend over the last 15 years. The Internet explosion has resulted in the creation of digital neighborhoods that attract like-minded citizens referred to as netizens.[5] Large numbers of individuals join these communities on a daily basis, and this could present e-business opportunities for hospitality enterprises.[6] Fifty-three million Americans currently visit online chat rooms at least once a month, according to Nielsen/NetRatings.[7] These groups include professional associations, social groups, and almost every community of interest. These groups are potential sources of customers and employees for hospitality enterprises. For instance, a resort chain seeking a computer programmer might find the perfect candidate at Linux.org, a virtual community of operating system programmers.[8] The online dating services industry alone had $1.14 billion in revenues in 2003, providing an excellent source of potential bookings for conferences, social gatherings, and cruises.

It is possible that hospitality enterprises will establish virtual communities to provide interactive services and information to clients and guests. These virtual environments will use electronic customer service avatars that will be available to provide information and answer questions via phone or PC 24 hours a day. Reservation call centers may be converted into virtual service communities that will provide round-the-clock interaction, as opposed to current centers, which are staffed only during business hours.

On-the-Job Training . . . Continued

As you step out to the loading dock, you witness Fred pacing back and forth, muttering to himself. You approach him carefully to see if there is anything you can do to help. Fred sees you coming and says to you, "Sorry for that outburst. This chef just drives me crazy." You say, "What did he do this time?" Fred responds, "The same thing he always does. He wants products for a thousand banquet meals beyond his forecast, and he wants it now. This guy can't forecast to save his life!"

"Is there anything I can do to help?" you reply. "Yeah," he says. "Convince that old man to retire or go back to grade school to learn how to count!" You suggest, "Why not let me talk with him?" Fred says in disgust, "Yeah, sure—do what ever you want."

You have always had a good rapport with Pierre, and so you stop by the chef's office to chat casually. At the right moment you suggest to Pierre, "I guess you and Fred had it out again." "Yeah," Pierre responds. "You know, it really isn't my fault or Fred's; it is the catering sales office." Pierre continues: "They book these pop-up meal functions, and no one finds out about them until they get the printed flash reports from their mailboxes. Fred doesn't check his printed mail until all his orders are placed each morning, and so he is usually the last person to know these things."

"Hmmm," you say. "This sounds like a systems problem." You quickly return to the purchasing office to chart the flow of information from the catering sales reps. You show your diagram to Fred.

"I have investigated this situation about the forecast," you begin with Fred, "and the problem seems to be with the sales reps, not the culinary team." You point to the diagram. "See, the sales reps take last-minute business for available space during business hours." You continue: "But they don't post it into their system until the close of business at 5 P.M., when your office is already closed for the day. An administrative assistant types up a flash report and places it into mailboxes at 9 A.M. the next morning. You start at 7 A.M. and don't check your mail again until the afternoon. They send someone to the chef's office to notify Pierre before you get to see the flash report. Pierre then calls you in a panic, and of course you get angry with him."

On-the-Job Training . . . Continued

Fred thinks about what you are telling him and responds, "So, it's sales' fault." You reply, "Let's not focus on blame. I think I have a solution to the problem. All we have to do is teach the sales reps to use the 'flash' feature on our automated communication system. We convince them to enter pop-up information at the time of booking that is transmitted to you and Pierre. Pierre will check it periodically and send you electronic versions of revised forecasts." You finish by saying, "When you arrive at seven in the morning, you will have the latest version on your desktop in time to place your orders."

Fred thinks for a minute. Then he smiles at you and says, "I guess you are learning something at that hospitality school. I am going to propose this to the food and beverage director immediately."

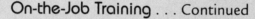

SUMMARY

The focus of this chapter was on e-business planning and problem-solving activities. Planning is a proactive activity, whereas problem solving is reactive in nature. Planning is focused on the future, whereas problem solving focuses on a current situation. The processes of planning and problem solving are virtually the same in regard to management and technology. In both cases a systems approach reminds managers to stay focused on the interdependent nature of subsystems and the organization as a whole.

DISCUSSION QUESTIONS

1. You are a manager who has just been assigned to run a hotel. You find out that the competition is fierce, the property management system is old, there are no point-of-sale systems in the restaurants, purchasing is done manually, there are many vendors in the local vicinity, there is a shortage talented labor available, and staff wages are higher than the rate in the local market. If you were to conduct a SWOT analysis, which of these factors would be categorized as external and which ones as internal? Which are strengths, weaknesses, opportunities, or threats?

2. A front-office manager at a hotel notices that guests' comment cards indicate slow check-in processes. How could this be a symptom of a people problem? A material resource problem? A systems problem? How would you go about determining the nature of the "real problem"?

3. You are a hotel manager, and you notice that the accounting office and property management system are independent of each other. Your possible alternatives are to scrap both systems and buy a new interfaced network, use the existing system and force front-desk agents to post data manually for the accounting office to use, or purchase network software and modify it to accommodate both systems. How would you evaluate each alternative from the cost/benefit, technical, and operational feasibility perspectives?

KEY TERMS

Brainstorming
Complexity
Cost/benefit analysis
Delphi technique
External environment
External scan
Internal audit
Internal environment
Management
Management by objectives (MBO)
Mission
Mission statement
Nominal group technique (NGT)
Nonprogrammed decisions
Operational feasibility
Opportunities and threats
Organizational objectives
Organizational value
Proactive approach
Problem
Productivity
Programmed decisions
Reactive approach
Risk
Strengths and weaknesses
Suboptimization
SWOT

Technical feasibility
Utility
Vision

REFERENCES

1. Jack Welch and John A. Byrne. (2003). *Jack: Straight from the Gut.* New York: Warner Books.
2. D. B. Bowes. (1996). Creating Globally Competitive Communities. *Industry Week.* 245:A1–A24.
3. R. Violino. (2004). BI for the Masses—Intelligent Communities. *Computerworld.* 38(25):38–39.
4. D. Robb. (2004). Taming Text. *Computerworld* 38(25):40–41.
5. Olga Kharif. (2003). The Net: Now Folks Can't Live Without It. *Business Week Online.*
6. John Hagel III and Arthur Armstrong. (1997). *Net Gain: Expanding Markets Through Virtual Communities.* Cambridge, MA: Harvard Business School Press.
7. To access the report "Surveying the Digital Future," visit the UCLA website at: ccp.usla.edu/pdf/UCLA-Internet-Report-Year-Three.pdf.
8. *Business Trends.* (2004):1(11), Willowbrook, IL.

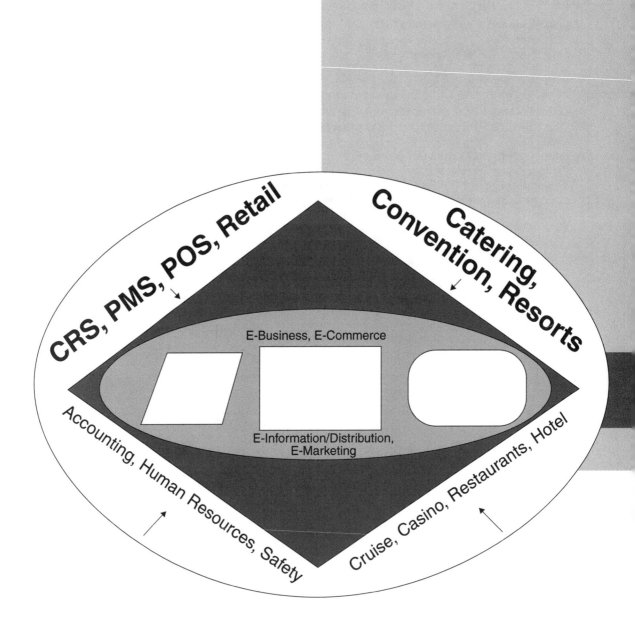

CRS, PMS, POS, Retail

Catering, Convention, Resorts

Accounting, Human Resources, Safety

Cruise, Casino, Restaurants, Hotel

E-Business, E-Commerce

E-Information/Distribution, E-Marketing

PART III

Hospitality
Functional
Applications

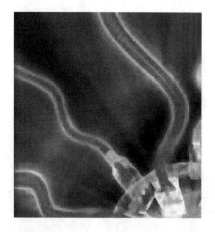

C H A P T E R
8

Computer Reservation Systems and Global Distribution Systems

CHAPTER OBJECTIVES

In this chapter you will learn to:

1. Identify the components of a central reservation system.
2. Identify the channels connected to a global distribution system.
3. Identify the current roles of travel providers and intermediaries.

On-the-Job Training

You are working as a part-time gate agent for a major airline at an international airport. Your job is to provide seat assignments, take head counts, scan boarding passes, and provide boarding announcements at various gates. Normally, two gate agents and a supervisor are assigned to each gate to perform those duties.

The other gate agents are older people who have worked for the airline for many years. Because of your status, you and the other part-timers are the last to be scheduled for working hours. There has been a rumor circulating among the other agents of impending layoffs because of the implementation of automated systems at each gate. The rumors claim that gate agent assignments will be reduced by 66 percent as a result of the new technology.

You are particularly concerned that these rumors may be true, since the part-timers will be the first to be laid off.

To be continued . . .

INTRODUCTION

Reservation An advanced booking to reserve space for a designated time and date.

In this chapter we look at the systems that are used for booking reservations at hotels and resorts, restaurants, car rental companies, air travel companies, and cruise lines. A **reservation** is an advanced booking to reserve space for a designated time and date. A dinner reservation at a fine-dining restaurant reserves a table for a specific number of people at a designated time. Reservations made at hotels and resorts are intended to reserve guestrooms for a number of "room nights." Travelers may book ahead to reserve seats on an aircraft and rental cars at their destinations. Cruise reservations arrange for staterooms and dining accommodations.

When you make a reservation, you are engaging in a business transaction with a hospitality enterprise to set aside space before your arrival. The nature of the transaction involves a commitment on the part of a guest/client to use space (a table, guestroom, car, airplane seat, or ship's cabin), with an agreement that the enterprise will make the space and related services available at a specified time in the future. Since the agreement is made before the delivery of hospitality products and services, a reservation is considered a **booking transaction.**

Before the time of a reservation, hospitality organizations maintain inventories of space for sale to guests and clients. The inventory for a resort may be 1,000 guestrooms, for instance. When a booking transaction occurs, a unit of inventory is set aside for future use, which deletes it from the inventory that is available at that date and time. Thus, a **reservation system** includes an inventory management base coupled with a direct transaction-processing component.

People have a natural tendency to visualize only computer-generated reservation systems; however, this is not always the case. Consider a small signature restaurant, for instance, in which a maitre d' stands at a podium before the opening for the dinner seating. He answers a phone call from a guest who would like to reserve a table for four at 8:30 P.M. The maitre d' glances at a plastic-covered schematic and notes that a window table has been reserved for 6:00 P.M. He assigns that table to the guest on the phone for an 8:30 P.M. arrival. He confirms that a table will be reserved for the party and bids the caller farewell. The maitre d's notation removes that table from the inventory for the remainder of the dinner seating. This scenario includes all the components of a manual reservation system. There is a chart of tables on the podium (inventory) and the

Booking transaction An agreement that is made with a hospitality enterprise before the delivery of products and services.

Reservation system An inventory management base coupled with a direct transaction-processing component.

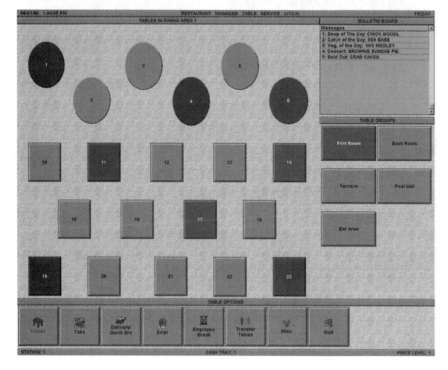

An electronic diagram of the restaurant can be one part of an electronic reservation system. (©Action Systems, Inc.)

maitre d' (transaction processor), who uses a tool to manage the inventory (an erasable marker). Of course, much more sophisticated systems exist in restaurants as well as in other hospitality operations.

ELECTRONIC RESERVATION SYSTEMS

Electronic reservation system (ERS) Consists of a database, a transaction-processing system, and an inventory management component.

The only difference between a fully manual reservation system and an electronic one is the use of a computer. Computerized reservation systems may be as small as a stand-alone single computer and as large as a global network. Regardless of size, the bare essentials of an **electronic reservation system (ERS)** include a database for inventories, a transaction-processing system with access to inventories, and an inventory management component to track inventory availability.

An ERS for a restaurant is contained within a point-of-sale system, which is a database and transaction-processing system used in restaurant and retail establishments. Independent hotels and resorts include an ERS as a single component of the overall property management system for the facility. Larger operations, such as hotel chains, car rental companies, and airlines, use centralized **computer reservation systems (CRSs).** The acronym CRS is used interchangeably to refer to both computer reservation systems and **central reservation systems.** In all cases, though, the term is applied exclusively to centralized computer reservation systems that contain a range of interfaces that include local area networks, metropolitan area networks, and/or wide area networks with a capacity for global telecommunication connections. Figure 8.1 depicts a CRS for a hotel chain.

Computer reservation system (CRS) An electronic system used to produce booking transactions.

Central reservation system (CRS) A centralized computer reservation system that contains a range of interfaces that include local area networks, metropolitan area networks, and/or wide area networks with a capacity for global telecommunication connections.

EVOLUTION OF CENTRAL RESERVATION SYSTEM NETWORKS

Electronic distribution systems (EDIs) Airline computer systems used to book reservations and track passenger loads across various flight routes.

The first attempt to use electronic reservation systems was enacted by competitors in the airline industry beginning in the late 1950s. During that time there was a lack of true competition among airline companies, which constituted a governmentally regulated industry until the 1970s. However, the carriers were seeking to establish systems to provide inventory control mechanisms, and that led to the creation of early versions of **electronic distribution systems (EDSs)** that were used to book reservations and track passenger loads across various flight routes. Those

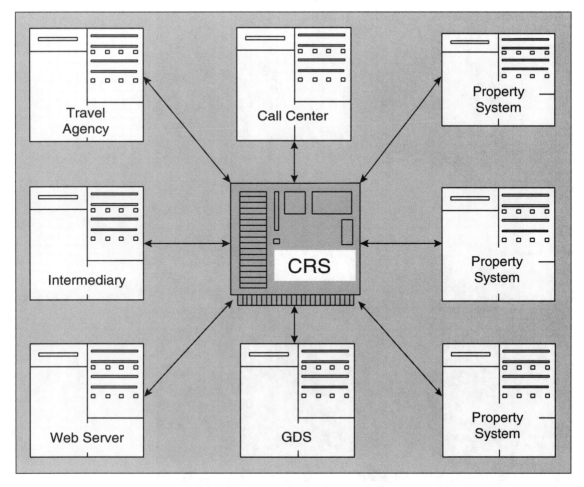

Figure 8.1 Hotel Central Reservation System

systems subsequently became more sophisticated as a result of technological developments that lead to mainframe computing networks. This caused the evolution from EDS to full-blown central reservation systems among major air carriers.

Since most flight reservations came through travel agents (TAs) before the 1990s, the airlines generously gave TAs access to the systems to provide direct bookings for prospective travelers and added travel-related services such as lodging accommodations for provider fees to help offset the capital costs of system development and maintenance. Eventually the airlines developed open platforms that resulted in the conversion of central reservation systems into full-service **global distribution systems (GDSs)** to provide a whole range of travel-related services through electronic switches and routers.

Global distribution systems (GDSs) A range of travel-related services provided through electronic switches and routers.

Like most airlines, some hotels now have electronic check-in capabilities that utilize a computer reservation system. (Courtesy of Cendant Corp.)

By that time most hotel companies had developed CRSs and paid the fees required for linkages to most global distribution systems. The availability of Internet commerce dramatically altered the original cooperative and collaborative system-sharing activities among all sectors of the hospitality and tourism industry. System developments were used to serve the needs of travel agencies and collaborative industry sectors through architectures that were open to providers yet closed to the general public until the 1990s. Suddenly the limited flexibility and the issue of fees for system access became an issue that caused various sectors to seek alternative means of electronic distribution. In particular, travel agents were adversely affected by policy shifts on the part of airlines that resulted in the demise of many offline TAs; this was an interesting paradox, since the evolution of GDS architecture was designed to accommodate that sector. By 2003 about 90 percent of all large corporations in all sectors had established Web-based distribution, for product marketing, distribution, and fulfillment. One report suggests that alternative distribution methods generated a four-year savings (2000–2003) for hospitality companies of $1.3 billion, which equates to 1.7 percent of industry profits in combined GDS and TA fees.[1] Figure 8.2 provides a description of Web-based interfaces among consumers, hotels, CRSs, and GDSs.

The traditional paradigm consists of consumers speaking with travel agents by phone to check availability and pricing and ultimately to book travel and lodging reservations. The TA would use direct access to a GDS

Figure 8.2 Web-Based Distribution Chains

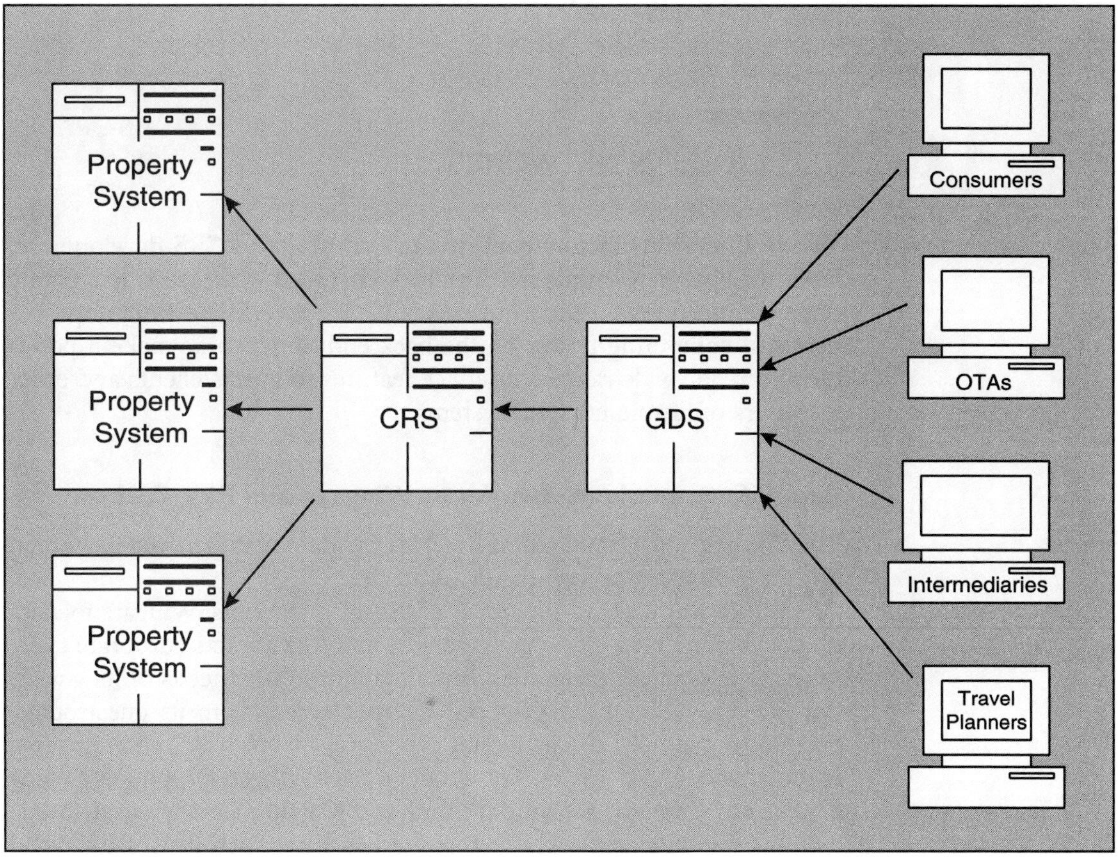

to perform those functions. The Web-based model permits consumers to investigate availability and pricing through search engines that link to numerous CRSs or an online intermediary with GDS interfaces. Once a "buy decision" is made, the customer will book with travel, lodging, and car rental enterprises directly through the website of the air carrier or intermediary (Expedia, for example). Airlines provide direct links to travel-related enterprise websites (lodging, ground transportation, etc.), whereas intermediaries use GDS and CRS interfaces for booking transactions.

From a database perspective, the computing power of early hotel CRSs followed a development pattern that was consistent with IT advances for general business applications. During the mainframe computing era, CRSs had the ability to store, manipulate, and sort the large numbers of data required of an inventory management system. The real competitive advantages for hotels emerged during the personal computing age that began during the late 1980s. PC interfaces permitted hotel chains to lower reservation costs through advanced automation and to add marketing research and yield management features to the systems.[2] These and other IT capabilities marked the advance into the modern state of CRS networks.[3]

MODERN NETWORKS

Two technological factors continue to contribute to CRS development. First, the Internet—more specifically, Web-based interfaces—is creating open architectures on the front end of CRS networks. Second, improvements in computing power on the back end of networks make it possible to provide wide ranges of service features to guests/clients and other end users of hospitality CRS systems.

Real-Life Example: Networks at Wingate and Ritz-Carlton

The Wingate and Ritz-Carlton hotel chains demonstrate these factors in practice as market differentiation strategies.

Both chains cater to the needs of business travelers: Wingate focuses on the value-conscious businessperson, and Ritz attracts corporate executives to its upscale properties. In recognition of the needs of its guests, Wingate provides free high-speed Internet access from its guestrooms, precluding the need to pay fees at cybercafés or business centers to stay in touch with home offices. This strategy gives Wingate properties a competitive advantage over Hampton Inns and Marriott Courtyards, two traditionally dominant players in this market. Ritz-Carlton uses back-end

The Wingate Inn has positioned itself strategically to provide business travelers with high-speed Internet access from its guestrooms. (Courtesy of Cendant Corp.)

technology to cater to its guests through a state-of-the-art guest history application that is interfaced with its CRS. The system tracks every specific preference of each hotel guest to ensure that personalized preparations are made for guest visits at any of its properties. Such a system was cost-prohibitive just a few years ago.[4]

Networking in Hospitality Operations and the Job of the CIO

The Internet and advances in computing power have generated opportunities to use technology in many areas of hospitality operations. The temptation is to employ technological applications for their own sake, which is contrary to the tactical deployment of IT strategies and solutions. The purpose of IT applications is to enhance productivity levels in hospitality enterprises. For this reason, hospitality organizations employ chief information officers as senior-level executives. The job of the CIO is to oversee the strategic planning and implementation of IT initiatives to ensure that technology contributes to the mission of the hospitality enterprise.

The CIO of a hospitality organization has a particularly challenging position relative to his or her counterparts in other industries because the hospitality industry is a mixed-functional business. The primary business of hospitality enterprises is to provide memorable face-to-face guest experiences through intimate service relationships (interactions). However, the industry also produces tangible products, which means that hospitality CIOs must be familiar with both service and manufacturing technology paradigms. This mixed-functional transaction processing is exemplified by electronic distribution systems such as CRSs and global distribution systems.

Mixed-Functional Transaction Processing and Global Distribution Systems

The original implementation of GDS technology revolutionized the distribution models of industry products and services even before the Internet explosion. Today GDS technology is still very much in use, although there is a new architecture of surrounding network nodes and access points.[5]

The majority of travel and lodging reservations were booked through offline travel agents and hotel call centers in the past. However, individual customers have direct online access to central reservation systems through the Internet in today's environment. So why have GDSs not become obsolete? The answer to this question contains many facets for consideration. The short answer would be that the GDS architecture is a brilliant design for all the travel-related sectors of our industry. These sectors include travel, lodging, and ground transportation enterprises.

Airlines and Global Distribution Systems

Airline companies put forth massive capital investments to develop global distribution systems during a time when nobody could have predicted the Internet revolution that is taken for granted today. The design was brilliant because those proprietary systems (owned by the airline companies) provided an open platform to view pricing and availability from all major carriers as well as all subscribing travel-related providers

through a single system. Popular U.S. owned GDSs include Sabre, Apollo, and Worldspan. Foreign-owned systems include Galileo and Amadeus. Airline corporations owned all these systems until the U.S. government forced them to divest the systems from their holdings about 20 years ago. The Civil Aeronautics Board has loosened this restriction, and the airlines maintain minority ownership of these systems.[6]

Users of GDSs view modern-looking screens that include point-and-click graphical user interfaces that are front-end interfaces built over the original back-end database structures. Traditional offline travel agents used to rely on generous commission payments from the airlines to perform GDS searches and booking arrangements for their customers.

Cendant Corporation provides travel distribution services, including car rentals (Avis, Budget), hotels (Ramada, Days Inn, Howard Johnson's), airlines (cheaptickets.com), and Galileo (providing electronic global distribution services). Its Trip Rewards program is the largest loyalty program in the industry. (Courtesy of Cendant Corp.)

Changes in the commission policies of airlines have forced many offline TAs out of business. However, online travel agents (OTAs) still conduct advanced searchers on GDSs for clients who are willing to pay for such services.[7] Most clients, however, are not willing to pay for these services, since there are many other options that permit them to perform their own searches for prices and availability of travel-related products.

In fact, the airlines are encouraging customers to access their CRSs directly through websites such as www.aa.com (American), www.continental.com (Continental), www.delta.com (Delta), and www.southwest.com (Southwest), among others. Today the airlines prefer to use the GDS platforms for efficiency measures such as aircraft scheduling, flight crew allocation, and flight coordination within "hub and spoke" routes.[8] They also use GDS interfaces to automate transaction processes that formerly were performed by ticket and ramp agents, such as check-in, boarding pass distribution, and baggage assignments. Automated transaction processing is a key strategic efficiency factor as airlines continue to struggle with price competition and escalating costs of resources such as fuel and payroll expenses.

The pioneers who developed GDSs never thought that these databases would evolve into the intranet servers that are used currently to streamline flight operations. Although GDSs have been internalized for airline applications, the owners of the systems still have an interest in providing transaction-processing services for potential guests of lodging enterprises.

This process is still within the domain of the remaining travel agents but increasingly is being taken over by intermediary organizations and mega-travel agencies such as American Express and Carlson. Currently, these agencies are engaged in survival strategies that eliminate the use of live agents by providing websites for online booking transactions. Clients may obtain information about destinations that includes restaurants, attractions, and entertainment options. These sites are designed for leisure travelers who are seeking getaway trips and vacations.[9] Once a purchase decision is made, clients may book all their travel-related activities through the site's portals. Certain intermediaries are affiliated with corporations that have an ownership stake in various GDSs.

GDS hotel distribution networks currently account for approximately 15 percent of hotel revenues.[10] Although they still serve large travel agencies by providing hotel bookings, GDS firms are slowly becoming their own intermediaries through ownership and alliances with online travel agencies. Sabre owns the intermediary called Travelocity, and Cendant, a hotel conglomerate, owns the popular consumer portals known as Cheap Tickets and Trip.com. Amadeus owns a wholesale company, and Worldspan is stepping away from the distribution business by shifting its role toward providing technology services to the travel industry.[11]

HOTEL DISTRIBUTION INTERMEDIARIES

Like all industries involved in electronic distribution, hotel distribution channels are in a state of flux in terms of mergers and acquisitions of intermediary organizations. There have been examples of collaboration as well as intense competition in recent times. Most popular intermediaries in the area of hotel distribution purchase blocks of rooms at various lodging facilities for wholesale prices. The intermediary firms then market the guestrooms on website consumer portals for sale at a markup, which still appears to be a discounted price to the customer. In a sense, these types of intermediaries are wholesale brokers that sell room nights to the general public for stays at various destinations. Some of the popular brokers are Expedia, Travelocity, and Hotels.com.[13]

In addition to possessing their own distribution channels, many intermediaries are linked with global distribution systems as well as CRSs owned by lodging and other travel-related entities. Dynamic changes in travel-related organization and intermediary ownership have made it difficult to track the linkage channels. At the current time, Sabre seems to be the dominant U.S. GDS providing linkages to TAs, OTAs, wholesalers, and lodging CRS systems. Galileo, a GDS that is owned by a consortium of European airlines, seems to be prominent in that market, and Travel Industry Automated Services (TIAS) appears to be the GDS of choice for the Australian and New Zealand markets. TIAS was developed through a collaborative venture among Quantis, Ansett, and Air New Zealand to replace linkages to the Galileo and Sabre systems. TIAS embraces a strategy of new technology innovations to provide enhanced client services, which recently included direct access links to the travel agency arm of American Express. A consortium of Asian airlines has developed a GDS called Abacus, which is also competing for market share in Australia.[14]

The Sabre Travel Network is the world's largest electronic network serving travel agencies, airlines, and travel suppliers. (Courtesy of Sabre Holdings.)

APPLICATIONS OF SPEECH TECHNOLOGY TO DISTRIBUTION SYSTEMS

Technology applications are in place to provide speech interaction between travelers and computers. It is possible that the agent on the receiving end of a phone call is not a person but a computer using natural-language-processing technology. Natural language processing is a form of speech technology that facilitates spoken dialogs between people and computers.[15] Human speech is used as inputs to databases to access information, prospecting, and transaction processing such as reservations and product purchases.

More than 50 years ago it was predicted that machines would fool people into thinking that they were interacting with another person.[16] This is a reality today with natural-language-processing technology in the early stages of development. Programmers use grammar-based approaches to build machine vocabularies that convert spoken words into text inputs used to process callers' requests. This type of programming has evolved over the last 10 years to permit machines to comprehend slang (such as "yeah" for "yes") and recognize various languages and accents. Grammar-based programming is as intricate as the languages and nuances of human communication processing. Modern programming uses statistical probabilities to enhance the ability of computers to achieve voice recognition and comprehension.

An example of statistical language programming in action is the Voice Tone system implemented by AT&T to handle customers' requests. A customer call handled by Voice Tone costs the company just 40 cents compared with an average cost of $4.50 per agent-handled call.[17] Similar cost savings are encouraging hospitality and travel organizations to adopt automated agent technologies, with airlines taking the lead in speech technology applications.[18]

Lodging, car rental, and travel intermediaries as well as foodservice operators are beginning to implement speech recognition technology in the United States and Europe. It may be argued that interactivity between hospitality guests and agents requires levels of intimacy that are beyond the capability of machines. However, many back-office functions are handled seamlessly through voice inputs to databases for transactions such as order placement, travel updates, and reservations. In fact, certain hospitality operations, such as quick-service restaurants, rely on relatively simple programming syntax options, such as toppings on a pizza. Limited-option interactions are more cost-efficient for speech recognition programming than are intricate dialogs such as the repair diagnosis used in the AT&T example.

The two most commonly used providers of speech recognition for the hospitality industry are Scansoft/Intervoice and Nuance. The initial applications for airlines were flight information and booking, but additional service enhancements using speech technology are being added continuously. Voice check-in service, seat assignment, and flight status are just a few of these services. Many large car rental companies (National, Dollar, and Thrifty, for instance) use the software to facilitate voice-automated reservation systems. Additionally, car rental companies are providing vehicles with voice-activated navigation and global satellite positioning systems. Marriott and other chain hotels as well as intermediaries such as Expedia.com and Travelocity.com use automated speech recognition and test to speech for online reservation systems. Railroads in the United States, Sweden, and Switzerland use voice recognition systems for passengers to check fares, book reservations, and follow schedules. Finally, the entertainment and foodservice sectors are embracing voice-activated technology for movies, shows, concerts, and home delivery services.

Many of the intimate interactions between guests and hospitality enterprises require face-to-face communications. However, a number of back-office transaction processing may be performed by voice-to-text database queries that are much more guest-friendly than the touch-tone tag that is still in use in many other service-related industries. As advances in technology development continue, it will become more difficult for customers to discern the difference between an agent and an automated machine. It would appear that the Turing test is becoming a reality.

On-the-Job Training . . . Continued

You begin to believe that the layoff rumors are true when you start to see workers from Travel Application Service Provider (TASP) Corporation arrive at the airport to automate one gate. You strike up a conversation with one of the TASP supervisors who is working on the project and find out from him that the company is installing the equipment at a few gates as an experiment for the airline. He tells you that a successful experiment will result in a contract to do an installation at all the gates. This is bad news as far as your job security is concerned.

You and the TASP supervisor hit it off, and you volunteer to help the crew for free during your off-hours. You tell the supervisor that the experience will help you with your coursework at a nearby college. He agrees and shows you how the system works.

You learn that the system combines check-in kiosks with automated voice announcements concerning boarding procedures. The package is tied into the airline's GDS. A small group of airline employees access the daily flight schedules and update the gate assignments as needed directly into the GDS. One gate agent then is assigned to each gate to handle the few manual boarding assignments (standby, for instance) and then plays the voice track of boarding announcements while scanning boarding passes. At the completion of the boarding procedure for the aircraft, the system provides an automated count, with the agent confirming the total by doing a physical count. The airplane doors then are closed, and the aircraft is ready for takeoff.

You spend about a month learning all you can about the system. Soon your job security fears are realized when the scheduling supervisor calls you into the office for a talk. Julie, the supervisor, advises you that the TASP system will be installed at all gates. As you brace yourself for the layoff notice, Julie says, "The TASP supervisor tells me you are becoming an expert in this system. How would you like to be assigned as a system data entry agent?" You respond with a look of surprise: "Really?" She replies, "Why not? You are already a member of our staff, and we won't need to train you on the system. In fact, you will probably end up training the others."

You quickly accept the new position and on the way home realize that your knowledge of systems has just saved your job.

SUMMMARY

This chapter looked at systems that are used for booking reservations at hotels, resorts, restaurants, car rental companies, and travel services. It was determined that a reservation system is a database that manages inventory and permits booking transaction processing. Reservation systems may be manual; however, most are electronic, which means that computer systems are involved in the reservation process.

Electronic reservation systems may be stand-alone machines or entire computerized systems. They may be interfaced with property management systems in hotels as well as point-of-sale systems in restaurants. Central reservation systems are computer systems that include a range of network interfaces that include LANs, MANs, and WANs. Early central reservation systems were developed by the airline industry and eventually became global distribution systems. Hotels later followed suit by developing their own CRS systems that interface with GDSs today.

The original reservations systems were accessed by industry insiders and travel agents to reserve accommodations for the traveling public. However, the Internet now permits consumers to conduct their own searches of flights and other travel-related services. More expansive services are being added to CRSs as technology becomes increasingly powerful. The technology systems that are used for reservations and other transactions fall within the jurisdiction of the chief information officer, a senior executive position with hospitality and travel-related organizations.

The role of GDSs and CRSs has changed the roles of consumers as well as those of the organizations that use them. Travel wholesalers, brokers, and other intermediaries are now prominent players in the electronic distribution of travel-related products and services. The industry expects that this dynamic organizational environment of collaboration and competition will continue to exist in the near future.

DISCUSSION QUESTIONS

1. Before the development of electronic reservation systems, hotels would book reservations manually. Identify the manual steps that were taken for this process.
2. Hotel central reservation systems are adding more features aimed at enhancing services every day. If you were a hotel manager, what types of services would you like to see added to the CRS for your organization? Use your imagination to answer this question.
3. Global distribution systems are undergoing many changes, as are the intermediaries that use them. Identify the major changes that have already happened and try to predict the future for these distribution channels.

KEY TERMS

Booking transaction
Central reservation system (CRS)
Computer reservation system (CRS)
Electronic distribution system (EDS)
Electronic reservation system (ERS)
Global distribution system
Reservation
Reservation system

REFERENCES

1. Bill Carroll and Judy Siguaw. (2003). The Evolution of Electronic Distribution: Effects on Hotels and Intermediaries. *Cornell Hotel and Restaurant Administration Quarterly* 44(4):38–49.
2. Marianna Sigala, Andrew Lockwood, and Peter Jones. (2001). Strategic Implementation and IT: Gaining Competitive Advantage from the Hotel Reservations Process. *International Journal of Contemporary Hospitality Management* 13(7): 364–371.
3. Shannon E. Martin. (2003). Knowledge Conversion Is the Key to Success. *Information Management Journal* 37(6):52.
4. Jeffrey S. Harrison. (2003). Strategic Analysis for the Hospitality Industry. *Cornell Hotel and Restaurant Administration Quarterly* 44(2):139.
5. Ibid.
6. Airline Computer Reservation Systems. (2003). *Regulation* 26(2):7.
7. Rex S. Toh and Peter Raven. (2003). Perishable Asset Revenue Management: Integrated Internet Marketing Strategies for the Airlines. *Transportation Journal* 42(4):30.
8. Jon W. Beard and Tim O. Peterson. (2003). Coming to Grips with the Management of Information: A Classroom Exercise. *Journal of Information Systems Education* 14(1):15.
9. Carroll and Siguaw. (2003).
10. Ibid.
11. Ibid.
12. Peter O'Connor and Andrew J. Frew. (2002). The Future of Hotel Electronic Distribution: Expert and Industry Perspectives. *Cornell Hotel and Restaurant Administration Quarterly* 43(3):33–45.
13. Linden Brown and Hugh Pattinson. (1995). Information Technology and Telecommunications: Impacts on Strategic Alliance Formation and Management. *Management Decision* 33(4):41–50.
14. Ibid.
15. Deborah Dahl. (2004). Is Natural Language Real? *Speech Technology* 9(3):34–36.
16. Turing. (1950). Computing Machinery and Intelligence. *Mind* 59:433–460.
17. L. Van Tichelen. (2003). Semantic Interpretation for Speech Recognition. *W3C Working Draft,* http://www.w3.org/TR/semantic-interpretation.
18. Nancy Jamison. (2004). Speech in the Travel Industry: Traveling with Speech Technology. *Speech Technology* 9(3):18–23.

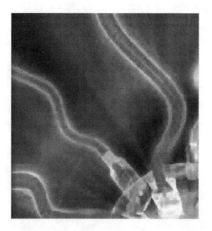

Property Management Systems and Point-of-Sale Systems

CHAPTER OBJECTIVES

In this chapter you will learn to:

1. Apply the hierarchy of data to hospitality systems.
2. Identify transaction-processing systems for hospitality organizations.
3. Identify process control systems for hospitality organizations.

On-the-Job Training

You have been working part-time at a large resort while going to school. Over the last two years you have worked in most of the rooms division departments, including the front office, the concierge office, housekeeping, reservations, and other guest services areas. This experience has given you a snapshot of rooms division operations. Your varied experiences have resulted in your being designated as a front-office trainer for new staff members.

While you are taking your lunch break, the human resources director approaches you in the staff cafeteria, and asks you to stop by her office at the completion of your shift. You agree and return to work at the front desk.

At the end of your shift you stop by to meet with the HR director. As you enter her office, you are surprised to see the corporate chief information officer seated and apparently expecting your arrival. The HR director introduces you to Dan, the CIO. As you shake his hand, he says, "I've heard a lot of great things about you." He continues: "It sounds as if you are learning just about every job in the hotel."

The HR director chimes in: "We have a special project that is both exciting and challenging." She continues: "Dan has selected our property as a prototype to chart the relationships of all systems in all our departments from the viewpoint of our guests. The findings will be used to establish a model for continuous guest satisfaction improvement to be implemented at all of our properties." She concludes by saying: "If you agree to do this project, you will be mentored by Dan, who has done every job there is in a hotel. Are you interested?" As you agree to work with Dan on the project, you experience mixed feelings of pride and trepidation.

To be continued . . .

INTRODUCTION

Most hospitality and tourism employees work with interfaces of systems that provide for transaction processing and process control in hospitality organizations. This chapter provides models that allow us to view descriptions of the systems we work with on a daily basis in hospitality organizations.

All systems consist of inputs, transformation processes, and outcomes. In hospitality information systems, inputs consist of data that are keyed into the system. This information is translated and manipulated by the transformation process mechanisms (computer processors) to yield usable information in the form of outputs.

TRANSACTION-PROCESSING SYSTEMS

Transaction-processing systems handle activities that occur between two or more parties. A potential guest will make a reservation for a hotel room, which is a **booking transaction,** or one in which an individual makes arrangements to use products and services at a future time. Booking transactions also occur in restaurants, health spas, airlines, and any other outlet that provides an opportunity for individuals to reserve space, products, or services. A booking transaction usually includes a **confirmation,** which is an agreement between the hospitality provider and the client that a product or service transaction will occur in the future. When services are rendered, as occurs when a licensed massage therapist works on a client for a reserved period of time, a **service transaction** is in progress. Service transactions also occur in restaurants during meal periods, in recreational facilities such as golf courses and tennis courts during the time of play, in transportation companies during transit, and in hotels during occupancy periods.

A **sales transaction** occurs when a customer or guest pays for the products and services that are rendered. The timing of the sales transaction varies with the traditional policies associated with the particular type of service. Payment for golf or tennis play, as well as for most recreational activities, occurs just before the guest participates in the activity. Airline and cruise reservations usually are paid in full before departure. Hotel reservations usually are guaranteed with one room night of payment, but full payment for the stay occurs at the time of guest check-in. The custom at restaurants is for the sales transaction to occur at the completion of the meal. In retail establishments the customer pays for purchased items just before leaving the retail outlet.

If a guest, customer, or passenger makes full payment before receiving the products or services, the sales transaction is labeled a **prepay transaction.** A **postpay transaction** is one in which the guest or customer pays upon the complete rendering of services. In some cases hotel guests may be asked to pay for products or services after checkout, which constitutes an **after-departure transaction.** When hotel guests are

Booking transaction Making a reservation at a hotel, resort, restaurant, or travel company.

Confirmation An agreement between the hospitality provider and the client that a product or service transaction will occur in the future.

Service transaction The actual time during which services are needed.

Sales transaction The process in which the customer or guest pays for products and services that are rendered.

Prepay transaction A sales transaction in which a guest, customer, or passenger makes full payment before receiving products or services.

Postpay transaction A sales transaction that occurs after a guest or customer receives products or services.

After-departure transaction A postpay transaction that requires billing after a guest or customer departs from the facility.

The timing of a sales transaction often depends on the type of service. In many foodservice operations the transaction occurs at the end of the meal. (©Action Systems, Inc.)

Cash in advance (CIA) A prepay deposit made by a guest who chooses not to use credit during a stay at a hotel or resort.

Tendering procedure An exchange of cash, use of a credit card, or posting to an internal credit ledger.

unable to establish credit at the time of check-in, there is usually a requirement for an advance deposit, which is referred to as **cash in advance (CIA).** Regardless of the nature of sales transaction process, all sales transactions are completed with a **tendering procedure,** in which there is an exchange of cash, use of a credit card, or posting to an internal credit ledger.

From a historical perspective, before the availability of electronic processing, all sales transactions were processed manually through handwritten postings of specific transactions. The first tabulating machine used for tendering procedures was the mechanical cash register. This machine used mechanical parts requiring no electricity to "ring up" a sale. The next wave of tendering machines was electronic cash registers, which used electricity to manipulate the internal mechanical processors in the machine. Eventually, the mechanical parts contained in the cash registers were replaced with transistors, which provided the capability for electronic cash registers to retain small amounts of "memory," similar to the functions of a current calculator. With this evolution came the ability to track electronically a few categories of numerical sales data that were used for basic bookkeeping reports through the preparation of **journal tapes,** which are printouts of sales transactions. Although this low-level technology reduced the need for manual transaction processing, machine-generated information was restricted to numerical transactions without more important sales information, such as items sold.

Journal tapes Cash register printouts of sales transactions.

Database interfaces are required for transaction-processing machinery to automate the booking, sales, and tendering procedures completely. Additional benefits of database interfaces include the provision of management reporting and the process control functions that are included among the procedures handled by current machines.

PROCESS CONTROL AND MANAGEMENT REPORTS

Process control functions are procedures that track the use of the material resources required to produce products and services. The range of process control functions varies with the sophistication levels of different systems. A fully automated process control feature links the procurement, inventory, requisition, and utilization aspects of raw materials. In some cases, such as freestanding restaurants, the process control features may include labor scheduling, payroll, and utilization analysis. Larger operations separate the scheduling and payroll aspects from the transaction-processing machinery, as there are more sophisticated types of systems for these functions. Those operations may, however, choose to retain labor utilization features, such as labor hours per output units, as part of the transaction-processing system. A database interface is required in all sophisticated transaction-processing machinery regardless of system configuration specifications.

Process control Procedures that track the use of the material resources required to produce products and services.

Management reporting functions include real-time and after-the-fact information resulting from data analyses of the transaction-processing and process control functions contained within the system. Management

Management reporting Real-time and after-the-fact information resulting from data analyses of the transaction-processing and process control functions contained within the system.

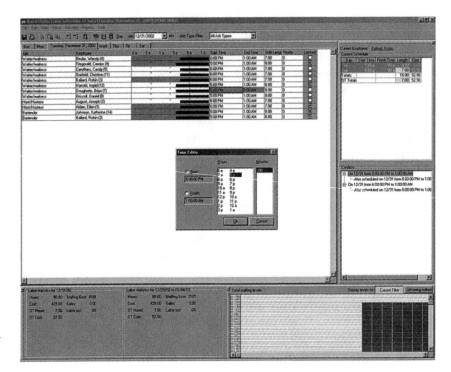

The management of employee scheduling is one aspect of process control. (©Action Systems, Inc.)

reports typically include transaction-processing information such as the following:

- Revenue volumes
- Sales details
- Sold items abstracts
- Time-of-sales tracking
- Sales summaries

Process control aspects of management reporting provide information concerning the following:

- Cost of goods sold
- Perpetual inventories
- Procurement orders
- Requisition tracking
- Labor utilization

All these functions require interfaces between the transaction-processing machinery and one or more databases.

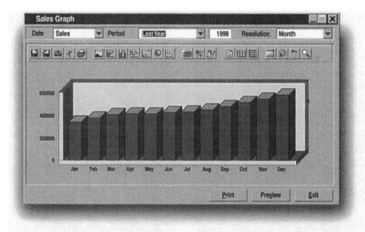

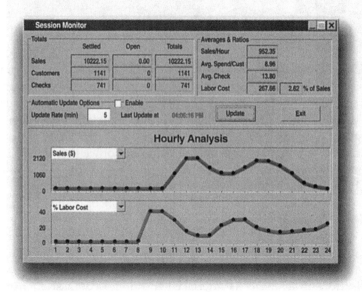

Revenue and sales information are management reporting functions. (©Action Systems, Inc.)

DATABASE INTERFACES

The transformational process of a database provides the ability to sort, tabulate, and manipulate data to produce information (outputs) that can be used for the management of a hospitality organization. The database structure and interfaces vary with the size and scope of the organization.

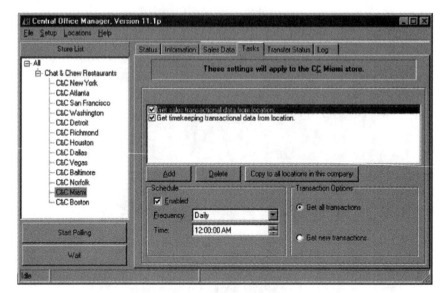

A restaurant chain or franchise can use a database interface to output information as part of the management reporting functions. (©Action Systems, Inc.)

For instance, a freestanding restaurant may rely on the services of a single database on the premises to produce required process control and management reporting functions. In contrast, a large resort may require an entire database management system to produce the same results on a much larger and more diversified scale. If that hotel were a chain affiliate, there would be remote databases in the corporate office that would interface with each property. A typical single database structure is shown in Figure 9.1.

Figure 9.1 provides a model that is used to demonstrate the hierarchy of data for a transaction-processing database. The database structure consists of characters, fields, records, and files within the database, which is used to store, sort, manipulate, and query data to produce useful information for management knowledge and decision making.

A collection of databases is interfaced through a database management system, as shown in Figure 9.2. End users work through each database that interfaces with each work area to input and extract data. Each work area database interfaces with a central database, the DBMS, which acts as a centralized warehouse for the entire operation—thus the term **data warehouse.**

Data warehouse Volume of information stored in a database management system configuration.

For instance, the central backbone or nervous system of a hotel, convention center, conference facility, catering property, bed and breakfast (B&B), hostel, or other lodging operation is called the property management system. PMSs are used at any physical plant that is in the business of selling space such as guestrooms, function rooms, and meeting rooms. These property operations vary in terms of volume and range of services.

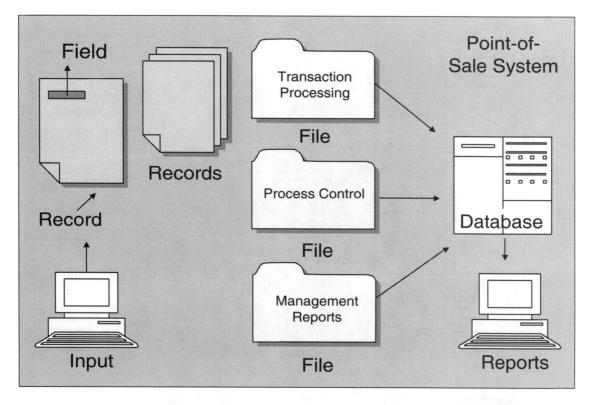

Figure 9.1 Single Database Structure

A small property with no food and beverage operations is considered a limited-service lodging facility. Similarly, small catering and conference properties with no lodging facilities are considered single-use operations. Although bed and breakfast operations include a preset menu food and beverages, the meals are part of the lodging package and the scope of such facilities is usually small (fewer than 100 guestrooms). Hostels, in contrast, usually provide dormitory-style accommodations to lower-budget travelers. Both hostels and B&Bs fall within the category of single-use lodging facilities. In all these cases the transaction-processing needs warrant a stand-alone PMS system that does not include multiple-transaction-processing interfaces. Figure 9.3 depicts a stand-alone PMS system.

Full-service hotels have varied forms of operations that include guestrooms, multiple food and beverage facilities, catering function and meeting rooms, and retail outlets, as well as conference or convention spaces in some cases. Also, these properties vary in terms of guest volume, ranging from midsized property (300 to 1,000 guestrooms) to a larger scale of over 1,000 guestrooms. Full-service resort properties

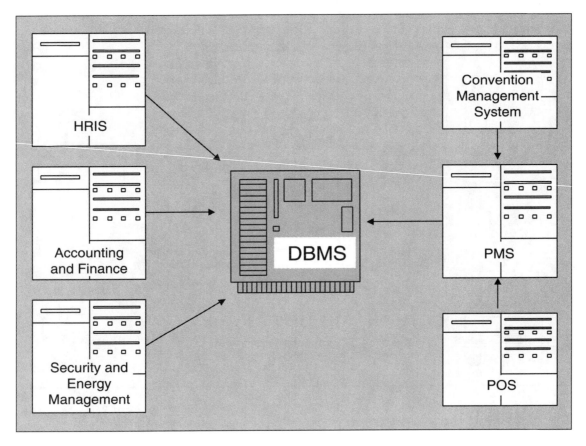

Figure 9.2 DBMS Warehouse

usually include a range of recreational facilities, including golf, tennis, a health spa, and/or water sports. These properties are self-contained villages that consist of numerous types of operations with varied transaction-processing requirements. Each outlet uses specialized machinery for transaction processing that is called a point-of-sale system. The configuration of each POS system will vary with the needs of the particular outlet. For instance, the transaction-processing procedures are different among restaurants, recreational facilities, and retail outlets. Since the PMS system is the backbone of such a property, that system becomes the hub **(server)** for interfaces with all the POS systems at a full-service hotel or resort. Figure 9.4 shows how a PMS for a full-service hotel acts as a hub for other aspects of the operation.

Server Computer that serves as the centralized processor for a network.

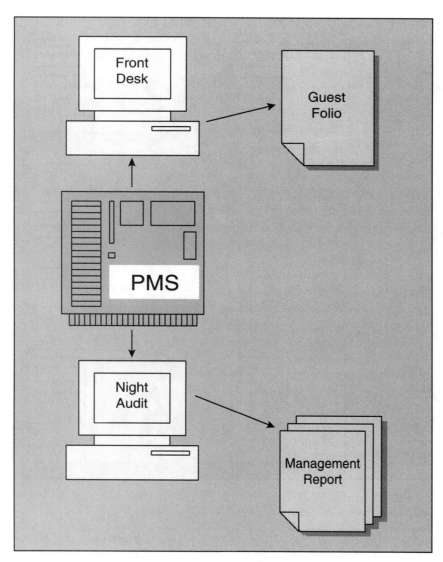

Figure 9.3 Stand-Alone PMS

PMS INTERFACES

Most individuals assume that the PMS is linked only to the front-office operations. That was the case until more expansive interfaces started to become available in the mid-1980s. Before that time the National Cash Register (NCR) Corporation dominated front-office hardware and

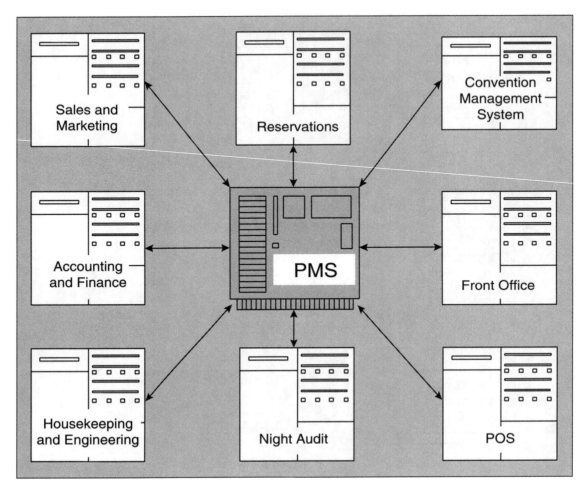

Figure 9.4 PMS Hub for a Full-Service Hotel

software. Practically every full-service hotel and resort used the NCR-4200 system for front-office operations, which was the extent of property management systems at that time. In the early 1980s hotels began to replace this system with dumb terminals connected to International Business Machine (IBM) Corporation mainframe computers. Software companies such as Hospitality Information Systems (HIS) provided IBM-compatible software to run front-office functions such as check-in/check-out procedures, guest history files, and folio management. Soon other providers began to compete for the industry-specific front-office software market written for the open IBM mainframe platform. This was the first initiative that used open platform information system processes designed for hospitality-specific applications. The impetus for this type of configuration was the perceived need to link front-office hotel functions directly with back-office accounting functions. Although this period marked a quantum leap toward open platform systems, interfaces between PMS and POS systems had not been established. One reason for the lack of linkages between the two systems was that POS hardware and software remained within the domain of proprietary systems that were dominated by companies such as Micros and Renkin. Figure 9.5 goes into the front-office operation for a closer inspection of the functions that are relevant to the core of a PMS system, which are interfaced with back-office accounting systems.

Note that the functions to the left of the front desk are back-office functions (behind the scenes), whereas those to the right are front-office (on stage for guests to see) functions. There are three points of guest interface. The first point of interface is by phone or the Internet to the reservations department, where guests inquire about availability and pricing to book guestrooms. The room rates quoted by the reservations agent are based on information that was input through the revenue management (sometimes referred to as yield management) system. The second point of guest interface occurs upon check-in and throughout the guest's stay and involves the front-desk personnel. During their stay guests may seek the one-to-one services of the concierge for information,

Figure 9.5 Hotel Front Office PMS System

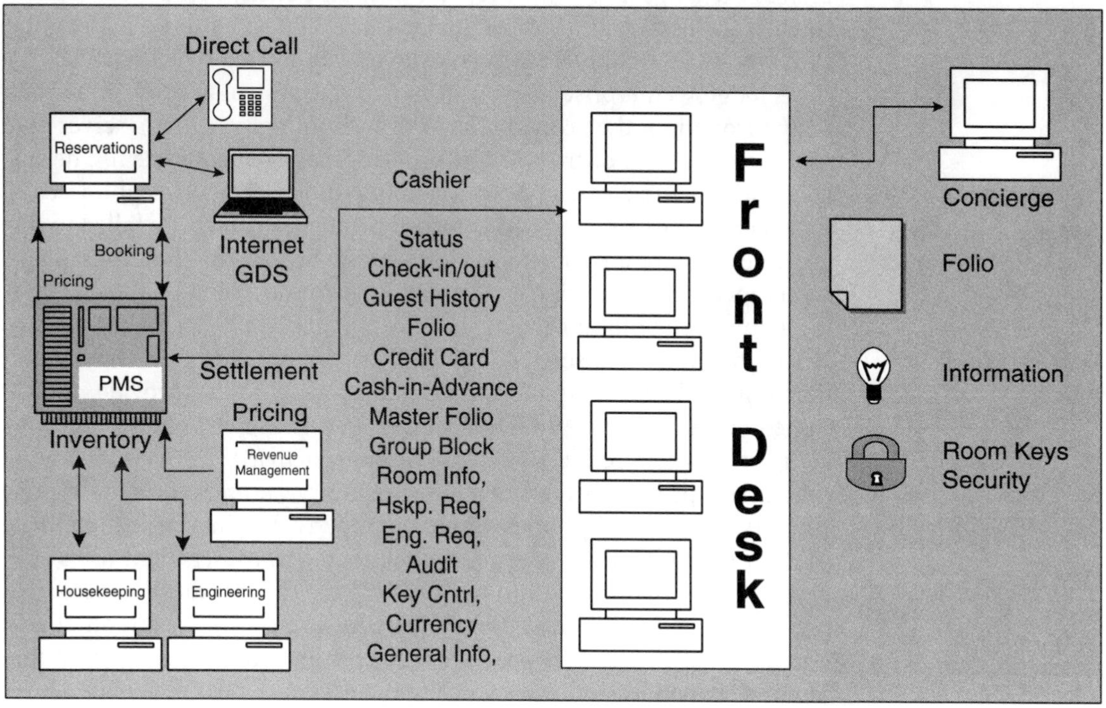

entertainment, child care, and other unique needs. These three points of guest interface are handled appropriately by a PMS system that is connected solely to the back office for accounting purposes. However, a full-service hotel or resort provides many more services than those which are accessed in the property's lobby, which is within the domain of the front-office managers and staff.

CALL ACCOUNTING SYSTEMS

The call accounting system tracks phone use throughout a hospitality enterprise such as a hotel or a resort. You can imagine the number of telephones in a 1,000-room resort, with a single phone extension for each guestroom in addition to lines for each of the outlets as well as for the administrative offices. A lodging establishment will purchase a phone switch that can cost millions of dollars from a telephone provider. The phone switch contains millions of wires that represent multiple phone connections. Hubs and routers are attached at various intervals to the phone switch, which usually is contained within an electrical room. The phone lines are run through a communications center called a public branch exchange (PBX). A PBX is an electronic switchboard that centrally routes calls to thousands of extensions. The PBX used to be manned by PBX operators, but hotels today mostly use automated switchboards.

A lodging enterprise uses a call accounting system to track phone activity throughout the property. The call accounting system is a server that interfaces the PBX board with the property management system. The call accounting system tracks both incoming and outgoing telephone calls for every phone extension. Calls placed from guestrooms are billed to the front desk folio for each room. Hotel guests believe that hotels earn ancillary income by charging exorbitant sums for outgoing phone calls ($1 for a one-minute local call, for instance). In actuality, most of those dollars go to the phone service provider, not the hotel. Phone systems for hotels involve large capital and operating expenses to provide an expected guest amenity. Additionally, most guests use cell phones for outgoing calls, which reduces guestroom phone activity mostly to incoming calls. A few properties have installed frequency-jamming devices to preclude the use of cell phones within a property. By the time a hotel has paid off its capital investment in phone switches, routers, and hubs, the property will require additional investments to upgrade the outdated phone system. Just as hotel operators never foresaw the invention of cell phones, telephone service providers underestimated developments in the Internet that allow it to carry voice transmissions.

TECH TALK

Advice from the Experts in Hospitality Information Systems

An interview with Del Ross: Director of Global E-Commerce Services for InterContinental Hotels Group

1. **What is your scope of responsibility?**

   My job is to develop, implement, and manage all strategic and tactical aspects of the company's consumer-facing Internet activities, principally including direct Internet reservations, PriorityClub.com, and Internet marketing. I am responsible for delivering approximately 7 to 10 percent of the total revenues for our hotels. I am currently delivering approximately $3 million per day in reservations through the company's branded websites.

2. **Has the nature of your work changed over the last couple of years?**

   Competition is fierce and comes from both direct competitors (Hilton, Marriott, etc.) and intermediaries (Expedia, Hotels.com, Travelocity). These competitive forces present two challenges: (1) maintain pace in re core functionality and features available to customers and (2) seek short-term competitive advantages through innovation wherever possible. In the last two years we have successfully implemented measures to reduce or eliminate customer piracy (forced intermediation) by our competitors through the assertion of intellectual property rights, aggressive search engine management, and legal action when required. In the next two years we will focus on developing functionality that will enable us to better serve our business and meetings customers through the direct Internet channel, while maintaining vigilant monitoring of competitive activity.

3. **What are the future prospects in terms of career opportunities for graduates with an interest in IT positions?**

   While my team includes a services delivery department which is highly technical in nature (principally application development, quality assurance, and project management), we are separate from our corporate IT department, which is chartered to develop and support our back-office processing systems. We will always be interested in discussing career opportunities with experienced, intelligent professionals but do not expect to expand our full-time staff significantly over the next several years.

   Our bias in service delivery is to source prebuilt, customizable solutions wherever possible and use in-house development only for core focus areas which cannot efficiently be outsourced or purchased.

(continued)

4. In your opinion, should nontechnical managers have a basic knowledge of IT and IS?

It is certainly useful for nontechnical managers (e.g., finance and marketing professionals) to have a basic understanding of the root capabilities of information technology and development processes, but in our model we require only that our clients and constituents have a very clear idea of the business requirements or objectives they would like us to address. The technology landscape shifts and changes far too rapidly for nontechnologists to maintain a working knowledge of solutions alternatives, so it is not feasible or effective to require an understanding of the latest technical innovations or approaches to problem solving and solution development.

5. Any final words of advice or prophecy for our future technologists?

Technology does not exist for its own sake, so innovations without applications are often doomed to failure irrespective of the nature of the innovation or its potential as a change agent. When pursuing the path of innovation, it is critical that the technologist begin with a problem or challenge that needs to be addressed or could be addressed far more efficiently. In so doing, the path of innovation may lead to new, unexpected benefits (e.g., the 3M Post-It story) irrespective of whether the original goal is met. Therefore, a balanced blend of pragmatism, perseverance, and opportunism is a key component of long-term success as a technology innovator.

We thank you for your advice, Del.

Jae Yeoung Lee conducted this interview. Mr. Lee is a manager at an InterContinental hotel and a graduate student at the Rosen School of Hospitality Management at the University of Central Florida in Orlando.

Some hotel operators are bypassing traditional phone switches by installing Voice/Internet Protocol (V over IP) systems. This technology is used by some homeowners to avoid phone service provider long-distance charges. V/IP phone systems require broadband access to an Internet server as well as telephone software used to route and handle calls over existing phone lines or wireless connections. The V/IP server may be maintained at the property level or outsourced to an Internet phone service provider. V/IP telephone service is digital and works as well as services provided by the phone company at a fraction of the cost. The initial capital investment is high, usually in the range of millions of dollars. However, the payback period is fairly short, since the per-call charges by the phone company are eliminated. The only downside is that the phone service is interrupted when glitches in Internet services occur, which is also true when traditional phone lines experience interruptions. An advantage of V/IP connectivity is the provision of high-speed Internet access as part of the phone system for each guestroom. V/IP systems may be interfaced with call accounting systems to track and bill for phone and computer use on guest folios. This protocol will be used in most hotels in the next few years.

OTHER SERVICES AND OTHER INTERFACES

During a guest's stay at a hotel there are numerous activities to partake in, including recreation (golf, tennis, water sports, etc.), restaurants, lounges, retail shopping, and in-room dining, to name just a few of the available amenities. Historically, guests would "sign" for these services on a hard-copy guest check and show a room key to verify their identity as a hotel guest. This procedure was used in the absence of interfaces between point-of-sale machinery in each outlet with the backbone system called the PMS. Today the procedures are different as a result of the existence of holistic transaction-processing systems that include interfaces between all POS machines and the centralized PMS.

In today's environment the guest simply presents a smart card at each of the hotel or resort outlets to have the charges posted directly to his or her folio through a POS system. Figure 9.6 shows the networking process for these transactions.

At the end of each 24-hour period, the night audit team compiles revenue figures from POS data networked through the PMS, along with direct entries to the PMS (room revenue), to generate a daily revenue report that is distributed to the hotel managers.

For each POS icon shown in Figure 9.6, there is a separate local area network that handles transaction processing within that outlet. The network (subsystem) can be as small as a single **terminal** for a small gift shop or as large as multiple connections in a restaurant or showroom. The LAN consists of terminals and printers that are arranged in a hub around a **master terminal.** In a hotel outlet, the master terminal provides the direct connection to the POS server, which in turn is linked to the PMS server.

In a freestanding restaurant, the master terminal also may be the server for the system. Chain restaurants may be connected to a remote server through a WAN or a MAN. The master terminal has the ability to collect all the data from the other terminals and produce various reports, such as sales, covers, and menu abstracts, among others. If the master terminal is connected to a POS server, the reports for all the outlets are generated from that single server. Figure 9.7 shows the POS network for a single restaurant.

Terminals Computers or other machines that function as nodes on a network.

Master terminal The terminal that controls all the other terminals in a POS LAN.

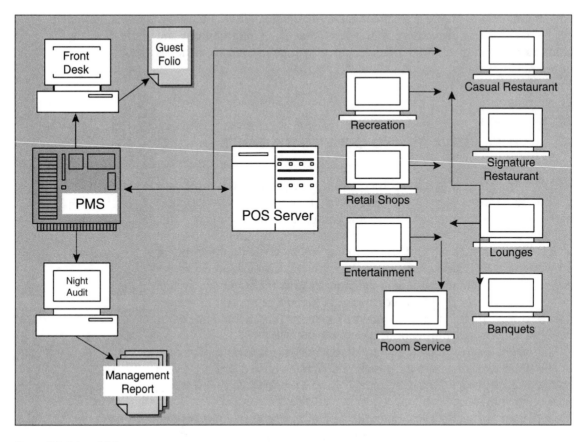

Figure 9.6 Point-of-Sale Network

The flow of data originates in the dining room and then is placed with the lounge and kitchen areas for production and ultimately service to the restaurant guests seated at the tables. The dining room terminals are located in front-of-house service areas. The food orders are transmitted to the kitchen production areas for preparation at the appropriate stations behind the culinary line. After the food orders are delivered, the remaining steps of service are provided and guest checks are tendered.

All the information from the dining room is "dumped" into the master terminal, which usually is located in a back-office area of the restaurant. The master terminal has the capacity to generate all the management reports for the restaurant. The server terminals also generate reports for use by the service staff. In some cases there are back-of-the-house components of the network to assist with culinary management functions, such as product usage, prepped items on hand, and labor production.

There are four possible options for information flow from the restaurant's master terminal. In a freestanding restaurant, the information flow

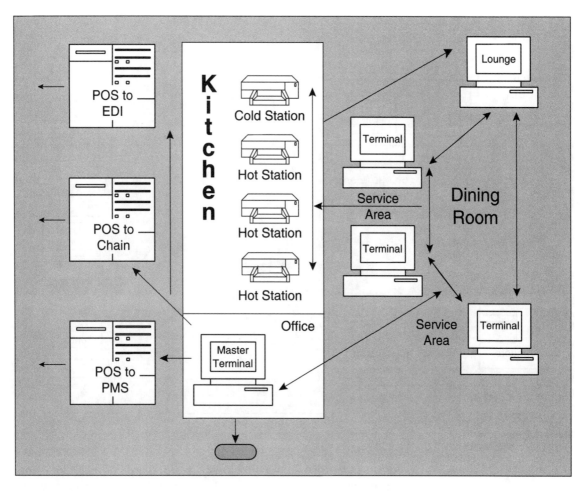

Figure 9.7 Restaurant POS Network

can terminate at the point of the master dump (symbolized by the terminator icon in the figure). A hotel restaurant will transmit information from the master terminal to the POS server, which ultimately will transmit the data to the PMS. A chain restaurant may transmit to a regional office or commissary. If an electronic data interface is established, information is transmitted to a purchasing location for comparison with inventories and converted into electronic orders for products from the vendors or the commissary.

Back-of-the-House Systems

Regardless of the structure of the business (hotel, freestanding or chain restaurant), Figure 9.8 shows the flows in an EDI system. The master terminals from the outlets connect to the inventory systems in the

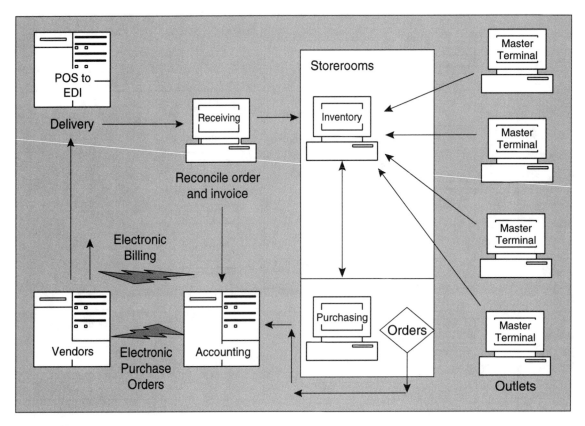

Figure 9.8 Restaurant/
Retail POS/EDI System

Par stock The predetermined levels of on-hand storeroom stock for each item before any stock requisitions.

Working stock Stock that has been requisitioned from storage for use in a work unit.

On-hand stock Stock available from storage areas.

Perpetual inventory An electronic means of tracking inventory movement in real time.

storerooms. Inventory items previously were requisitioned from the storerooms for use in each outlet. If the requisitions are electronic, the storerooms have the capacity to maintain a perpetual inventory, meaning that they have continuous counts of items requisitioned from stock. The master terminals report the use of stock items at the end of business, and those figures are compared with the perpetual inventory. This permits the storerooms to forecast usage for the next business period.

The calculation equation for the storerooms is **par stock** (standard levels) minus requisitions (**working stock** in the outlets), which equals **on-hand stock.** The difference between stock on hand and par stock equals the amount it is necessary to reorder, which the purchasing office will follow in the absence of EDI and **perpetual inventory** systems. However, with EDI, par levels may be reduced to near zero in some cases because electronic interchanges with vendors produce just-in-time inventories. In Figure 9.8, the storerooms know how much stock was requisitioned for the outlets and how much was used in the outlets, indicating the amount of working stock in the outlets for the next business period. Based on this information plus the next day's demand, the storerooms may forecast the next day's usage and report that figure to the purchasing department for the placement of stock orders with the vendors. The purchasing director establishes purchase orders (POs) to notify the vendors of each purchase amount. The POs are sent through the accounting office and transmitted electronically to the vendors.

The vendors process the orders for delivery to the property. The receiving agent at the property inspects the incoming orders to ensure that they meet specifications and that the invoice amounts are correct. The stock then is entered into inventory in the storerooms, and the invoices are confirmed with the purchasing and accounting offices, which notify accounts payable to accept the electronic billing totals from the vendors. Payment is scheduled for electronic distribution to complete the purchasing cycle. Meanwhile, the outlets requisition the materials needed for the new business period, and the perpetual cycle continues. The cycle includes purchasing, accounting, storeroom, and receiving as separate functions to ensure "checks and balances" that keep all the parties honest. Also, when usage versus sales in the outlets is monitored, exceptionally high levels of usage will generate exception reports; these are "red flags" for managers to investigate discrepancies, which may indicate theft or waste at the outlet level.

Wireless POS Options

The historical shift from electronic cash registers to POS systems provided new productivity challenges for restaurant service staff members. When electronic cash registers were in use, a server would take the order at tableside by writing the items on a notepad called a dup-pad (duplicate pad) or captain's pad (named after restaurant captains who used to be the only people who took orders from guests in fine-dining establishments). Those pads were small notebooks with perforated sheets of paper containing carbon copy pages beneath the regular pages. Once an order was completed, the server would enter the kitchen and place carbon copies of what was written at appropriate stations along the culinary "line." With this task completed, the server would go about providing dining room services to restaurant guests until another party was seated, which required that a new order be placed.

When restaurants shifted to POS systems, the written versions of guests' orders were entered through a keypad or touch screen into a "precheck" terminal that would transmit orders to printers in the lounge and kitchen areas. The production staff would use the printouts (called chits) as guidelines for order processing. Alhough this process enhanced productivity for service bartenders and culinarians, it created new problems for members of the wait staff. Since the precheck terminals had to be hardwired to other parts of the POS system, only a limited number of these expensive machines were made available to the servers. This created a bottleneck of groups of servers waiting in line to access each precheck machine. For years restaurant managers had to learn to live with this scenario. Today, however, there is a cost-efficient alternative to limited numbers of hardwired precheck machines for order entry.

Wireless technology has become a reliable means of telecommunications for POS systems through the use of radio or microwave frequencies. A number of hotel and resort restaurants have installed wireless transceivers provided through platforms such as Bluetooth Technology that permit restaurant servers to perform order entry directly into personal digital assistant palmtops at the same time the guests place their orders. This eliminates long lines of servers waiting at precheck machines in discrete areas of the restaurant. Wireless LAN technology may be used for indoor dining rooms as well as for outside areas such as poolside "tiki-bar" restaurants. For instance, the Gaylord Palms resort in Orlando uses wireless systems for its indoor and outdoor restaurant and lounge outlets. Darden restaurants, a chain with freestanding restaurant brands such as Red Lobster and Olive Garden, is using wireless systems in its newest theme concept, Seasons 52. It is expected that within a short time traditional precheck machines will be replaced by PDAs with wireless connections in all restaurants, and this will save service steps.

Handheld and monitor POS systems are used commonly in restaurants. (©Action Systems, Inc.)

Seasons 52 is a new restaurant franchise that will operate with a wireless system. (Courtesy of Darden Restaurants, Inc.)

Catering and Convention POS Systems

Catering facilities are in the business of providing prearranged food, meeting, and entertainment functions for hosted groups of people. Convention and conference centers are in the same business but provide those arrangements on a much larger scale. The arrangements for a function are made before the prearranged date of the event, with the final details confirmed at least 72 hours before that date. The majority of transaction-processing functions occur during the time between original guest inquiries and booking arrangements (menu selection, facility setup, decor, entertainment, etc.). A deposit is made when the arrangements are completed. Next, the guaranteed guest count is communicated by the host of the party three days before the function. Finally, the function takes place and the host pays the catering facility a remaining balance at the end of the event.

Although some catering facilities are stand-alone operations, the majority are located within full-service hotels and resorts. Traditionally, catering offices used databases to track the progress of event management from prospecting, to sales, to planning, to the completion of a function. The software for these functions is a somewhat modified sales and marketing database program. Catering facilities consist of meeting rooms and ballrooms that are configured individually to meet the needs of an event for a specific client.

Traditionally, function room schematics were drawn manually on paper to depict the setup of a particular function, as traditional software packages were not readily available to perform this function until recently. Today there are application service providers (ASPs) that use powerful workstations to provide digital representations of the configurations for each meeting room and ballroom. For instance, the catering director for a resort will establish a contract with an ASP such as the Matrix Corporation to have all the measurements and room specifications at the resort digitized into a graphical design database. The database will reside at the ASP location and be accessed and manipulated by catering personnel from the resort to provide catering clients with digital representations of room specifications for a particular event.

Let's say a client is booking a wedding at a resort. The client will sit with a catering sales manager who will access the ASP database from her office. The client will describe how the ballroom should look for the wedding. The sales manager will manipulate digital pictures of tables, flowers, buffet tables, cake and gift tables, the stage, the dance floor, and the like, until the computer shows an image of the perfect room for the client. The client may think that the workstation database resides at the resort. However, the powerful server used to create the design is located at the ASP office, and the catering sales manager is manipulating the figures through online analytical processing, which means that the work is being done online.

Because digital design software is complicated and expensive and requires heavy-duty computing power, most resorts do not have the resources to provide this service in-house. Application service providers invest in the technology and share it among a number of clients to help offset the cost of sophisticated processing. ASPs such as Matrix provide services for convention and conference centers as well as catering facilities at hotels and resorts.

On-the-Job Training . . . Continued

It has been about six months since you agreed to work with Dan. As you prepare to enter the boardroom for your project presentation, you take a moment to reflect on these experiences. You and Dan have charted every system in the hotel to determine its ultimate effect on guest satisfaction. You now have a thorough understanding of all hotel systems, including accounting, procurement, inventory management, and transaction processing as well as PMS and POS interfaces. Now is the moment of truth as you are introduced as Dan's copresenter.

Once the initial butterflies settle, you proceed with your charts and graphs that depict simplified versions of each system. The executives seated in the room are intrigued by your conclusive list of recommendations for continuous improvement. For a moment, you feel as though you were educating the experienced veterans in your audience. The attendees respond with excited applause as you thank them for their attention.

Afterward, it's just you and Dan seated in his office. He gives you one of those knowing smiles as he congratulates you for an outstanding presentation. He concludes by saying, "So, are you ready to start the implementation phase of our new plan?" You are totally flattered by your mentor's new offer.

SUMMARY

This chapter brought together information from various transaction-processing configurations to present information technology applications in hospitality settings. The examples that were presented mostly focused on hotel, restaurant, and retail systems. However, similar networks are used in other areas of the hospitality/tourism industry operations to enhance efficiency and effectiveness as a way to improve productivity levels.

DISCUSSION QUESTIONS

1. Consider the various transaction-processing systems for hotels, resorts, travel organizations, and restaurants. In your opinion, are these systems more complex than those used in other industries, such as retail? Why or why not?

2. How important are the process control aspects of transaction processes? What types of controls would you want to have available if you were a manager in a hotel or restaurant?
3. We know from this chapter that there are various types of transactions (sales, booking, confirmation, service, and tendering). Are any of these transactions more important than the others? Why or why not?
4. Toward the end of the chapter we discussed wireless network applications to transaction processing. Can you think of any areas other than restaurant service that would benefit from this technology? Give a few examples.

KEY TERMS

After-departure transaction
Booking transaction
Cash in advance (CIA)
Confirmation
Data warehouse
Journal tapes
Management reporting
Master terminals
On-hand stock
Par stock
Perpetual inventory
Postpay transaction
Prepay transaction
Process control
Sales transaction
Servers
Service transaction
Tendering procedure
Terminals
Working stock

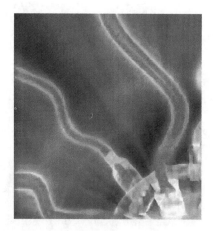

CHAPTER
10

Accounting Control and Production Systems

CHAPTER OBJECTIVES

In this chapter you will learn to:

1. Identify the interfaces of accounting information systems with other operating areas of hospitality enterprises.

2. Identify the processes of accounting, finance, and procurement systems.

3. Identify the processes used in each of the three production processes in hospitality organizations.

On-the-Job Training

As part of your management training program you are assigned to work as a supervisor for the banquet setup crew at a medium-size conference hotel. That crew is responsible for setup, breakdown, and cleaning for the meeting room, ballrooms, and prefunction areas of the conference center.

After just a few months you realize that employee turnover for your work crew is high. Exit interviews suggest that crew members are leaving the hotel for other jobs because of a lack of work hours. The banquet business is sporadic. Some days you need all the help you can find, but on others you don't have enough tasks to justify keeping most of the staff members on the time clock. You are wondering how to solve this dilemma, which apparently has baffled other supervisors for some time.

To be continued . . .

INTRODUCTION

This chapter examines the systems used to support the front end of hospitality operations. The primary focus of frontline hospitality operations is face-to-face interactions with guests that result in memorable service experiences. During those interactions we seamlessly perform transaction processing from the first point of contact through the time when we bid our guests farewell.

The back offices of the operation support the frontline staff members who interact with the guests. At the same time the back-office systems generate reports about the events that occur at the front end of the organization. A two-way flow of information is required for back-office functions to perform their duties. Figure 10.1 provides a snapshot of information flows for back-office operations.

Information from front-end transaction processing is sent to the back office for distribution to the shareholders. At the same time, resources are procured by back-end functions for distribution to the frontline staff members. The majority of back-office functions fall under the jurisdiction of the accounting and finance department.

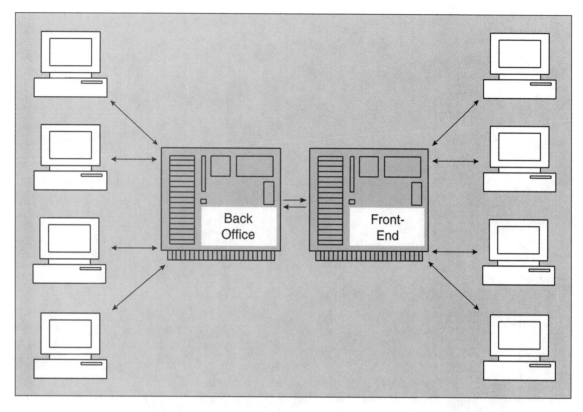

Figure 10.1 Back-Office Operations Information Flow

ACCOUNTING AND FINANCE FUNCTIONS

Accounting functions were the first to use computer systems during the mainframe era in the 1970s. The first versions of spreadsheet applications programs were generated during the PC revolution of the 1980s. Today all accounting functions are automated through **accounting information systems (AISs),** which consist of computer networks used to report business transactions and economic events that occur within a hospitality enterprise. The AIS is linked with all transaction processes that include a payment component at both ends (back and front) of the organization. Figure 10.2 shows the locations of these transactions. **Supply chain transactions** occur as part of the procurement processes that are used to acquire material resources for use in the hospitality enterprise. **Sales transactions** involve payments for products and services rendered

Accounting information systems (AISs) Computer networks that are used to report business transactions and economic events that occur within a hospitality enterprise.

Supply chain transactions Part of the procurement processes used to acquire material resources for use in a hospitality enterprise.

Sales transactions Payment for products and services rendered by the organization.

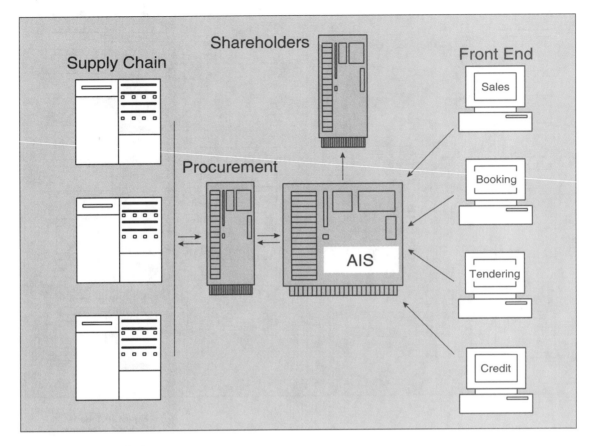

Figure 10.2 Location of AIS Transactions

Booking transactions
Reserving space for future use, which may include a confirmation deposit rendered to a hotel or full payment for a cruise or flight at the time the reservation is transacted.

Tendering transaction
After-the-fact payment for products and services rendered.

Cash settlement transaction After-the-fact payment for products and services rendered.

Credit transactions Sales are posted to an account that includes terms and conditions for future cash payment.

by the organization. In our business there are a few variations involving payment portions of sales transactions. **Booking transactions** reserve space for future use, which may include a confirmation deposit rendered to a hotel or full payment for a cruise or flight at the time the reservation is transacted. **Tendering transactions** or **cash settlement transactions** involve after-the-fact payment for products and services rendered. Examples would be the checkout procedure at a hotel and payment for noninclusive incidentals during a cruise. **Credit transactions** occur when sales are posted to an account that includes terms and conditions for future cash payment. For instance, clients may have established house charge accounts at restaurants or city ledger accounts with hotels. The AIS is linked automatically with any transaction that involves a monetary exchange at both the supply chain and sales ends of the hospitality organization.

Traditional Accounting Processes and Reports

Historically, accounting processes and reports were generated through manual systems that required the employment of many clerical and bookkeeping workers in the business offices of hospitality organizations. The mainframe networks of the 1970s provided electronic depositories of accounting information that still required the services of keypunch operators for data entry processes. Computer research laboratories developed very large scale integration (VLSI) transistor components that resulted in the proliferation of powerful personal computers that were used to perform accounting transaction processing in the mid-1980s. The drawback at that time was the gap that existed between PCs and mainframe computers that could not communicate with each other. When PCs replaced pencil and paper transaction processing, the data were entered into freestanding computers that had no platform for telecommunication.

The development of local area networks in the late 1980s provided linkages of freestanding PCs with centralized accounting databases. Although this was a large move forward in terms of database integration, the data entry and transaction-processing portions of the accounting function still required the services of numerous accounting clerks.

Accounting Databases and Their Components

The hub of an accounting database is the **general ledger (GL),** a journal that consolidates data received from other journals that contain data from specialized accounting functions. Figure 10.3 provides a picture of the journal entries that provide inputs to the general ledger.

The **accounts receivable (AR)** ledger tracks entries pertaining to credit transactions with clients who owe payment to the hospitality enterprise at a future point in time. Sales transactions with hotel guests who have city ledger accounts are posted to accounts receivable, and noncredit sales are reported as cash settlements of daily revenues. Credit transactions with vendors and suppliers also occur on the supply chain end of a hospitality organization. These purchase transactions are recorded in the **accounts payable (AP)** ledger to track the payment of bills owed to suppliers of material resources such as goods, equipment, and supplies. The **payroll (PR)** account is used to monitor the payment of salaries and wages as well as deductions that are placed in accounts to pay federal, state, and local payroll taxes and benefit contributions. Accounts payable and payroll are examples of expense accounts, whereas accounts receivable is a revenue account. Additional expense accounts include sales tax, debt service, and other accounts used to monitor expenses incurred by hospitality enterprises.

General ledger (GL) A journal that consolidates data received from other journals that contain data from specialized accounting functions.

Accounts receivable (AR) A journal that tracks entries pertaining to credit transactions with clients who owe payment to a hospitality enterprise at a future point in time.

Accounts payable (AP) A journal that tracks the payment of bills owed to suppliers of material resources such as goods, equipment, and supplies.

Payroll (PR) An account used to monitor the payment of salaries and wages as well as deductions that are placed in accounts to pay federal, state, and local payroll taxes and benefit contributions.

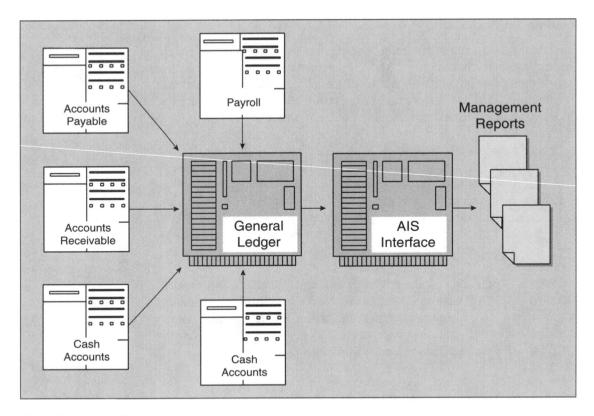

Figure 10.3 Inputs to the General Ledger

Accounting Information Systems

In the current state of accounting information systems, technology is used to provide online transaction processing and data entries for databases. Modern databases have advanced inquiry and documentation processing that yields automated financial reports. Before the development of this technology, hospitality managers in all operating departments were required to produce manual postings of revenues and expenses for the accounting offices. Modern AIS systems enhance the productivity of operating managers by saving time that previously was spent providing information to business offices. The managers may use this saved time to supervise the execution of hospitality services, which is their primary directive. The automation of AISs has eliminated the need for most data entry and clerical accounting positions and has enhanced productivity in operating departments. Figure 10.4 shows the interfaces that constitute a modern AIS.

Modern AISs place accounting functions at the center of hospitality operations. This is accomplished through the establishment of seamless

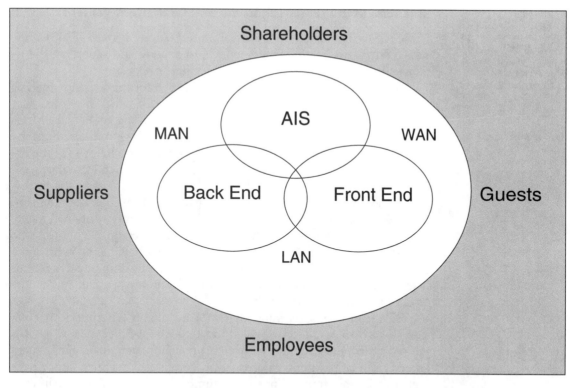

Figure 10.4 The Modern AIS Interface

connectivity to the operating areas of the enterprise. This is in contrast to the older systems described above, in which the accounting functions were placed at the back end of operations. The older paradigm forced operations personnel to support the accounting system through information inputs. The modern AIS paradigm positions the accounting function in its proper place as a support system for the operations.

The connectivity at the hub of the AIS consists of a LAN that is used to network work units within a single physical plant. Metropolitan area networks and wide area networks may be interfaced for direct connectivity to regional and home offices. Back-end extranets provide access that allows vendors and suppliers to engage in automated business transactions with a hospitality enterprise through electronic data interchange architecture. Front-end extranets may be made available to clients and guests on the Internet to facilitate online financial transactions through secure payment servers. Intranets may be interfaced with the system to provide two-way employee portals that can be used to exchange financial information. Portal outputs consist of management financial reports based on system query criteria. Portals also may be used for department managers to input financial data such as operating budgets and cost/revenue forecasts.

Financial Management Systems and Cash Management

Financial management system (FMS) Uses mathematical models to analyze and report on the financial planning aspect of a hospitality enterprise.

Cash management The balance of receipts and disbursements of cash flows for an organization.

Some AIS systems include **financial management system (FMS)** components that use mathematical models to analyze and report on the financial planning aspect of a hospitality enterprise.

Financial management systems provide information and analysis concerning an enterprise's management of money, which is of particular interest to shareholders and corporate executives. The goal of an FMS is to maximize the management of financial assets. **Cash management** involves the balance of receipts and disbursements of cash flows for the organization. The first phase of cash management is the collection process for accounts receivable on the books. The goal of this process is to collect all the funds that are owed to the organization through the extension of credit. A second factor focuses on the aging of accounts receivable, which is a measurement of the time it takes for credit clients to settle their debts. The goal of AR is to collect all the money that is owed to the company in the shortest period of time after the posting of each debt. It is fortunate that hospitality organizations place only a small percentage of sales into accounts receivable.

The majority of sales transactions for hospitality enterprises are considered cash transactions in which most clients pay their bills with cash or credit card. For the hospitality enterprise, however, this is not a guaranteed form of payment, as credit card companies may not honor payments on certain transactions for a number of reasons. Also, credit card companies charge points for each merchant transaction, which discounts the amount of cash received from each of these sales transactions. Merchant discounts and dishonored settlements have a negative impact on the cash position of a hospitality enterprise. Cash management also is concerned with the disbursement of cash reserves through accounts payable.

Accounts payable consists of debit accounts or money owed to other businesses that support the supply chain of a hospitality organization. The terms and conditions of those accounts are based on time and money. Terms of payment may include a discount for early payment and interest added for late payments to the supplier. Cash management seeks to maximize the amount of cash on hand by calculating the present and future values of money disbursements used to pay expenses. This calculation determines the most suitable amount of time that should elapse before an AP payment is processed. Other financial management strategies include investment management as well as capital and operational budgeting processes.

Capital-intensive Large amounts of capital dollars are spent on the assets of hospitality enterprise.

From the perspective of asset management, hospitality organizations are **capital-intensive.** This means that large amounts of capital dollars are spent on the assets of a hospitality enterprise. Lodging companies make huge investments in real estate acquisitions, which include the construction and design of quality properties. The same is true for theme parks, which make additional capital investments in state-of-the-art technologies to provide attractions to entertain their guests. Airlines continuously purchase new aircraft, and companies in the cruise business commission new vessels to expand their fleets. The recreation sector invests heavily in the development of clubhouses, golf courses, sports facilities, and full-service health and wellness spas. Restaurant chains purchase premium real estate to build stores in highly populated locations. Financial management systems provide forecasting tools that are used to calculate returns on investments, interest rates, asset appreciation, and terms of capital financing and amortization.

Hospitality operations are **labor-intensive,** which means that payroll expenses are extremely high relative to other service industry providers. This makes sense in light of the fact that our primary product is face-to-face guest interactions. FMSs contain models to perform ratio analysis to

Labor-intensive Payroll expenses are extremely high relative to other service industry providers.

It is important to conduct analyses of labor expenses in the hospitality industry. (©Action Systems, Inc.)

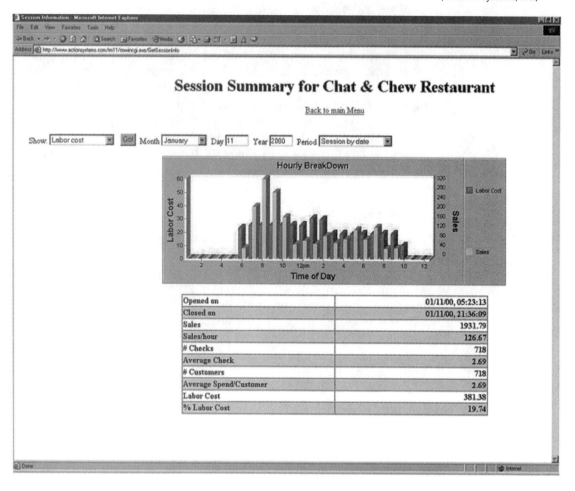

measure units of labor expenses in relation to units of production. For instance, hotels calculate employees per guestroom ratios and restaurants measure labor units per plate production. These and other ratios are used in budget forecasting and planning activities to control labor costs.

PROCUREMENT SYSTEMS

Procurement system
System used for the purchase of material resource made available through the supply chain of a hospitality enterprise.

Procurement systems are used for the purchase of material resources that are made available through the supply chain of a hospitality enterprise. Most purchasing departments use some form of computer automation to perform certain procurement functions. A few hospitality organizations, such as the Walt Disney World (WDW) Corporation, have implemented full-scale Enterprise Resource Planning systems. An ERP is a centralized system that provides completely automated material resource acquisition and allocation services throughout an organization. In the case of Disney, the "Project Tomorrowland" endeavor will result in the centralization of resource distribution for worldwide operations by 2007. This endeavor is the result of a collaborative effort between WDW and SAP Solutions, a dominant applications service provider corporation. The project could result in a scalable prototype used for ERP applications being made available to many hospitality enterprises in the near future. Most hospitality organizations, however, use systems that are somewhat less inclusive than global ERPs. Figure 10.5 shows a depiction of common procurement systems for hospitality organizations.

Purchasing

Purchasing agents or purchasing managers
Hospitality procurement professionals.

Hospitality procurement professionals usually are referred to as **purchasing managers** or **purchasing agents.** These individuals are responsible for acquiring material resources for a hospitality enterprise in a timely and cost-efficient manner. A process called sourcing is the means by which purchasing professionals identify the vendors that provide resources that meet the specifications of a specific hospitality organization. The purchaser will base procurement volumes on operational forecasts used to determine resource use. Once the volume levels have been determined, the purchaser will secure pricing bids from a number of purveyors (vendors). The purchaser then will issue a **purchase order (PO)** to each selected vendor. The PO is an authorization for accounts payable to pay for a specific invoice after the goods are received by the hospitality organization. In most cases the PO is generated electronically from the accounting office.

Purchase order (PO)
Authorization for accounts payable to pay for a specific invoice after the goods are received by a hospitality organization.

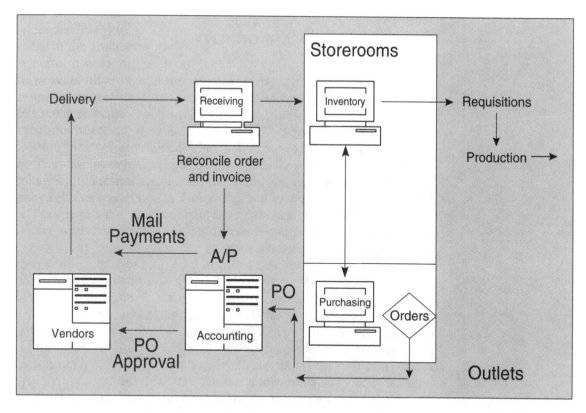

Figure 10.5 Common Procurement Systems

Delivery

The next step in the procurement process is for vendors to deliver the products to the hospitality enterprise. The person in charge of receiving purchased items usually is called a **receiving agent.** The receiving agent works independently from the purchasing agent to ensure **checks and balances,** a procedure for separating the order and entry points for purchases. The receiving agent verifies counts and quality specifications of items that arrive at the receiving dock and signs invoices for items that meet those specifications. Once the items are received, the invoice is transmitted to accounts payable and the new stock is forwarded to the appropriate storage areas and counted as inventory. Operating departments requisition items from inventory (stock) for use in their areas.

Receiving agent The person in charge of receiving purchased items.

Checks and balances A procedure for separating the order and entry points for purchases.

INVENTORY MANAGEMENT

Three parts of the inventory management process take place in the storage areas. The established level of inventory on hand for each item is called par stock. Items that are requisitioned for operating areas are deleted from the par stock. The difference between par stock and items on hand is the order amount that is sent to the purchaser. A perpetual inventory is an electronic process of accounting for storeroom transactions in real time. A perpetual inventory will track items that are entered into inventory to reestablish pars. It also will track each requisitioned item and remove it from on-hand inventory and then calculate order volumes. The order volumes are distributed electronically to the purchasing office, which begins the procurement process.

A perpetual inventory system also may be used to automate the procurement process. The purchasing office of a hospitality enterprise could establish an electronic data interchange interface through an extranet for access by suppliers (vendors). This permits purchasing agents to review electronically generated reorder levels to make additions and deletions that are based on forecast fluctuations. Once the purchaser is satisfied with reorder levels, the request for bids is transmitted electronically to selected vendors. Vendors respond with electronic bids, with the best bid receiving an electronic PO from the purchasing agent. Next, the items are delivered and go through the receiving and storage process. Invoices are approved, and accounts payable electronically transmits funds to pay the invoices at appropriate times. Figure 10.6 depicts a perpetual inventory system that is linked to procurement and accounting processes through an EDI.

TRACKING TECHNOLOGIES

Advances in chip and satellite technologies offer enhanced productivity in the areas of procurement and inventory management. Radio frequency identification (RFID) technology uses stationary signal detectors to scan tagged items at close distances. Pallets of items may be scanned at the receiving dock of a hospitality enterprise to update inventory systems in real time. This technology is just beginning to be used in large retail establishments such as WalMart stores.

RFID technology has profound implications for the tracking of food products. For instance, the beef industry is considering the use of RFID tags and scanners to track cattle from ranches to meat-processing plants

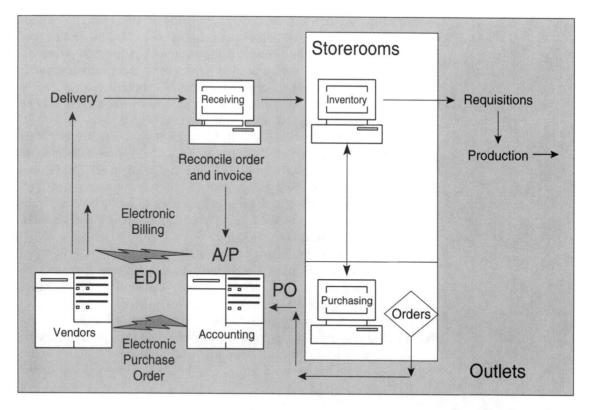

Figure 10.6 Perpetual Inventory System Linked through an EDI

in the wake of concerns over food-borne illnesses. The technology also may be used for asset protection by tagging furniture, fixtures, and equipment (FF&E) to prevent pilferage. Some security firms tag cash drop boxes that self-destruct when stolen. When RFID technology is coupled with PDA/telephony, inventory managers may access real-time updates on inventory items that require reordering as well as identify surpluses that may be used to market specialty items to reduce stock. These technologies link production systems with procurement and inventory management systems.

Modern RFID tags are small and concealable. They may be worn on identification badges and coded to permit access to restricted security areas. This technology also may be used to track individuals within the workplace. For instance, a housekeeping employee at a resort may be tracked throughout the hotel to determine which guest areas he or she entered at specific times. Some people consider this an invasion of privacy, but others contend that most individuals are willing to wear tracking devices in this technologically driven society.

Some theme parks and attractions use RFID wristbands to track children who are visiting a park. This permits any child who becomes separated from a guardian to be located instantly within the park grounds. These wristbands also may be used to debit prepayment transactions as individuals enter various attractions. There is entertainment value to RFID technology in that automated and customized visitor tours may be activated as a guest passes a scanner at an attraction or site.

The only limitation to current RFID technology applications is that they are restricted to distances of about 25 miles. Broader-scale tracking of assets and individuals may be accomplished through Global Positioning Satellite (GPS) systems like those in many automobiles. GPS applications provide enhanced guest experiences as well as security features in various recreation sectors, such as national parks, golf courses, skiing, hiking, and mountain climbing.

A company in Florida is marketing a $200 verichip that may be worn or implanted inside people.[1] These chips have been used for pets for some time. Each chip carries identification information as well as space to encode other information, such as medical history or biographical data. The company actively markets the devices in countries that lead the world in kidnappings. The chip is the size of a grain of rice and may be attached to a bracelet or implanted just under the skin. Security chip technology is coming to rapid fruition in the area of international travel via electronic passports and visas.

OTHER TECHNOLOGY-BASED TRENDS

Earlier chapters stated that the personal computer has had a tremendous impact in various aspects of people's personal and commercial lives. More than a billion personal computers are in use around the globe, with millions more added each year, according to certain estimates (e.g., International Data Corporation).[2] These machines are instrumental in annual increases in U.S. productivity of around 4 percent per year. The initial explosion in Internet use, e-commerce, and telecommunications is directly attributable to the PC revolution. Recent computing advances may make the traditional desktop computer obsolete in the near future.

We already have discussed the potential of telephony as a new wave of computing for business and entertainment. Many electronic devices, such as notebook computers, PDAs, and MP3 players, are used by many people today. Other developments in technology may set the stage for the post-PC generation of computing, according to *Business Trends* magazine.[3]

Microchip design has evolved continuously since the invention of the original 286 series processor. Chips are smaller and more powerful as a result of recent systems-on-a-chip designs. These chips are being embedded in a number of electronic devices, including smaller cell phones and PDAs, as well as a number of home and business appliances. The proliferation of wireless communications technologies, originally through cell phones and more recently through PDAs, has created a more mobile workforce. According to a *Red Herring* magazine report,[4] more than 60 million workers maintain digital home offices, with more workers choosing to be telecommuters each year. Laptop computers have become untethered, with many users using home access points and hotspots that are becoming available in restaurants, hotels, and airports.

Digitization of video, audio, and telephone communications and photography are providing remote transmissions of these media across noncomputer hardware devices such as cell phones and DVD players. In fact, these devices are converging into single small appliances such as teleputers. The result of these and other developments will be self-contained information systems possessed by workers, travelers, and guests of hospitality enterprises. This provides evidence that managers in our industry must be aware of technological advances for the purpose of anticipating guest needs as well as the continued enhancement of enterprise productivity enhancements.[5]

WIRELESS CONNECTIVITY

In earlier chapters we talked about the high costs associated with wired networks. Wireless fidelity (Wi-Fi) provides connectivity by using wireless frequencies that are run through routers (access point transponders), and the cost of this hardware has been reduced greatly in recent years. Wi-Fi may become a cost-efficient alternative for proprietary networks as well as high-speed Internet connectivity. It is estimated that in four years, 50 percent of businesses and homes will be using Wi-Fi connectivity, up from 12 percent today.[6] According to a Goldman Sachs survey, corporate CIOs rank Wi-Fi as one of their top three priorities for technology purchases.[7] Just a few years ago businesses were reluctant to embrace this technology. However, this has changed because of improved security features and the continual downward spiral of costs.

Standard Wi-Fi protocols refer to the 802.11 standard established by the Institute of Electrical and Electronic Engineers (IEEE). Recently, the market has been flooded with newer standards, including WiMAX, Mobile-Fi, ZigBee, and Ultrawideband (UWB). This variety of technologies promises to bring wireless networking to every area of life, from cars and homes to hospitality enterprise buildings. Venture investments in these technologies have topped $4.5 billion, and some of these products are starting to hit the market.[8] The technology has major marketing implications by giving small towns in developing nations broadband Internet access.

UWB is a short-range connection that spans about 60 feet, which is much less than the range of Wi-Fi, which covers spans of hundreds of feet. However, UWB moves data quickly and may be used to replace current USB connections and for access to information from any room in a building. This protocol also will facilitate the passing of connectivity among noncomputer appliances such as DVD players, TVs, and stereos. Cell phone companies have upgraded their hardware to handle Wi-Fi as well as UWB technologies.

WiMAX is a possible alternative to broadband and cable piping, as it may span 30 miles for a single hotspot. This is similar to the range of Wi-Fi, but with a much broader area of coverage. Using the 802.16 standard, this technology could replace small area phone and telecommunications systems. WiMax antennas placed on buildings may replace connectivity over telephone lines. Cell phones may be configured to use these signals.

The ZigBee technology uses low-powered microsensors to communicate information across short distances. These sensors are powered by long-life batteries, making them very energy-efficient. This technology may replace the Bluetooth systems that are used currently for wireless PDA-to-computer interfaces in hotels and resorts. For instance, housekeepers may use ZigBee transponders to upload room status reports to computers at the front office of a hotel for real-time inventory control.

THE IMPACT OF TECHNOLOGY ON EMPLOYMENT

It has been argued that developed societies have repeated the same steps of commercial development since the industrial revolution of the 1920s. One author suggests that every technology revolution goes through three phases: (1) speculative exuberance, (2) crash, and (3) strong build-out.[9]

These phases may be applied to computer technology, as evidenced in the dot-com boom and bust that has led to the current wave of creating real value through technology solutions. The key contribution of technology to value creation is the availability of tools and services for productivity enhancement. The immediate outcome associated with productivity growth usually declines in labor use. This is particularly true for jobs that may be automated by technology, such as call center workers and order takers. At the same time, the hospitality industry is experiencing a labor crisis in which fewer qualified workers are available for larger numbers of positions. Some suggest that the overall workforce is shrinking as a result of the aging of the U.S. population. It could be suggested that aging populations create increased demand for products and services, in particular those provided by the hospitality industry.[10] In this case, the same trend both creates increased demand and shrinks the workforce.

The hospitality industry is in the first wave of a technology build-out that is focused on automating back-office functions in various sectors of the industry. The next wave will be focused on automating aspects of product, maintenance, and repair production systems. This will involve the use of robotics to perform tasks that currently are performed by semiskilled and unskilled workers. The majority of positions in the hospitality industry will be filled by those who provide guest services, service managers, and production technicians over the next 20 years. According to the Bureau of Labor Statistics, the fastest growing positions over the next 10 years will be computer specialists (software engineers, technicians, and network administrators), executive and middle managers (in service industry sectors), and workers in the personal, health, and wellness services.[11]

According to *Business Trends* magazine, we may expect the steady shrinkage of companies' workforces along with the increased buying power of baby boomers. An increase in upstart technology firms and an increasing reliance on knowledge management systems in most commercial enterprises also will hold true for the immediate future.[12] Finally, there will be an increasing trend of automating manual labor tasks across a wide range of industries.

PRODUCTION SYSTEMS

So far we have discussed systems that enable accounting, procurement, receiving, and inventory management functions. Many of the items requisitioned from inventories are used as raw materials to produce tangible products. Hence, it makes sense here to take a look at systems that facilitate the product production process, but first we will discuss the types of tangible items produced by various sectors of the industry.

The most obvious tangible products are produced by fine-dining restaurants in the form of delectable cuisine platters with artistic visual appeal. Quick-service restaurants (QSRs) are in the volume food production business, as are banquet and catering facilities. Full-service hotels include food and beverage outlets that provide a complete range of dining services. Similar foodservice amenities are available at theme parks, attractions, and recreation and social clubs as well as meeting, entertainment, travel, and event venues. Food and beverage services are part of almost every sector of the hospitality industry. The creation of food and beverage items requires a **product production** system that provides for the conversion of raw materials (ingredients) into finished products (meals and consumable beverages). Any tangible item that is produced from raw materials is considered a product.

Other hospitality production systems are used to repair or maintain existing products. For instance, a hotel guestroom is an existing product. It is taken out of inventory while it is occupied and replaced into inven-

Product production
Provides for the conversion of raw materials (ingredients) into finished products (meals and consumable beverages).

An inventory control system allows a hospitality business to keep better control of costs and purchasing. This is especially important in foodservice, where much of the inventory (food) has a limited life span. (©Action Systems, Inc.)

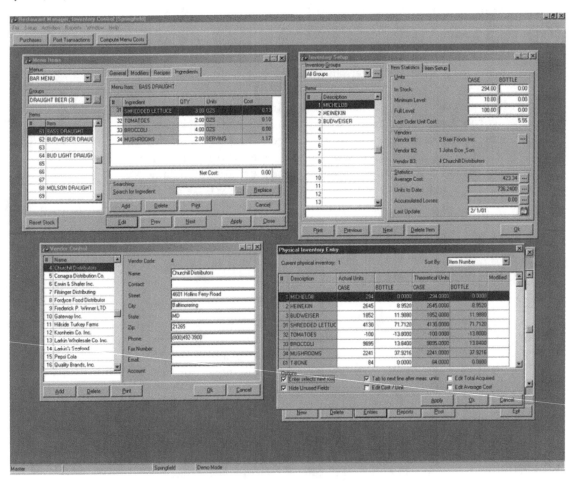

Public areas of a hotel, such as the lobby, are part of the lodging product and require upkeep and maintenance as part of product production. (Courtesy of Cedant Corp.)

tory when it is vacant and clean (ready for check-in). If the shower in a guestroom is malfunctioning, the room is taken out of inventory and labeled as an "out-of-order" room. Only when repairs to the shower are completed may the room be placed back into inventory. Public areas such as the hotel lobby are also part of the lodging product and must be kept to the standards expected by guests. The outside grounds of a hotel require cleaning and landscaping because they exist for the aesthetic enjoyment of the guests. All these areas require production processes that do not create new products; instead, those processes are used to maintain and repair existing products.

In cases involving lodging, foodservice, a clubhouse, theme parks, attractions, and meeting and event venues there are physical plant facilities and outside areas (grounds) that must be maintained and repaired continually. Air and sea travel organizations must maintain aircraft equipment and vessels as well as terminal and gate areas. A **maintenance production** system puts an occupied space into a state of readiness for reoccupation by customers, clients, passengers, or guests. A **repair production** system converts an out-of-order physical space into one that is ready to be occupied by guests, clients, passengers, or customers. All production systems are based on a productivity model similar to the one shown in Figure 10.7.

Maintenance production
Converts an occupied space into a state of readiness for reoccupation by customers, clients, passengers, or guests.

Repair production
Converts an out-of-order physical space into one that is ready to be occupied by guests, clients, passengers, or customers.

Figure 10.7 Production Systems Productivity Model

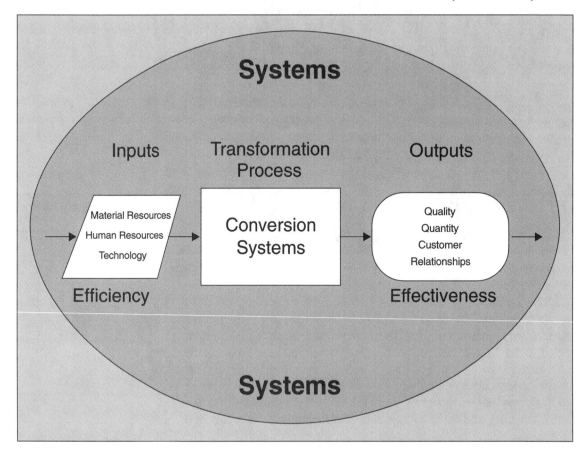

Material resources include raw materials, tools, equipment, and supplies that are used for product conversion. Human resources are inputs of human capital in the form of workers who have the knowledge, skills, and abilities to perform the conversion process. In the case of product production, workers transform raw materials into finished products. Workers also may use raw materials such as replacement parts in the transformation process that occurs during repair production. Maintenance production usually requires the use of tools, equipment, and supplies to enact the transformation process to produce outputs. All production systems produce outputs that result from the completion of transformation processes. Outputs are measured in terms of quality and quantity. Quality is measured in terms of compliance with established standards for outputs; quantity refers to the number of outputs produced per work unit.

Hospitality operations are engaged in mixed-function activities, which is not the case in most other industries. Most companies are in the manufacturing or distribution businesses. Hospitality enterprises are involved in both functions on a daily basis, which is why we are a mixed-function business. Manufacturing organizations use two types of electronic systems that also are used in factories where production lines produce products. **Computer-aided manufacturing (CAM)** systems provide automated assistance to workers on the factory floor. Some manufacturing firms use computerized systems to automate large portions of the overall production process. These **computer-integrated manufacturing (CIM)** systems provide electronic manufacturing planning, organizing, processing, and control of production lines in a production setting.[13]

The production processes in hospitality organizations are on a much smaller scale than those found in factories. **Computer-aided production (CAP)** systems provide electronic assistance to workers in small-scale production processes in some hospitality enterprises. Examples of CAP are notable in the foodservice production areas of restaurants and hotels. For instance, there was a time when a restaurant server would write orders on a pad and then walk to the kitchen to distribute orders at hot and cold line production areas. This process has been automated with interfaces between the precheck machines attached to the restaurant's point-of-sale system and printers in the production areas. When a server enters an item on the precheck POS machine, the order is transmitted to printers in the production areas; this keeps the server from having to walk through the kitchen to drop off written order slips. CAP replaces manual aspects of the production process with computer automation. Most CAP system processes are involved with the transfer of information used to facilitate a production process. The next step for hospitality organizations is to automate aspects of the actual work performed as part of a production process.

Computer-aided manufacturing (CAM) Systems that provide automated assistance to workers on the factory floor.

Computer-integrated manufacturing (CIM) Systems that provide electronic manufacturing planning, organizing, processing, and control of production lines within a production setting.

Computer-aided production (CAP) Systems that provide electronic assistance to workers in small-scale production processes in some hospitality enterprises.

In many restaurants today, the wait staff's POS system interfaces with the precheck machine in the kitchen, allowing the chefs to prepare a customer's order. (©Action Systems, Inc.)

Computer-integrated production (CIP) Systems that use electronic automation to perform tasks involved in the production process.

Computer-integrated production (CIP) systems use electronic automation to perform tasks involved in the production process. Most CIP systems for hospitality production areas are still in the research and development phase of development. However, in a short time we should witness these systems being used in hospitality operations. For instance, the technology currently exists to automate the fry stations fully in quick-service restaurants. Portion-controlled baskets may be lowered automatically into deep fryers for a specific period of time and then raised and turned to pour the contents onto a production table for seasoning and packaging. Sensors may monitor packages removed from the tray to determine when to drop the next basket of uncooked fries. This technology was developed in laboratories some time ago, but it is not used widely in

QSR outlets. We may see automated fryers in most stores when the cost of the technology drops below the labor costs for fry cooks.

The technology to automate product, maintenance, and even some repair production processes already has been researched in laboratories. Also, most of the technology that can be used for CIP systems is not really new. For instance, the automated vacuum cleaners sold in stores for home use were developed by students at the Massachusetts Institute of Technology (MIT) in response to a challenge to produce an automated maintenance tool at a unit cost under $150. The vacuums are self-propelled and use sensors for free-range roving or remote control responses. They use a form of technology called **mobile optical robotics,** which are self-moving machines that perform tasks, with visual sensor capabilities. This technology has been widely available at moderate costs since 1995, yet most hospitality organizations fail to recognize its applications to production operations. This is one area where you will be able to enhance productivity as a future hospitality manager if you remain aware of technologies that are applicable to the production operations in our industry.

Advanced production robotics includes artificial intelligence reasoning agents coupled with fuzzy logic and programmable logic controllers (PLCs) that are connected through neural networks. These robotics systems are already used in large-scale manufacturing settings, and the technology will be available to our industry in short order. Automated procurement, inventory management, requisitioning, and process control systems are used currently by many hospitality enterprises. The introduction of advanced robotics to hospitality production systems will further automate the resource allocation and transformation processes required to produce outputs. At that point we will be positioned to simplify and integrate all the production system components of the inputs and conversion processes used to yield finished products (outputs). Managers in a specific operational area will use integrated electronic tools for production planning, transformation, and control processes within a single system called a **production execution system (PES).** The goal for PES implementation in hospitality operations will be to automate the production transactions that take place behind the scenes to afford our workers more time to engage in guest interactions, which is the core function of our industry. Hospitality managers who embrace such technologies will be in the business of using *higher tech* to create *higher touch* with our customers, clients, passengers, and guests.

Mobile optical robotics
Self-moving machines that perform tasks; have visual sensor capabilities.

Production execution system (PES) An integrated system of electronic tools for production planning, transformation, and control processes.

On-the-Job Training . . . Continued

You have been pondering your staffing dilemma for a few days with no viable answers coming to mind. You meet Liz, a highly experienced housekeeping manager, for lunch. As you dine, the conversation turns to your dilemma. Liz tells you, "Oh, yeah, turnover has been very high among banquet setup workers for some time now." She continues: "The former supervisors just tried to react to the problem by always hiring new workers. It's sad. They would no sooner train a new staff member than he would quit for a job with more stable hours." Liz's comments are not encouraging.

After a lull in the conversation, as Liz pokes her dessert with a spoon, she matter-of-factly mentions, "Of course, I know the solution to your problem." You laugh and say, "If you have all the answers, why does the problem persist?" She replies, "Because no one around here understands the concept of maintenance production synergy." She casts an indignant glance in your direction. "I don't even know what that means, let alone understand it," you reply.

Liz quips, "Neither does anyone else." After a long silence you look at her and say, "Well, are you going to enlighten me, oh, sage?" "Well," she jokes, "I'll give you the benefit of my years of experience just this once." She sets her dessert aside and pulls a napkin toward her. She starts drawing on the napkin while she says, "This is my department, where we clean public areas and guestrooms. The guestrooms must be cleaned on a rigid schedule, but this is not true of the public areas. We clean those areas during our downtime. All we have to worry about is making sure every area gets cleaned every day, but it doesn't matter what time of day."

You give her an incredulous stare and say, "I fail to see the science here." "Ha," she says, as she continues to draw. "Here is your work crew, who are always in 'hurry-up-and-wait' mode." "True," you reply. "So," she says, "we can combine certain activities in your area with public cleaning activities in my area. Since your work is time-sensitive, we build in my public area cleaning needs with your workers' schedules during your downtimes." She continues: "Then we simply transfer the hours to the appropriate departments."

On-the-Job Training . . . Continued

You think as you stare at her napkin drawings. After a while you say, "If we collaborate this way, you will need fewer public area cleaners assigned to your department and I will be able to provide full-time hours to my guys to do the same work they do in banquet areas." Liz smiles at you and says, "You got it. That's synergy, when our mutual outcomes exceed the sum of our staff." But then you ask, "How come you never did this before?" Liz responds, "Your predecessors were territorial. They never realized that collaboration creates win-win outcomes."

As you head back to your department, you begin to plan your new alliance with Liz.

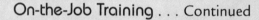

SUMMARY

This chapter looked at many of the back-end functions that support hospitality operations as well as those used to produce tangible items for guests. The chapter began with the accounting function that supports all the financial transactions that occur in a hospitality enterprise. We recognized that accounting processes indirectly serve our clients and guests as well as the shareholders and front-line workers of the organization. We tracked the evolution of accounting systems from their origins in manual processing up to the modern accounting information systems that are used to automate these functions in hospitality enterprises.

We differentiated between accounting and finance functions by noting that financial management systems produce information that is used to maximize the use of financial resources, such as investments and interest accumulation. We took notice of the interfaces between procurement practices and the accounting office. We found that automated procurement processes are used commonly to integrate resource acquisition and receiving and storage functions as well as inventory management and requisitioning processes. This led us to a discussion of the production processes that occur in hospitality enterprises.

Since the hospitality industry is mixed-functional, we came to the realization that we engage in interactive services as well as tangible item production processes. We identified three types of production that occur in hospitality operations: product, maintenance, and repair production systems. We considered examples of these processes as they occur in various sectors of the industry. We concluded with the current and future states of automated production systems that may be applied to hospitality enterprise operations.

DISCUSSION QUESTIONS

1. Put yourself in the shoes of an operations manager for a hotel before the implementation of an AIS. What accounting-oriented activities would you have engaged in then that have been eliminated from your daily routine with today's systems?
2. There was talk throughout the chapter about the enhancement of productivity in hospitality enterprises. How would automated procurement, inventory management, and requisitioning activities enhance productivity for operations managers?
3. What does "higher tech for higher touch" really mean? Use your imagination to identify ways you might use this concept as a manager for a hospitality enterprise.

KEY TERMS

Accounting information systems (AISs)
Accounts payable (AP)
Accounts receivable (AR)
Booking transaction
Capital-intensive
Cash management
Cash settlement transaction
Checks and balances
Computer-aided manufacturing (CAM)
Computer-aided production (CAP)
Computer-integrated manufacturing (CIM)
Computer-integrated production (CIP)
Credit transaction
Financial management system (FMS)
General ledger (GL)
Labor-intensive
Maintenance production
Mobile optical robotics
Payroll (PR)
Procurement system
Production execution system (PES)
Product production
Purchase order (PO)

Purchasing agents or purchasing managers
Receiving agent
Repair production
Sales transaction
Supply chain transaction
Tendering transaction

REFERENCES

1. *Business Trends.* (2004). 1(11), Willowbrook, IL.
2. Ibid.
3. Ibid.
4. Ibid.
5. Peter F. Drucker. (2002). *Managing in the Next Society.* New York: St. Martin's Press.
6. Olga Kharif. (2004). Wi-Fi's Growing Pains: How the Wi-Fi Future Might Look. *Business Week Online.*
7. Alex Salkever. (2004). Wi-Fi's Growing Pains: Before Wi-Fi Can Go Mainstream. *BusinessWeek Online.*
8. Heather Green. (2004). No Wires, No Rules. *BusinessWeek.*
9. Harry S. Dent. (1993). *The Great Boom Ahead: Your Comprehensive Guide to Personal and Business Profit in the New Era of Prosperity.* New York: Hyperion.
10. *Business Trends.* (2004). What They Don't Want You to Know.
11. Alex Salkever. (2004). Wi-Fi's Growing Pains: Before Wi-Fi Can Go Mainstream. *BusinessWeek Online.*
12. Ibid.
13. J. A. O'Brien. (2000). *Management Information Systems: Managing Information Technology in the E-Business Enterprise,* 5th ed. Boston: McGraw-Hill Irwin.

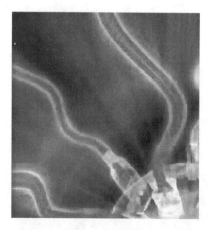

Marketing and Human Resources Management Systems

CHAPTER OBJECTIVES

In this chapter you will learn to:

1. Apply the four Ps to interactive marketing systems.
2. Identify the steps involved in marketing and sales systems.
3. Identify the functions of human resources management systems.

On-the-Job Training

You are about one month into your assignment with the human resources department at a luxury resort. Your last assignment was to spend three months in the sales and marketing department, where you learned a lot while making many new friends. You enjoy working with the human resources practitioners as well. However, there is one activity that you find stressful.

Members of departments in operations as well as those in human resources and marketing are being forced to collaborate on a customer relationship management project. You feel uncomfortable attending these meetings because the participants from all three areas cast blame on each other and never seem to agree on anything.

This afternoon, another one of those dreaded meetings is scheduled. You are not looking forward to attending, but you know it is part of the job.

To be continued . . .

INTRODUCTION

This chapter looks at the systems used to support the function of marketing and human resources management in hospitality enterprises. These functions involved mostly manual processes until the late 1990s. Today many of the manual systems have been electronically automated, resulting in higher levels of efficiency and effectiveness for both of these support functions.

Marketing strategies provide the key drivers for all operational processes that produce outputs for the hospitality enterprise. Human resources management is focused on the input portion of hospitality organizations. Figure 11.1 shows the relationship of these two functions within the productivity structure of an organization.

We can see in the figure that the success of a hospitality organization hinges on the relationships between the functions of marketing and human resources. *Marketing* is most simply defined as the acquisition and maintenance of guests, clients, and customers. **Acquisition** occurs when new guests are encouraged to use the services of a hospitality enterprise.

Acquisition When new guests are encouraged to use the services of the hospitality enterprise.

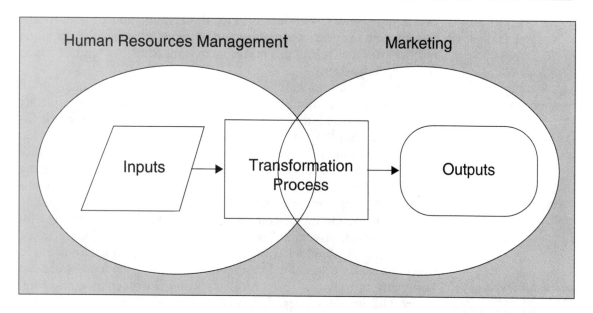

Figure 11.1 The Relationship between HRM and Marketing

Maintenance is the practice of generating a significant pool of repeat guests who become frequent users of the services provided by a hospitality facility. *Human resources management* is focused on the acquisition and maintenance of employees. Clearly, sound practices in human resources management result in appropriate numbers of skilled employees to provide services and products to new and returning guests. At the same time, successful marketing systems provide a significant customer base that attracts the best employees to seek positions with a specific hospitality operation. Thus, one can see that the marketing and human resources management functions are engaged in a **symbiotic relationship** in which each function benefits from the performance of the other function.

Symbiotic relationship
Each function benefits from the performance of the other function.

MARKETING SYSTEMS

Before we begin our discussion of systems, we must understand the factors associated with marketing processes. Marketers use the term *product mix* to identify the specific services and products provided by hospitality enterprises. We know that services consist of interactions and products consist of transaction processes that should be seamless to the guests; this of course constitutes the magic of our business. The interaction/transaction-processing moments create the overall guest experience that results from

Four Ps Product, price, placement, and promotion.

our facilities and service levels. Thus, the combination of transactions and interactions generates the creation of memorable experiences in the minds of our guests, and this makes them want to visit us again at a later time (repeat guests).

The marketing process is driven by the **four Ps:** products, price, placement, and promotion. As we already have discussed, hospitality products consist of interactions and transactions in our sector of the industry, including lodging, travel, recreation, entertainment, foodservice, events, and meetings. The customer pays a *price* for our *products,* which are provided at the *place* of our business facilities. *Promotions* are marketing activities (advertising, etc.) that encourage prospective guests to try our products. E-commerce systems have a tremendous impact on marketing strategies by permitting customers to engage directly in the discovery of products, prices, places, and promotions through the use of electronic media. Hence, technology is responsible for creating an environment in which guests have access to information concerning the four-Ps of most hospitality operations. This process is called **interactive marketing.** Figure 11.2 provides a description of marketing processes in hospitality organizations that are open to interactive access points.

Interactive marketing An environment in which guests have access to information concerning the four Ps of most hospitality operations.

Synchronous management practices A process of two-way real-time feedback loops concerning the planning, execution, and evaluation of product and service processes.

As can be seen in the figure, marketing should exist in collaborative harmony with the operations of a hospitality enterprise. This means that hospitality operations and marketing should engage in **synchronous management practices,** a process of two-way real-time feedback loops concerning planning, execution, and evaluation of product and service processes. How do senior managers make this happen? The collaborative relationship should become part of the corporate culture, which is driven by the mission for the enterprise. Operations managers should have marketing experience, and marketing managers should have experience in operations. They should collaborate on each function of organizational management, including planning, organizing, influence, and control. From the control perspective, the managers in each area should be evaluated on the basis of the same performance criteria. This thinking is consistent with systems theory, the key driver of technology applications in organizations.

From a marketing perspective, the key differentiator between products and services has to do with tangibility: sensory perception such as sight, touch, smell, and hearing. A product may be perceived with the physical senses, which makes it a tangible entity. Services, of course, are intangible, since they are not physical products. Hospitality operators engage in product, maintenance, and repair production processes. The outcomes of these processes are tangible: a meal, a clean guestroom, or a fully operating aircraft. The services that occur during production processes are intangible, yet these interactions create the memorable experiences for guests, clients, and customers.

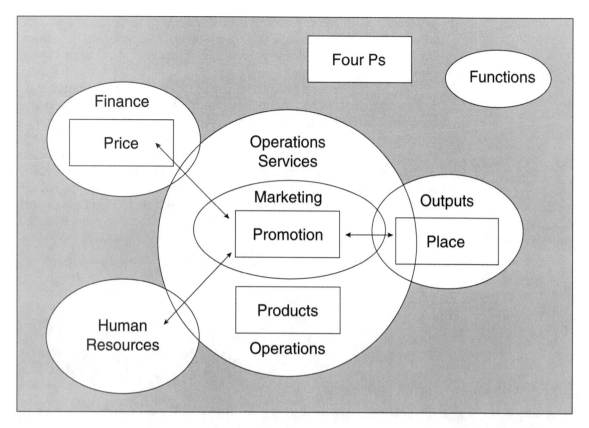

Figure 11.2 Interactive Marketing Processes

The key factor of influence for hospitality marketing systems is the realization that all transactions and interactions occur during the period of customer product consumption. In hospitality operations, there is no time lag between production and distribution processes (place). Most companies in other industries either produce (product) or distribute (place) products for consumption at a later date.

Interactive marketing systems include processes that occur before, during, and after a customer confirms a "buy decision" concerning our services and products. The buy decision results in a booking transaction, which is an agreement to use the services of a hospitality enterprise at a future time. Before making this decision, a customer uses the Internet or other intermediary services to conduct a search of the four Ps concerning specific hospitality services and providers. Next, the consumer becomes a guest of the hospitality enterprise and experiences interactions and transactions relative to his or her expectations concerning the four Ps. These experiences sometimes are referred to as "moments of truth," in which the service staff will meet, exceed, or fail to meet the perceived expectations of each guest.[1] Marketing systems provide consumers with three phases of processing: search, booking, and service transactions. Figure 11.3 provides a depiction of these phases as they occur in a linear set of processes.

The search process makes information available to potential customers (prospects) who are shopping around for hospitality products and services. The promotion aspect of the four Ps is the key driver for search-processing systems. The underlying strategy of search system development is to provide easy access and seamless navigation of information categories to educate a prospect about the things a specific hospitality enterprise has to offer. Search processes are driven by databases that are interfaced with two access points. The first point of access is a company

Figure 11.3 Three Phases of the Marketing System

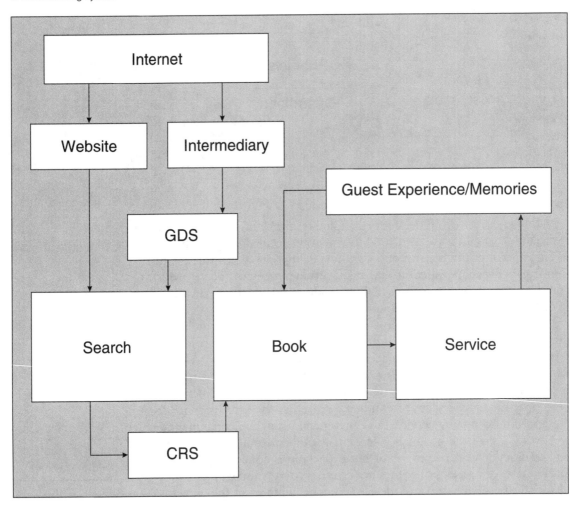

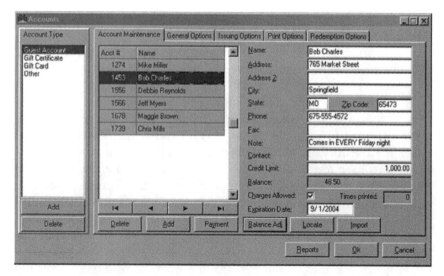

Guest history data are a useful tool for targeted marketing campaigns. (©Action Systems, Inc.)

website that is widely available for entry by the general public. The second access point consists of global distribution system and central reservation system interfaces that are made available to intermediaries such as online brokers (Orbitz, for instance) and travel agents. A database resides at the hub of the two points of access. This database is located at the front end of the database management system for the hospitality enterprise.

Although there are many new and improved overlays, such as graphical user interfaces for GDS and CRS systems, they still lack the appearance standards that are associated with public-domain Web pages. Webmasters are responsible for the design of visually appealing and technically functional websites that provide individual shoppers with direct access to a hospitality company's promotional information. Individual shoppers enter the World Wide Web (WWW) through an Internet Service Provider and then access a search engine (Yahoo!, for example) to start a search for hospitality products and services. Hospitality enterprise websites must be readily accessible through all the popular search engines to entice visits from the general public. Also, the websites must provide a searcher with valuable information with as few navigational clicks as possible. If an individual finds a website slow or cumbersome, he will jump quickly to the site of a competitor.

At some point a Web surfer will be ready to purchase specific hospitality products and services. This is the point called the buy decision. There will be a link to the company's CRS on the website. Once the surfer clicks on the link, she will be taken to the CRS to complete a booking transaction, which is a promise to use the services of that company at a future time. The transaction will be completed when the surfer provides credit card information over a secure payment link to place a deposit or full payment. At this point the booking phase (phase 2) of the marketing process is complete. The third and final phase of the marketing process will take place during the customer's experiences with the hospitality enterprise.

Some hospitality firms integrate sophisticated data collection processing concerning guest preferences from point-of-sale and property management systems. In the lodging sector, this information is channeled into a guest history file, which may be used to enhance personalized services for repeat guests. The collected data also may be used for future targeted marketing campaigns, which are strategies that focus on appealing to specific market profiles. The Ritz-Carlton chain uses guest history files to both enhance services for repeat guests at each of its properties and to target certain categories of senior corporate executives for special incentive programs.

Targeted marketing strategies are one example of direct marketing programs, in which a hospitality enterprise communicates directly with potential clients, guests, and customers. In the past, direct marketing campaigns were costly endeavors that provided small returns on investment. The current state of technology, however, has increased both the efficiency and the effectiveness of direct marketing programs. Modern direct marketing strategies employ database structures and telecommunications to reach intended audiences of potential buyers.

Most large hotel chains, for instance, use database management systems with numerous interfaces that are connected through wide area networks for data collection activities. These databases automate data collection and the sorting of information according to geographic, demographic, psychographic, and other relevant variables that may be used in making marketing decisions. Standard Query Language interfaces provide data-mining capabilities that permit marketers to perform data analyses that are used to generate marketing strategies and tactics. Modern marketing systems use technology to accumulate large volumes of data through automated processes that greatly reduce the costs associated with marketing research. Also, information technology processors provide timely and accurate data analyses to enhance the decision-making effectiveness of marketing executives. These decisions translate into marketing strategies that can be used to guide the sales efforts of hospitality enterprises. IT makes it possible for marketing departments to establish *customer relationship management (CRM)* systems, a holistic approach to the acquisition and maintenance of guests, clients, and customers.

Marketing and sales are separate but related functions in hospitality organizations. Marketing strategies support the sales force in each enterprise. The sales process consists of three functions: prospecting, qualifying, and closing activities. Prospecting is the process of generating a pool of interested potential buyers. The next step is to qualify individuals from the prospecting group as those with the intention to purchase the services and products of the hospitality enterprise. The final step is to get a qualified prospect to make a buy decision, which is called "closing the sale." Sales to individual (transient) buyers have been automated by current technology systems in most hospitality sectors. Sale professionals still deal on a personal level with group sales clients with the help of automated systems. Internal marketing occurs during guest and traveler interactions and is the function of every employee associated with a hospitality enterprise.[2] For this reason, the human resources management function takes primary responsibility for internal marketing strategies.

HUMAN RESOURCES MANAGEMENT

Human resources management (HRM) is a strategic approach to facilitating the acquisition and maintenance of employees who have the knowledge, skills, attitudes, and abilities (KSAAs) needed to support the mission of an organization.[3] HRM is based on a philosophy that considers workers human capital, which means they are organizational assets that provide returns on investment. Various functions are associated with human resources management, including recruitment, selection, training, development, employee relations, compensation, legal compliance, and performance management systems.

Human resources management (HRM) A strategic approach to the acquisition and maintenance of employees who have the knowledge, skills, attitudes, and abilities (KSAAs) needed to support the mission of an organization.

The purpose of employee recruitment practices is to establish a large pool of applicants for an open position in a hospitality enterprise. The task of making hiring decisions from a given applicant pool is called the selection process. The next step in the employment process is for employees to be trained to do their current jobs. Development is a type of training that is provided to prepare individuals for future promotional opportunities, such as management positions. The goal of the human resources office is to retain all employees who meet or exceed performance expectations, a process called retention. Employee relations are the process through which HR practitioners communicate with employees to ensure that job and work life satisfaction exists at a level that encourages employee retention.

Compensation administrators are responsible for policies concerning wages, salaries, benefits, and perquisites. There is a dynamic legal environment surrounding employment relationships that requires HR professionals to take proactive steps to ensure legal compliance to protect the assets of a hospitality organization. Finally, human resources practitioners are responsible for the administration of employee performance management systems that set performance standards, evaluate actual performance, and provide reward systems for high performers in a hospitality enterprise. In essence, hospitality human resources practitioners are responsible for the people management system in our labor-intensive industry. The primary managerial tool for effective human resources management is the ability to communicate effectively with individuals and groups at every level of the organization.

Human Resources Information Systems

Human resources information system (HRIS) A management information system that is used for human resources management applications.

One form of communications in practically all organizations is provided by a digitized system of interfaces that convert data (facts) into usable information that is called a management information system. An MIS that is used for human resources management applications is referred to as a **human resources information system (HRIS).** You may recall from our earlier discussions of productivity that resources include people, materials, technology, and finances.

In the world of MIS, the input side of the productivity model consists of "data resources." As is the case with any set of resources, data must be managed for efficient and effective allocation and utilization as inputs to the transformation process, which yields outputs in the form products and services. In the case of MIS, the outcome (product or service) is "information" that can be used for managing organizational processes. As is the case with most organizational functions, human resources management has specific informational processing needs. Hence, an MIS for HR is referred to as an HRIS.

Why is an HRIS a form of communication? The HRIS process converts data into information that is used to produce reports and other outputs that are shared with multiple parties. Thus, the HRIS will use data to create information (sender/encode) and then transmit that information (channel, media) to individuals with a need to know that information (decode/receivers), with a conclusive mechanism for responses to that information (feedback loop). It is safe to say that all management information systems, including HRIS systems, are communication systems.

A database is an integrated collection of logically related records (objects) that are sorted into files. Therefore, a human resources database consists of records that are related to employment activities (personnel actions and applicant flow data), compensation (salaries, wages, benefits, and perquisites), job analysis (job descriptions and job specifications), and training/development files to track the preparation of individuals who are eligible for promotion. Figure 11.4 shows the relationships of data items in an HRIS.

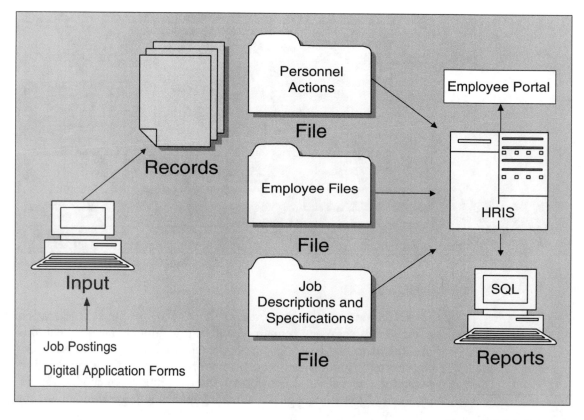

Figure 11.4 Data Relationships within an HRIS

Note that data are input into the HRIS, which requires the completion of fields that include sorted records, with the information from the records divided into files. For instance, the name of a new employee would be placed into the "name" field of a "personnel action form," and that name would be replicated as a field on a record for each of the four files. Hence, after the new employee's name is entered, an employment, compensation, job analysis, and training record exists in each of the files. If the employee is promoted, that personnel action form will trigger only the employment, compensation, and job analysis file since a promotion will result in a higher pay grade (compensation file) with a new job description (job analysis file) and a change in title (employment file). In another scenario, let's say the employee completes first-aid and cardiopulmonary resuscitation training. The input in this case triggers the training file (list of completed training) and the employment file (additional credential for an employee). The job analysis file and the compensation file will not be updated unless this training results in a change of duties or pay level.

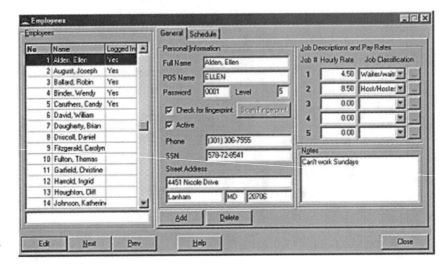

Employee information in an HRIS database allows for easier generation of reports. (©Action Systems, Inc.)

All this information is stored in the human resources information system database. When human resources practitioners need to manipulate the data to generate reports, such as an Equal Employment Opportunity Commission report, they select certain fields on a report generator screen to sort and format the data into a conceptual report. Standard Query Language is a software application commonly used for this manipulation process.

In addition to traditional administrative functions facilitated by an HRIS, there are many newly developed communication processes that permit access to certain database areas directly by employees. The process that facilitates this form of interaction is called an intranet, which replicates the Internet by providing search engine capability to help users find and enter information. Additionally, extranet interfaces to the Internet are used commonly for employment purposes, including job postings, digital job application forms, and other recruitment and selection processes. Employee portals are becoming common "one-stop shops" for employee communications, access to records, and B2E services. This aspect of employee relations is a new and exciting component of human resources interaction. Finally, many hospitality corporations may construct enterprise resource planning programs similar to the global project under way at the Walt Disney World organization. The goal of an ERP is to centralize all sourcing, acquisition, and allocation of resources for use throughout a corporation. ERP will present further changes to the practice of human resources management, including the outsourcing of certain HR functions.

On-the-Job Training . . . Continued

It is 1:30 P.M., and you have been listening to the bickering among participants from marketing, human resources, and operations for about 30 minutes. This time the argument is between the rooms division manager and the marketing director concerning the booking of complimentary room nights as trade-outs for free media advertising. Of course, the argument has nothing to do with CRM, but it is common for the participants to go off on these tangents. The complaint from the rooms division manager is that the trade-outs are displacing actual room revenues. The marketing director's argument is that the promotional value exceeds the value of lost room revenues.

Since you already have worked in rooms division and marketing, you have an understanding of both sides of the argument, and you think the discussion is childish. After listening for a while, the human resources director says, "We have been through this a million times. Why can't you guys just come to an agreement?" The marketing director replies, "Corporate policy places a cap on the amount of dollar credit per room that can be used for promotional trade-outs." The rooms division manager nods in agreement. After some thought, the HR director says, "It's a shame these promos don't benefit the employees." She continues: "If that were the case, I have some unused funds in the employee benefits budget that I could allocate."

After some silence, you decide to contribute. You say, "I have an idea." Everyone stares intently at you, since you are not one to talk much in these meetings. The HR director urges you to continue. "Well," you say, "I am working on a project that uses the employee portal to announce discounts for products and services to our staff members." You continue: "Maybe we could get the word to the other media business advertisers that we have over 2,000 employees who would be willing to buy their products and services at a discount." You conclude by saying, "We could advertise the discounts for free through our employee portal and subsidize the media trade-out account from our employee benefits budget."

There is a long pause as everyone digests what you have just stated. The HR director speaks up: "That sounds like a triple win to me: The employees win, rooms division wins, and the marketing department wins." Everyone nods in agreement.

Finally, the discussion gets back on track.

SUMMARY

This chapter looked at both the marketing and the human resources management functions of hospitality organizations. We realized that both do practically the same thing with two different groups of constituents. Marketing is the acquisition and maintenance of guests, whereas human resources management is the acquisition and maintenance of qualified employees who ultimately provide services to the guests.

We learned that marketing involves research, decision making, and strategic planning. Database systems with telecommunications interfaces have enhanced the effectiveness and efficiency of marketing functions. Data collection and data analysis are two of the functions of marketing research. DBMSs facilitate the collection of huge amounts of data representing geographic, demographic, psychographic, and other pertinent variables used for marketing plans and decisions. SQL interfaces provide data analysis of large masses of data through data-mining techniques. The four Ps of marketing are product, price, place, and promotion. We discovered that the Internet and other customer intermediaries provide direct access to search, book, and use hospitality services based on reviews of the four Ps for targeted companies. This open access has enhanced the return on investment associated with direct marketing strategies, including target marketing campaigns.

Sales and marketing are related but different functions. The sales process is mostly automated in current hospitality environments for transient clients. Sales professionals still interact personally with group clients; however, many aspects of the prospecting, qualifying, and closing sales functions are partially automated. Every staff member of a hospitality enterprise shares responsibility for internal marketing, which is provided through interactions and transactions while a guest is using the products and services. This led to a discussion of human resources management and its role in the internal marketing process.

Human resources management is based on a philosophy of human capital and functions that stresses contributing to the strategic direction of the hospitality enterprise through the management of people. The job of human resources practitioners is to attract, select, and retain individual workers who have the knowledge, skills, attitudes, and abilities (KSAAs) needed to perform as hospitality professionals.

We investigated the workings of a special type of management information system used by human resources practitioners called a human resource information system. The core of an HRIS is a database used to help practitioners perform the functions of employment, compensation, job analysis, legal compliance, and employee relations documentation.

SQL interfaces are used to query the HRIS database to extract data for analysis and management reports. We discovered that telecommunications interfaces provide direct employee and applicant access to the employment side of the organization through intranets and extranets. More hospitality organizations are developing employee portals, and it is predicted that future HRIS systems will become part of overall ERP initiatives designed for hospitality enterprises.

DISCUSSION QUESTIONS

1. In this chapter we discussed the "synchronous relationship" of marketing and operations systems. In your own thinking, how would this work in a hospitality enterprise such as a hotel, restaurant, or convention center?
2. We talked about "interactive marketing." What does this mean from a systems perspective? Who is interacting with whom? How are they interacting? Why are they interacting? What is the reason for them to interact?
3. We discussed how systems help marketers with the four Ps. How does this work?
4. Human resources management drives the internal marketing for a hospitality organization. Which HRM functions contribute directly to internal marketing?

KEY TERMS

Acquisition
Four Ps
Human resources information system (HRIS)
Human resources management (HRM)
Interactive marketing
Symbiotic relationship
Synchronous management practices

REFERENCES

1. Karl Albrecht and Ron Zemke. (1985). *Service America! Doing Business in the New Economy.* Homewood, IL: Business One Irwin, p. 6.
2. Robert D. Reid and David C. Bojanic. (2005). *Hospitality Marketing Management,* 4th ed. Hoboken, NJ: Wiley.
3. D. V. Tesone. (2004). *Human Resource Management in the Hospitality Industry: A Practitioner's Perspective.* Upper Saddle River, NJ: Prentice-Hall.

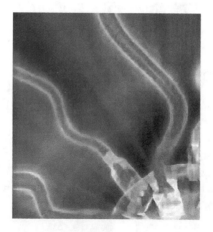

Safety, Security, and Physical Plant Systems

CHAPTER OBJECTIVES

In this chapter you will learn to:

1. Identify techniques that are used to secure data resources.

2. Identify technology applications that are used to provide safety and security for guests and others.

3. Identify technology applications for the management of physical plants.

On-the-Job Training

You are doing an internship with the information technology department of a casino hotel. The property uses an open platform e-mail system that resides on a server at the corporate office. Lately there has been a problem concerning excessive spam reaching many of the e-mail users. Some of those e-mails have contained executable attachments containing viruses that have attacked a number of individual computers. The technology manager at the property reacts appropriately when viruses attack a computer and is waiting to no avail for the corporate office to fix the problem proactively.

This situation is a little embarrassing to you, since everyone knows you are the technology intern. You have been taking a lot of good-natured ribbing from the other employees. It is all in good fun, but you wish the problem would get resolved, because you are tired of being the brunt of technology jokes.

To be continued . . .

INTRODUCTION

Managers in all sectors of hospitality enterprises have certain duties and responsibilities concerning guests, workers, and others who come in contact with the organization. One of those duties is to ensure the welfare of the company's assets as well as that of the individuals associated with the hospitality enterprise. **Security** is the practice associated with taking steps to protect the assets of a hospitality organization. **Safety** practices ensure the well-being of individuals, including guests, workers, and others who interact with a hospitality enterprise. The words *safety* and *security* often are used together to refer to the protection of valuable resources, possessions, and property (assets) as well as people.

Technology managers are responsible for the protection of data resources in the same way that security personnel engage in activities to protect physical assets and prevent harm to individuals. Continuous advances in technology provide assistance to individuals who are responsible for securing resources, physical property, and the safety of individuals. These topics are addressed in the first portion of this chapter.

Security The practices associated with taking steps to protect the assets of a hospitality organization.

Safety The practices that ensure the well-being of individuals, including guests, workers, and others who interact with a hospitality enterprise.

Physical plants consist of facilities used by hospitality enterprises to house the services provided to the guests of an enterprise. Physical plant management includes the functions of maintenance, repairs, and energy utility. We already have discussed maintenance and repair production processes and technology applications. Toward the end of this chapter we will discuss technology applications that assist with the management of energy resources, which are very expensive for certain sectors, such as hotels and resorts.

Physical plants Facilities used by hospitality enterprises to house the services provided to the guests of the enterprise.

DATA RESOURCE SECURITY

Today's hospitality organizations have access to local and global networks. Although these networks provide rapid and far-reaching communications, there is a need to protect data resources from unauthorized access. All network security problems have to do with outgoing and incoming data transmission. Most proprietary networks have built-in *firewalls* that limit user access to various servers through the use of permissions that are granted to each user. Secure connections, such as those used for credit card payments, use data **encryption** techniques that scramble incoming data, which are decrypted when they reach the payment-processing receiver. This prevents unauthorized access points from using sensitive data, such as credit card information, that may be diverted during transmission. The same technique can be applied to e-mail networks to keep intruders from reading sensitive information. Common Internet secure connections include the Secure Sockets Layer (SSL) and Private Communications Technology (PCT) developed by Netscape and Microsoft, respectively.[1] When a user sees a Universal Resource Locator (URL) that has https:// in the address line, this indicates that the user is accessing a secured server. Those letters stand for Hyper Text Transfer Protocol Secured.

Encryption Techniques that scramble incoming data, which are decrypted when they reach the receiver.

Most publicly accessed Internet servers place **cookies** in a file on a user's browser software. A cookie is a small set of text data that tracks access to various servers. Cookies permit commercial enterprises to track a user's surfing habits on the Internet. Another feature of Internet servers is the use of universal operating system programs that are embedded in websites. The most popular operating system for website programs is called **Java.** This is a universal program that runs small programs called *applets* within Web environments known as the Virtual Java Machine. Java is completely portable, which means it will run on personal computers as well as Macintosh machines. Netscape originally created it for Web users. Java loads its programs onto the computer of the user. However, safeguards

Cookie A small set of text data placed in a file on a user's browser software that tracks access to various servers.

Java A popular operating system for website programs.

ActiveX A Web operating system program that is more robust than Java but has fewer protections attached to downloaded programs.

Computer virus A program that is embedded in an executable program that can harm a user's machine by deleting, freezing, or rearranging files on a home computer.

Macro An embedded set of instructions contained in documents or spreadsheets.

Hackers Remote users who gain unauthorized access to computers.

Distributed network A network that is controlled remotely through indirect interfaces with many computers.

Identity theft Unauthorized access to information used to steal the identity of the user.

built into the software prevent any downloaded program from doing harm to the user's machine. Microsoft's Internet Explorer uses an operating system program called **ActiveX** that is more robust than Java but has fewer protections attached to downloaded programs.

There are few reasons for individual users to be concerned with the downloaded programs that are sent to a computer. The first concern involves **computer viruses.** A computer virus is a program that is embedded in an executable program that can harm a user's machine by deleting, freezing, or rearranging files on a home computer. Computer viruses are transmitted as e-mail attachments containing executable files as well as through *infected* portable disks that have been used in a public-use machine (the library, for instance). Another means of transmitting a virus is through a **macro,** an embedded set of instructions contained in documents or spreadsheets. The best defense against incurring computer viruses is to load a copy of antivirus software onto each machine and update it frequently, as new virus codes are developed continuously. Another safeguard is to turn off the macro feature on spreadsheet and word-processing software.

Another potential security breach occurs when remote users gain unauthorized access to computers, a practice performed by **hackers.** Hackers attempt to bypass security measures such as firewalls, filters, and encryption devices to enter servers as well as personal computers. Most hackers focus on the networks of large corporations and government agencies to gain access to guarded information. Others download operating systems onto home and office personal computers to control those computers remotely. A hacker who gains access to personal computers is able to set up an unauthorized **distributed network** that is controlled remotely through indirect interfaces with many computers. This provides the hacker with a free network that may be used to process information by controlling many computers owned by unsuspecting users. In addition, the hacker has access to all the files on a personal computer, which may provide information that can be used to steal the identity of the user, a crime known as **identity theft.**

Home computer users can connect to the Internet through phone lines, digital subscriber services, wireless connections, and cable modems. A phone line connection is open only during the time of the dial-up session. When the session is completed, the user hangs up the phone, which breaks the open connection. This is not the case with the other three connectivity architectures. When you plug your computer into a cable or subscriber modem, the connection is always on, even when the computer is turned off. This gives a hacker an opportunity to control your computer remotely and access all the data that reside on that machine. Wireless connections are even more vulnerable, as they transmit through airwaves. A hacker need only match the wave frequency to gain access to a computer that uses a wireless connection. This is why many users of broadband and wireless connections install firewall software. However, proficient hackers have the ability to break through firewalls to gain unauthorized access to computers.

A third security concern has to do with direct access from and to computer users within a hospitality organization. Many e-mail systems are susceptible to junk mail (spam) sent to broadly generated e-mail lists. Still another security concern involves workers who abuse corporate computers to surf the Web in search of non-work-related sites. **Filtering** software may be used to restrict incoming and outgoing access on computers. Most e-mail programs have filtering features that restrict the access of spam to specific mailboxes. Outgoing filters, sometimes called censorware, prevent the use of *blacklisted* key words and URLs or may permit the user to access only *whitelisted,* or condoned, sites.

Filtering Software used to restrict incoming and outgoing access on computers.

COMPUTER PRIVACY AND WORKER SURVEILLANCE

Virtually every white-collar hospitality worker is a user of digital computers and telecommunications, and this provides opportunities for employees to use the equipment for personal entertainment during working hours.[2] Electronic monitoring systems are used by approximately 40 percent of all networked organizations to trace, block, or queue illicit telecommunication connections from computers in workstations. Since organizations are responsible for protecting their digital environments from offensive transmissions, numerous workers at organizations have been discharged for downloading pornographic or violent e-mail messages. These actions are considered justified as protection against offensive environment harassment claims, as is evident in legal settlements reached by Microsoft and Chevron for $2.2 million resulting from sexual harassment lawsuits filed by workers who found those downloads offensive.[3] Many employers now feel compelled to monitor worker transmissions in the name of legal protection, with some taking the application further by using surveillance mechanisms to check on employees' performance.

Employers use various software packages to monitor worker keystrokes, mistakes, job processing, and transaction production in a specific period of time. In addition, employers have the ability to track time away from computers, idle time, and the viewing of files stored on disks. As for monitoring employees who move about during the workday, "active badges," which are credit-card-size transponders built into identification badges, provide infrared transmissions to strategically placed receivers that log a worker's whereabouts into a database.[4] This method seems to be a cause of consternation on the part of privacy rights activists.

It appears that ethical debates concerning the digital tracking of employees within organizations fall within two single-sided categories. From the workers' perspective, the arguments center on invasion of privacy that minimizes human respect and dignity; agents for employers maintain their stance on their "need to know" this information for purposes involving liability and managerial responsibility. Interestingly, published debates have not matured to include holistic points of view concerning the discourse presented by each of the dissenting parties.[5] Although some people argue the United States provides limited protection for the privacy rights of employees, there are reports of more stringent privacy protection in the European Union.[6] Regardless of national setting, it is apparent that the same technology used for data storage and communication to enhance productivity is also useful for surveillance of the workforce. Beyond the nature of digital media for storage and communication are applications requiring digital data manipulation.

For instance, scientific investigation uses digital means to collate and work with data in the process of making new discoveries in the areas of biology, chemistry, and physics, such as DNA replication, which would be an impossible task without digitized representations of chain reactions.[7] At the same time, new forms of digitized input technologies permit access to data that are beyond the realm of keyboard entry. An example exists in the area of biometrics, which provides input mechanisms that include magnetic resonance imaging as well as retinal, fingerprint, blood, urine, and facial impression scans.[8] Although some of these devices are not newly developed input mechanisms, they are becoming more cost-efficient with the passage of time; this is consistent with Moore's law.[9] These devices, when coupled with data management systems, can provide means for external and internal identification of individuals, including genetic composition and hence physical predisposition. Nanotechnology developments, currently being conducted in research laboratories, provide the potential for data collection beyond the reach of biometrics.[10]

Nanotechnology goes beyond the limitations of electronic digitization through submicroscopic chemical technology with the capability of human ingestion. It is feasible at this time to use ingested "nanobots" (submicroscopic nano-level robotics) to explore the genome of an individual from an internal perspective.[11] It is apparent that this advanced and noninvasive technology holds immense promise for the future of biochemical diagnosis and treatment in the field of medicine. However, it also presents the potential for employers to measure internally and possibly reprogram the chemical composition of prospective employees. The balance between worker privacy and invasive technologies will present challenges for hospitality managers in the near future.

SAFETY AND SECURITY SYSTEMS

During the last 10 years technology applications have enhanced safety and security programs in hospitality organizations while reducing the numbers of personnel required for maintaining safe and secure facilities. Most hospitality-sector organizations sanction departments to ensure the safety and security of individuals and corporate assets. These departments are called *security, loss prevention,* or *public safety* departments. The functions of these departments include life and property protection, emergency medical services, disaster response, and accident prevention.

Safety and security services are provided for two reasons. First, it is the ethical responsibility of hospitality enterprises to protect life and property. Second, a legal duty is placed on hospitality facilities to provide reasonable levels of security. This standard varies by state. However, in the event of an unfortunate incident, an individual could have standing under civil law to engage in litigation against a hospitality corporation on the basis of the tort doctrine called breach of security. The legal test for most hospitality enterprises in one state traditionally was based on the ratio of the numbers of security patrol officers per shift to the crime and disaster statistics for the area surrounding a hospitality facility. Modern technology has rendered this approach an obsolete measurement of facility security practices.

Current advances in database management systems, telecommunications, smart cards, and digital video peripherals are used in security operations to a large extent. The applications of this technology are aimed at surveillance, tracking, and data collection functions relative to security functions. Wireless networks provide reasonably priced means for security personnel to set up small and inconspicuous Web cams (cameras) in strategically determined locations throughout the public areas of a facility. The cameras digitally record activity in each zone and transmit the time-lapsed shots to a database in a central dispatch office. An officer monitors the sector videos in real time (as they are happening) to alert patrol officers to respond to any irregularities. The stored videos are used for evidentiary documentation of any security incident that may have occurred in each sector. Time-lapsed videos of patrol officers conducting rounds also are entered into the database. Before the availability of this technology, patrol officers inserted *time keys* at designated stations to document their rounds.

Smart lock installations are electronic locks attached to doors that provide access to public and administrative areas of a facility. They are interfaced with the database to facilitate the locking and unlocking of doors at times entered into the database schedule from the dispatch center.

Safety and security systems are important in today's environment. (Courtesy Corbis Digital Stock.)

Each lock also has card access for patrolling officers to enter secured areas manually. Smart cards use one of two architectures. The smart feature is provided by either a computer chip or code. One method is to embed the chip on the card. Another means is to code the card to communicate with a chip that resides in the lock. Security access usually uses the first method, and the cards are somewhat expensive. Guest keys at hotels usually employ the second method, with the use of much more reasonably priced disposable cards that are coded at the front desk during check-in. In a typical scenario a hotel guest will use a coded card that is read by the smart lock to access a guestroom. Security officers will use cards that bypass the smart lock code to enter the same guestroom. This is an electronic version of a master key.

When smart card technology is linked with a database, the numbers of entries to each secure area are logged with dates and times.

Hotel guest keys generally are coded during check-in. (Courtesy of PhotoDisc, Inc.)

Administrative personnel, such as housekeeping and engineering staff members, are tracked as to times of entry to guestrooms and other restricted areas. A single smart card will serve as an employee timekeeping, access, and house charge device. As was mentioned earlier in this chapter, smart cards also may be used to track an employee's movements through unsecured areas of a facility.

The gaming sector of the hospitality industry is always the first to embrace state-of-the-art security technologies. Every inch of a casino floor is monitored both in real time and through digital recordings. Hotel areas of casinos are closely monitored and have a prominent security presence. Surveillance crews operate monitoring equipment above the ceiling of a casino in an area called a *catwalk*. The surveillance cameras in the catwalk are powerful enough to read the serial number on a dollar bill. Every motion that occurs on each table game is observed by the *eye in the sky* (the catwalk monitors).

Gaming security takes special care to preclude undesirable individuals from entering the casino floor in a fashion similar to that used by airport security to prevent terrorists from entering an aircraft. Casinos define undesirable individuals as certain types of criminals as well as card counters and other *cheats*. Casino surveillance has access to huge centralized databases containing photographs of undesirable individuals. Facial recognition software compares images of casino guests to the facial characteristics of individuals in the database. When a match is found, security patrol officers will confront the individual and remove him from the casino floor; this results in probable prosecution for trespass.

Airport security is experimenting with facial recognition software at gate security checkpoints. In this case the database used for comparison contains photos of known terrorist and flight-risk criminal individuals. Immigration authorities are engaging in digital fingerprinting of international travelers going from specific destinations to the United States. The purpose of this measure is to use the data to monitor travel patterns and profile individuals who may pose travel risks on air carriers. Additionally, the government is experimenting with voluntary flight security-status profiles with the intent to establish databases that will contain information concerning all individuals who use air travel. Of course, as was mentioned earlier in this chapter, these practices must balance the security personnel's need to know information with the traveling public's right to privacy.

Cruise vessels have engaged in the practice of photographing each passenger for some time. The digital photos are entered into a database and used for comparison with the facial features of individuals upon reentry to the ship from ports of call. This practice is intended to prevent unauthorized embarkation onto vessels.

PHYSICAL PLANT SYSTEMS

Physical plant management deals primarily with the functions of building maintenance, repair, renovation, and energy utility. The technologies employed as part of physical plant (facilities) management are similar to those used in the safety and security function. Facilities managers use databases to schedule and rotate normally scheduled preventive maintenance (PM) activities. The need for building repairs comes to the attention of engineering personnel in the form of *maintenance requests*. Before current developments in telecommunications, these requests required the completion of a manual form that was hand carried to the engineering department. Today, these requests are transmitted through computer and radio networks in real time, with workers dispatched immediately to respond to high-priority requests.

The telecommunications scheme for repairs and maintenance uses a combination of voice transmissions, regular computer networks, and in some cases wireless computer transmissions. The wireless architecture is beginning to include the use of handheld personal digital assistant computers. For instance, the housekeeping and security staff in a hotel will log and prioritize maintenance and repair records onto a PDA while making rounds. *Hot-spot* transponders are located in certain zones, say, a location on each guestroom floor. The staff member connects the handheld device to the transponder *(hot-synch)* in the nearest zone to transmit the requests to the engineering department's computer. This system uses Wi-Fi wireless technology such as schemes provided by Bluetooth Technologies.

Some hospitality enterprises, such as hotels and theme parks, use large amounts of energy from utilities such as electric and water companies. Engineering personnel are charged with the responsibility to conserve the use of energy to lower the cost of monthly utility bills. The basics of energy management are focused on keeping the cooling, heating, and plumbing equipment in optimum working condition. Additionally, steps are taken to discourage wasted energy on the part of guests and workers. The technology used for energy management may be minimal, such as relay switches on sliding balcony doors that turn off the air-conditioning (A/C) unit when the door is open. A simple step like this can result in savings of thousands of dollars on the monthly utility bills and preserve the condition of A/C and air-handling units.

The capability of a facility to use technology applications for energy conservations is limited by the age of the buildings in the physical plant. Older buildings were constructed before the development of energy-saving features that require extensive amounts of wiring. Wiring costs are reasonable at the time of building construction. However, the cost of laying wire in existing buildings is extremely high and can be disruptive to the operation.

Newer buildings are prewired with energy conservation technologies in mind. For instance, these buildings include motion detectors attached to lighting fixtures that automatically extinguish lights when there is no movement in a room. When a person enters the unlit room, the motion detector will turn the lights on. This feature is common in newly constructed administrative offices and other work areas in a hospitality physical plant. Another feature available in newly constructed buildings is centralized temperature control monitors. For instance, a central monitor will alter the temperature in unused hotel meeting facilities and ballrooms. Workers enter the schedule of use for meeting rooms into the central PC. The computer alters the temperature to hospitable levels just before a scheduled function and returns the temperature to a cost-saving level after the completion of the function. This type of technology requires communication between a computer and the smart chips embedded in utility units.

Utility applications of smart chips are in their infancy. However, they are being refined rapidly to automate many *detection-and-response* routines. The more common examples of this technology are found in automobiles. Household appliance smart chips have the capacity to learn the habits of occupants. For instance, a smart chip may be embedded in a household thermostat that tracks adjustments during various times of the day. If the occupant turns up the thermostat every evening at 10, the smart chip will make the adjustment automatically. This example and many others employ the technologies that will create *smart houses* in the near future.

On-the-Job Training . . . Continued

For a little while you assumed that the solution to the virus and spam problem had to be implemented from the corporate office, since it was in control of the e-mail server. Even though property-level technology administrators did not have total control of the server, they did have administrative permission to modify certain parameters across the property level.

You were reading through an e-mail manual one day and turned to a section on filters. You learned that you could modify the appearance of e-mail subject lines based on certain parameters. You also learned that you could set up routines to view file attachments to all e-mails at the property level. With this new knowledge, you decided to experiment.

You set up a routine that looks for e-mails that are broadcast to more than four users. You set up a routine that adds the letters "PMX" to the front of the subject lines of those e-mails. Next, you set up a routine that searches for executable file attachments, as designated with an "EXE" extension, and adds an autodelete code. Finally, you set out to test the routines you wrote.

Sure enough, any e-mail that was sent to more than four users appeared with the letters "PMX" in front of the subject line. Also, any e-mail that was received was scanned for an "EXE" file, which was deleted as soon as it reached the property e-mail account.

The remaining steps were easy: First, you sent an e-mail showing all users how to filter PMX subject lines from their mailboxes. This caused all spam to be filtered directly into the trashcans of the users. The second step was to program a message that was sent to each user who was the target of an EXE attachment. The notice told those individuals that such a file was detected and eliminated.

In a short period of time most spam and all viruses were eliminated at the property. Your fellow workers still joke with you, but now they call you Dr. Death. That is just fine with you.

SUMMARY

This chapter provided a snapshot of technology applications in the safety, security, and physical plant management functions of hospitality enterprises. We discovered that this assists security personnel in providing for the welfare of individual as well as protecting the assets of a hospitality facility. The pricing of these technologies is reasonable to the point where security professionals may perform their duties effectively with fewer workers. The key technologies applied to safety and security operations include telecommunications, database management systems, and video peripherals. Some operations, such as casinos, use state-of-the-art technologies to protect their organizations. Airports and cruise line operations also employ relatively sophisticated security procedures. Technologies similar to those used in property security are used for physical plant management.

Physical plant management is focused on repairs, maintenance, and energy utility in hospitality facilities. Databases, wireless communications, and smart chip technologies assist physical plant staff members with these functions. Technologies for energy conservation are more limited in older buildings because of wiring constraints. Newer structures are prewired to take advantage of commonly available smart chip technology. The houses and buildings of the future increasingly will use smart chip technology.

DISCUSSION QUESTIONS

1. This chapter discussed both ethical and legal duties to provide safety and security services for hospitality enterprises. If you were a hospitality manager, what would be your position concerning security functions? What technology applications might you consider to ensure the safety and protection of assets in your organization?
2. We talked about a few techniques that are used to monitor hospitality employees. We also discussed applications of future technologies for this purpose. Are we going too far as employers in terms of invading the privacy of our workers? Why or why not?
3. We noticed that gaming operations employ state-of-the art security technologies. We also discovered that airport security is just starting to experiment with some of these technologies. Why do you think casino security is more advanced than airport security?
4. Use your creativity to develop the smart hotel of the future. What features would you include if you had unlimited funds and technology?

Key Terms

ActiveX
Computer virus
Cookies
Distributed network
Encryption
Filtering
Firewalls
Hacker
Identity theft
Java
Macro
Physical plant
Safety
Security

References

1. Harley Hahn. (2000). *Harley Hahn Teaches the Internet,* 2nd ed. Indianapolis: Que Corporation.
2. D. V. Tesone. (2004). The Changing Face of a Constant Issue: Emerging Privacy Issues. *Journal of Applied Management and Entrepreneurship.* 10(2):119–124.
3. D. E. Corbin. (2000). Keeping a Virtual Eye on Employees. *Occupational Health & Safety.* 69(11):24–28.
4. J. M. Mishra. (1998). Privacy in the Workplace? *S.A.M. Advanced Management Journal.* 63(3):4–16.
5. G. S. Alder. (1998). Ethical Issues in Electronic Performance Monitoring: A Consideration of Deontological and Teleological Perspectives. *Journal of Business Ethics.* 17(7):729–744.
6. L. B. Pincus. (1997). Private Parts: A Global Analysis of Privacy Protection Schemes and a Proposed Innovation for Their Comparative Evaluation. *Journal of Business Ethics.* 16(12/13):1237–1261.
7. C. Ruby, Y. William, and J. Bryan. (1999). High Penetrants, Over Weight, and GlucoCorticoid Receptor Variant: Case-Control Study. *British Medical Journal* 318:1337–1342.
8. A. Stikeman. (2001). Recognizing the Enemy: Face Recognition Technology Could Soon Become an Integral Part of Security Systems. *Technology Review* 104(10):48–50.
9. D. Lawrence. (2001). Echelon and the Legal Restraints on Signals Intelligence: A Need for Reevaluation. *Duke Law Journal* 50(5):1467–1469.
10. Self-Assembled Tubes for Electronic Devices. (2002). *USA Today.* 6(1):6.
11. D. Rotman. (2001). Nanotech Goes to Work. *Technology Review.* 104(1):62–65.

Glossary

A

Accounting   Financial transactions, including accounts payable, accounts receivable, payroll, journal entries, ledgers, banking, and cashiering.

Accounting information systems (AISs)   Computer networks that are used to report business transactions and economic events that occur in a hospitality enterprise.

Accounts payable (AP)   A journal that tracks the payment of bills owed to suppliers of material resources such as goods, equipment, and supplies.

Accounts receivable (AR)   A journal that tracks entries pertaining to credit transactions with clients who owe payment to a hospitality enterprise at a future point in time.

Acquisition   When new guests are encouraged to use the services of a hospitality enterprise.

ActiveX   A Web operating system program that is more robust than Java but has fewer protections attached to downloaded programs.

After-departure transaction   A postpay transaction that requires billing after a guest or customer departs from the facility.

AI   See *Artificial intelligence.*

AIS   See *accounting information systems.*

Application programs   Software packages designed to perform functions required by end users.

Application-specific programs   Software programs designed for single-purpose-use.

Architecture topology   Configuration of network nodes.

Artificial intelligence (AI)   The blended disciplines of computer science, biology, psychology, linguistics, mathematics, and engineering.

B

B2B   Transactions involving business-to-business interactions.

B2C   Transactions involving business-to-consumer interactions.

B2E   Transactions involving business-to-employee interactions.

Back end   Contains interfaced components designed to provide e-commerce services to end users.

Bandwidth   The range of frequency for the transmission of data.

Bits per second (BPS)   Volume of data transmitted through a telecommunication channel to determine the speed of the medium.

Booking transaction   An agreement that is made with a hospitality enterprise before the delivery of products and services.

Brainstorming   A group activity used to generate creative ideas to solve problems.

Broadband   A channel with transmission speeds in excess of 256,000 BPS.

Business functions   Include marketing, human resources management, accounting, and operations.

C

C2C   Transactions involving consumer-to-consumer interactions.

Capital-intensive   Large amounts of capital dollars are spent on the assets of a hospitality enterprise.

Cash in advance (CIA)   A prepay deposit made by a guest who chooses not to use credit during a stay at a hotel or resort.

Cash management   The balance of receipts and disbursements of cash flows for an organization.

Cash settlement transaction   After-the-fact payment for products and services rendered. See also *Tendering transaction*.

Central processing unit (CPU)   The collection of boards, chips, and cards that process information.

Central reservation system (CRS)   A centralized computer reservation system that contains a range of interfaces that include local area networks, metropolitan area networks, and/or wide area networks with a capacity for global telecommunication connections.

Checks and balances   A procedure for separating the order and entry points for purchases.

Chief information officer (CIO)   The executive-level individual responsible for the information technology and information systems within an organization.

CIO   See *Chief Information Officer.*

Client/server architecture   Network configuration that permits data input and exchange by end users as well as information specialists.

Closed system   An entity consisting of related parts that is not influenced by outside forces.

Code   Programmed instructions for performing computer functions.

Complexity   The number of variables influencing a problem.

Computer-aided manufacturing (CAM)   Systems that provide automated assistance to workers on the factory floor.

Computer-aided production (CAP)   Systems that provide electronic assistance to workers in small-scale production processes in some hospitality enterprises.

Computer hackers   Individuals who attempt to gain unauthorized entry into databases, often for destructive purposes.

Computer-integrated manufacturing (CIM)   Systems that provide electronic manufacturing planning, organizing, processing, and control of production lines within a production setting.

Computer-integrated production (CIP)   Systems that use electronic automation to perform tasks involved in the production process.

Computer network   Several terminals that are linked together for a common purpose.

Computer programmers   Individuals who write code for computer instructions, using program languages.

Computer reservation system (CRS)   A centralized computer reservation system that contains a range of interfaces that include local area networks, metropolitan area networks, and/or wide area networks with a capacity for global telecommunication connections.

Computer software   The term used to describe the code that permits a computer to perform a number of functions as required by the end user.

Computer telecommunications   A general category that includes computer communications from remote locations.

Computer virus   A program that is embedded in an executable program that can harm a user's machine by deleting, freezing, or rearranging files on a home computer.

Confirmation   An agreement between the hospitality provider and the client that a product or service transaction will occur in the future.

Cookie   A small set of text data placed in a file on a user's browser software that tracks access to various servers.

Cost/benefit analysis   Determines economic/organizational feasibility.

CPU   See *Central Processing Unit.*

Credit transactions   Sales are posted to an account that includes terms and conditions for future cash payment.

CRM   See *Customer relationship management.*

CRS   See *Central reservation system.*

Customer relationship management (CRM)   A holistic system of advertising, promotion, and target marketing; market research; and forecasting using electronic data mining and analysis to generate long-term guest/customer loyalty.

D

Database administrator (DBA)   The individual responsible for overall database management system performance, including development, interrogation, maintenance, and applications.

Database management system (DBMS)   A group of individual databases that are linked together.

Data mining   The process of drilling through information contained in a data warehouse to access specific information.

Data warehouse   A centralized group of databases.

DBA   See *Database administrator.*

DBMS   See *Database management system.*

Decision support systems (DSSs)   Provide electronically generated statistical support to justify or nullify what managers intuitively apply to making decisions.

Delphi technique   The distribution of questionnaires that are recycled until a consensus is reached.

Digital video disks (DVDs)   Video and audio compact disks read by lasers; have replaced videotape media.

Distributed database   A database that is accessed over a network to more than one user.

Distributed network   A network that is controlled remotely through indirect interfaces with many computers.

DSS   See *Decision support systems.*

Dumb terminals   Monitors used to enter data and read information from a mainframe computer.

E

E-commerce   The shorthand term used to describe electronic commerce, which consists of transactions and interactions over computer telecommunications networks.

EDI   See *electronic data interchange.*

Electronic commerce   Transactions and interactions that occur through computer telecommunications networks.

Electronic data interchange (EDI)   Permits the electronic exchange of inventory information, purchase orders, invoices, and funds transfers to settle accounts.

Electronic distribution systems (EDSs)   Airline computer systems used to book reservations and track passenger loads across various flight routes.

Electronic reservation system (ERS)   Consists of a database, a transaction-processing system, and an inventory management component.

E-marketing   Electronic networks used for the promotion and placement of products and services.

Employee application interfaces (EAIs)   B2E information systems aimed at maximizing employee productivity.

Encryption   Techniques that scramble incoming data, which are decrypted when they reach the receiver.

End users   Individuals who use computers for work or play.

Enterprise resource planning (ERP) The overall information system used to maximize resource utilization in the transformation process and manage output generation.

ERS See *Electronic reservation system.*

External customers Guests, passengers, and clients.

External environment Factors that are outside of a hospitality organization that influence the performance of that enterprise.

External scan The process used to collect and analyze data from outside an organization.

Extranet A private communication channel for corporate outsiders such as guests, vendors, and other customers to access an organization's limited network areas; has a configuration that resembles that of the Internet.

F

Filtering Software used to restrict incoming and outgoing access on computers.

Financial management system (FMS) Uses mathematical models to analyze and report on the financial planning aspect of a hospitality enterprise.

Firewall Computer communications processor that filters all network traffic to provide a safe transfer point for access into a network and transmission to other networks.

Four Ps Product, price placement, and promotion.

Freeware Software that is available to the public at no charge.

Front end Points of access for e-commerce end users, including customers, employees, and business affiliates.

G

General ledger (GL) A journal that consolidates data received from other journals that contain data from specialized accounting functions.

General-purpose application program An application program that performs generic functions that may be used for a number of different outcomes by the end user.

Global distribution systems (GDSs) A whole range of travel-related services provided through electronic switches and routers.

Graphical user interfaces (GUIs) Templates linked to the operating system of a computer that provide point-and-click navigation to access the machine's applications and utilities.

GUI See *Graphical user interfaces.*

H

Hackers Remote users who gain unauthorized access to computers.

Hierarchy of data The range of data items from the smallest to the largest visible unit.

HRIS   See *Human resources information system.*

HRM   See *Human resources management.*

HTML   See *Hypertext Markup Language.*

Human resources (HR)   Recruitment, selection, development, and retention of employees.

Human resources information system (HRIS)   A management information system that is used for human resources management applications.

Human resources management (HRM)   A strategic approach to the acquisition and maintenance of employees who have the knowledge, skills, attitudes, and abilities (KSAAs) needed to support the mission of an organization.

Hypermedia databases   Databases containing hypertext formatted information from the Internet.

Hypertext Markup Language (HTML)   A code used to generate Web pages.

I

Identity theft   Unauthorized access to information used to steal the identity of a user.

Information system (IS)   Relationship of the information technology components used to produce, store, share, and distribute information for use by the people affiliated with an organization.

Information technology (IT)   Hardware and software used to process information for organizations.

Input devices   Instruments used to enter data into a computer, such as a keyboard.

Integrated software packages   Customized bundling of compatible software applications.

Interactive marketing   An environment in which guests have access to information concerning the four Ps of most hospitality operations.

Interdependence   The mutually beneficial relationship among systems and subsystems.

Intermediaries   Organizations that purchase blocks of hotel rooms for resale to travelers, often at discounted rates.

Internal audit   The process used to examine and analyze the business functions of an organization.

Internal customers   Employees who serve other employees who serve external customers; otherwise referred to as support staff.

Internal environment   The inside operations and business functions of an organization.

Intranet   A private communication channel for employees to access an organization's networks; resembles the Internet.

IS   See *Information system.*

IT   See *Information technology.*

J

Java   A popular operating system for website programs.

Journal tapes   Cash register printouts of sales transactions.

L

Labor-intensive   Payroll expenses are extremely high relative to other service industry providers.

M

Macro   An embedded set of instructions contained in documents or spreadsheets.

Mainframe computer   The largest category of computer; used mostly for data storage and large-volume transactions.

Maintenance production   Converts an occupied space into a state of readiness for reoccupation by customers, clients, passengers, or guests.

Management   The process of accomplishing the objectives of an organization through the activities of others.

Management by objectives (MBO)   A process of top-down shared goal setting.

Management information system (MIS)   The conversion of data into information for use by the members of an organization to serve its guests or customers. MIS links information technologies with information systems to support enterprise transactions and interactions.

Management reporting   Real-time and after-the-fact information resulting from data analyses of the transaction-processing and process control functions contained in the system.

Marketing   The management of the pricing, placement, and promotion of products and services provided by a specific hospitality enterprise.

Master terminal   The terminal that controls all the other terminals in a POS LAN.

Microcomputers   Small, self-contained computers that include desktops, laptops (notebooks), and personal digital assistants.

Midrange computers   Midsize computers used as network servers and as workstations to perform specialized high-powered functions.

MIS   See *Management information system.*

Mission   The current purpose and philosophy of a hospitality organization.

Mission statement   A printed paragraph or so depicting the purpose of a hospitality organization.

Mixed-function industry   Hospitality business sectors that are both manufacturers and service providers.

Mobile optical robotics   Self-moving machines that perform tasks; have visual sensor capabilities.

Modem (modulator/demodulator)   Used to convert communication signals from digital to analog and back to digital.

N

Network computers (NCs) Personal computers with limited internal components designed exclusively for using the Internet.

Network nodes Terminals connected to a network.

Nominal group technique (NGT) Assures all participants equal participation in decision making by consensus measurements.

Nonprogrammed decisions One-of-a-kind decisions that lack a formal structure.

O

Object-oriented programming (OOP) A high-level programming language that universally recognizes all data fields.

On-hand stock Stock available from storage areas.

Online analytical processing (OLAP) The ability to process information online as opposed to downloading it to a computer.

Open platforms Operating systems that support commonly used hardware and application software packages.

Open system An entity consisting of related parts that is influenced by outside forces called the external environment.

Operational feasibility The willingness on the part of end users to use the system in operations.

Operating system Software that manages computer resources, files, applications, and tasks.

Opportunities and threats Things from the external environment of an organization that can have either positive or negative outcomes.

Organizational objectives Targets for performance in a hospitality organization.

Organizational value The perception on the part of stakeholders (guests, employees, shareholders, and the community) of the viable success of a hospitality enterprise as a marketplace competitor.

Output device A unit that displays processed information.

Outputs Products and services that are measured in terms of quantity and quality.

P

Par stock The predetermined levels of on-hand storeroom stock for each item before any stock requisitions.

Payroll (PR) An account used to monitor the payment of salaries and wages as well as deductions that are placed in accounts to pay federal, state, and local payroll taxes and benefit contributions.

Peripherals Hardware components that are attached to computers.

Perpetual inventory An electronic means of tracking inventory movement in real time.

Physical plant Facilities used by hospitality enterprises to house the services provided to the guests of an enterprise.

PO   See *Purchase order.*

Portal   A location on a telecommunications network for access by all the members of a special-interest group.

Postpay transaction   A sales transaction that occurs after a guest or customer receives products or services.

Prepay transaction   A sales transaction in which a guest, customer, or passenger makes full payment before receiving products or services.

Primary storage   Machine memory that is coded onto silicon chips within the CPU.

Proactive approach   Involves strategic planning aimed at preventing problems from arising in the future.

Problem   An adverse situation concerning actual performance in relation to standards for performance.

Process control   Procedures that track the use of the material resources required to produce products and services.

Processor   A silicon chip that converts data into information.

Procurement system   System used for the purchase of material resources made available through the supply chain of a hospitality enterprise.

Production execution system (PES)   An integrated system of electronic tools for production planning, transformation, and control processes.

Productivity   Outputs (products and services) divided by inputs (resources).

Productivity model   Consists of inputs, transformation processes, and outputs.

Product production   Provides for the conversion of raw materials (ingredients) into finished products (meals and consumable beverages).

Programmed decisions   Decisions that are routine and highly structured.

Proprietary systems   Hardware and software that are owned by a specific vendor that do not permit interfaces with commonly used operating systems.

Purchase order (PO)   Authorization for accounts payable to pay for a specific invoice after the goods are received by a hospitality organization.

Purchasing agents or purchasing managers   Hospitality procurement professionals.

R

RAM   See *Random access memory.*

Random access memory (RAM)   Temporarily stored memory that operates application programs.

Reactive approach   Involves organizational interventions to fix problems that exist in the present.

Read only memory (ROM)   Permanently stored memory that handles the machine functions of a computer.

Receiving agent   The person in charge of receiving purchased items.

Repair production   Converts an out-of-order physical space into one that is ready to be occupied by guests, clients, passengers, or customers.

Reservation   An advanced booking to reserve space for a designated time and date.

Reservation system   An inventory management base coupled with a direct transaction-processing component.

Resources   The people and things that are required to produce a product or service.

Risk   The probability of a negative consequence associated with a decision.

ROM   See *Read only memory.*

S

Safety   The practices that ensure the well-being of individuals, including guests, workers, and others who interact with a hospitality enterprise.

Sales transaction   The process in which the customer or guest pays for products or services that are rendered.

Secure electronic payment systems   Encrypted payment transactions that protect credit card information from access by unauthorized individuals.

Security   The practices associated with taking steps to protect the assets of a hospitality organization.

Server   Computer that serves as the centralized processor for a network.

Service transaction   The actual time during which services are rendered.

Software suites   Bundled packages consisting of various software applications.

Stakeholder groups   Guests (customers/clients), employees, shareholders, and the community (suppliers, neighbors, industry colleagues, society, etc.).

Stand-alone machines   Computers that are not connected to a network of other computers.

Standard query language (SQL)   A program for users to interrogate a database to extract useful information.

Strengths and weaknesses   Things a company does well and things it could do better within the internal environment of an organization.

Suboptimization   Conflicts between smaller goals and larger goals.

Supply chain management (SCM)   A system of information interfaces with sources of supply for material resources.

Supply chain transactions   Part of the procurement processes used to acquire material resources for use in a hospitality enterprise.

SWOT   Situational analysis of strengths and weaknesses within an organization as well as opportunities and threats from outside the organization.

Symbiotic relationship   Each function benefits from the performance of the other function.

Synchronous management practices   A process of two-way real-time feedback loops concerning the planning, execution, and evaluation of product and service processes.

T

Technical feasibility   The ability of hardware and software to provide a business solution.

Telecommuting   Employees using intranets to perform their jobs from their homes or other remote locations.

Telephony   A blending of telephone and computing technology.

Tendering transaction   After-the-fact payment for products and services rendered. See also *Cash settlement transaction.*

Tendering procedure   An exchange of cash, use of a credit card, or posting to an internal credit ledger.

Terminals   Computers or other machines that function as nodes on a network.

Transformation process   All the systems that are used to convert resources into outputs (products and services).

U

Utility   A measurement of the consequences associated with an action.

V

Vendors   Organizations that provide materials, equipment, and supplies to a hospitality company.

Vision   The future direction of a hospitality organization.

W

Working stock   Stock that has been requisitioned from storage for use in a work unit.

Workstation   Highly specialized midrange computer used for high-power functions such as CAD, CAM, and computer animation applications.

WORM   See *Write once, read many.*

Write once, read many (WORM)   Drives on a personal computer that have the ability to write data onto a compact disk.

Index